Thank you for reading this book!
Our intention is to provide you with inspiration from REAL people who have experienced extraordinary things—just like YOU to serve as inspiration and hope. We dedicate this book to the entrepreneurial spirit, to families struggling in myriad ways, to young people daring to dream big but might feel a little lost or unsupported.

We encourage colleges and high schools to **read this book**, as well as clubs and networking groups, corporations and entrepreneurs and anyone who **dares to think differently**, dream bigger and wants more than what sometimes seems possible. It is all possible,and we want to encourage you to follow your dreams because **YOU** are destined for greatness. We all are!

To get discount copies of our book inquire at forbes@forbesfactor.com

In our hearts FOREVER
YOU are missed! RIP

Lari Thomas

Dedication

Forbes Factor is a true labor of love and I am SO grateful for my students and friends that have made this journey, the trip of a lifetime. I'm humbled by your honesty, willingness to play full out and strive so hard to support a cause greater than ourselves.

With deep love, admiration and sincere appreciation, I dedicate this book to my wonderful family and especially Ryker and Makenna, my twins who have been the wind beneath mommy's wings... your love has allowed all of us fly!

If you are a friend of mine, you know it and there are too many of YOU to single out by name. I dedicate this book to YOU, whoever you are and wherever you are. I am YOU. A dreamer, a schemer and TEAMER!~ We are in this together and our rising tides shall lift all boats!

Forbes Riley

The Forbes **FACTOR**

Profits from the sales of this book will be donated to the LEAP FOUNDATION

LEAP Week is a 6-day program at UCLA designed to help young adults reach their maximum potential.

LEAP attendees experience workshops, small group exercises, and mentor sessions that give them the foundational life skills and confidence needed to achieve their goals.

Scholarships for students that demonstrate academic excellence and financial need.

For more info on getting involved to help support visit:

www.LeapFoundation.org

L E A P

Children are 10% of our population but 100% of our future!

Dr. Bill Dorfman - Celebrity Dentist and co-founder of LEAP. He's helped thousands of patients smile for over 20 years. Featured on shows like ABC's Extreme Makeover and CBS's The Doctors, he is passionate about helping create bright smiles and bright futures!

Meet The Authors

Aaron Hills

Ann McIndoo

Ashonda Claxton

Cody Iverson

Emily Letran

Forbes Riley

Jose Elizondo

Joshua Self

Julianna Stark

Kinzey Ray

Kipling Solid

Lari Thomas

Maria Loya

Maria Lucassen

Mariano Padilla

Shelly Stucchi

Stacey Saintz

Tim Hodgkiss

"WE FORBES'D IT!"

Bob Martinez

Chuck LaDouceur

Cindy Mirkamali

Jerid Fenderson

Jim Cassidy

John & Doris Vallee

Justin Holland

Justin Yanagida

Kevin Cabriales

Leah Holmes

Lisa Paul Heydet

Makenna Riley

Pat White

Renee Barnes

Robbin Fortier

Tucker Wells

Tyronda Richardson

Daphne Street

SPECIAL **FREE** BONUS
Gift for YOU!

www.Free**Gift**fromForbesRiley.com

Enjoy my Video Training Series & Resource Guide"
designed to show **YOU** how to leaverage your
expertise, achieve your goals fast and create true
abundance!

FREE
$797
VALUE

Table of *CONTENTS*

FOREWORD

Foreword by LES BROWN
The World's Best Motivational Speaker

Many of us never realize our greatness because we get sidetracked by secondary activities. We spread ourselves too thin, never saying no to anything or anyone. We spend our entire lives doing everything else but taking care of ourselves.

Henceforth, decide to take some time to work on you; you deserve that. Your life deserves some prime time. You are the master of your own show, so you decide what roles to cast. Take the effort to invest great energy in yourself. Don't be too busy, don't get caught up in the rat race. Take out time to attend seminars, classes, grow your gifts and invest in yourself. Concentrate on building up yourself, for if you don't, you will make a settlement. Most people are settling with less than what they deserve.

I want YOU to "Forbes" feeling good about yourself. Develop a health plan. Good health is good wealth. Furthermore, live life with energy and passion. Make a conscious decision to be lively. Be happy, you have a lot

to be thankful for. Avoid faces that will make you lose your happiness. Learn to stand up for yourself, fill your mind with positive thoughts and energy. Sometimes you have to shut up yourself.

More so, in many instances, you will get scared and your mind will go blank on you. Watch your inner dialogue, it will determine the quality of your life. Sometimes the enemy is not outside of us, but it is within us. Whenever you are about to do something and the voice in your head says "you can't do it, you are not qualified" just say watch me.

The biggest challenge you can have is you.

Every day, ask yourself "what do you want out of life" what do you want out of the job, career, relationship, what will make you happy. You have to ask yourself questions. How will you know when you got it? Be specific, don't be vague by saying "I just want to be happy".

Once you begin to determine what you want, write it down. Read it three times a day, that is; morning, noon and night. It will cause you to focus. When the negative thoughts tell you that you can't do it, that will make you focus. It will discipline your thinking. you are going to become so creative, ideas will pop up. Reading it everyday gives you imaginative thoughts that will lead you towards your main goal.

Entrepreneurs reading this book will truly understand that nothing is impossible.

I have been a personal friend and fan of Forbes Riley for many years and I encourage you to seek her out, attend her trainings and truly learn to manifest YOUR best life ever.

That's my story and I'm sticking to it.

INTRODUCTION

by FORBES RILEY

"You are the sum of the obstacles you overcome." This has been a defining motto of mine throughout my life and each year it seems that this quote takes on a different and deeper meaning.

Whether it was dealing with being bullied for wearing braces for 8 years as a kid, for being overweight, a crooked nose, and frizzy hair or having a father who spent 3 years in the hospital, enduring 15 operations, or suffering through the murder of a young man I helped raise for 12 years— I've learned that the most difficult times have given so much to me.

As I periodically look back at the mountains I've climbed and the rapids I've crossed, I realize that each challenge changed me: I've suffered but endured, questioned yet found salvation, lost my way and circled back again with the help of friends, mentors, masterminds and trainings. I've become more compassionate, more confident, more thoughtful, more vulnerable and most grateful.

Forbes Factor was born from this and now uplifts and transforms people around the world.

The name "Forbes" has been important to my family, not because we are heirs to the Forbes Magazine Empire, because we're not; it was given to us long before Malcolm Forbes claimed publishing fame. My Jewish Grandmother found it impossible to allow her son to go into engineering college with the last name of Feinstein, so she looked through the yellow pages and randomly chose Forbes.

Legally, with my dad's last name and my first given name, I was born Francine Forbes, then married a Riley. As women, society invites us to drop our last names in marriage. Well, being the disrupter I've always been, I dropped my first name and took his last name.

The new name, Forbes Riley, was born! That was 27 years ago, now the name seems to have a life of its own.

At one of my earliest motivational speeches, I shared my tales of defying convention. Always using the backdoor to manifest my wildest dreams, from touring the world with no money to hanging out with wild cheetahs in Africa. Starring in movies and tv shows, to establishing my own fitness empire and manifesting success with my signature fitness creation, SpinGym! I talked about growing up with no money and yet I manifested skiing, scuba diving and even learned to fly an airplane. Truly mastering "What You Want and Why You Want it"... and then getting it without hesitation through perseverance and the principles we teach at Forbes Factor called Dream It, Believe it, Achieve it.

Right after that speech there was a raffle drawing with 250 women in attendance. Karen, a woman I had been coaching for years, began ranting that she needed to win the prized necklace because it would be the ideal compliment to her mother of bride dress... and she just had to have it. Imagine the 250 to 1 odds... So the drawing begins, and the emcee shouts... KAREN, winner of the jeweled necklace... we were all stunned. Then she turns to me with a HUGE grin on her face and exclaims, "Ha, I Forbes'd it!" And thus the myth of "Forbesing" your dreams into reality was forged.

So I ask you... What Have You **Forbes'd** Lately?

What Have You **Forbes'd** Lately?

My name is Aaron Hills, and I Forbes'd some of my wildest dreams... so far! It's all about learning from your failures until you achieve success. Now, success is defined differently, person to person, so find your definition and seek to obtain it in all that you do. Progress in this world happens when people are willing to think beyond what is currently available and then set forth to make it happen. Don't let failure or setbacks stop you, continue to find a way, so the whole world benefits from YOUR contribution.

Shoot for the

MOON

By Aaron Hills

My love for the stars, planets and the "great beyond" charted the course for my career as a pilot and has allowed me to live the life of my dreams. The passion I have for flight and space exploration has propelled me through some of the toughest times in my life, as I learned valuable lessons along the way. In fact, the most profound lesson I have learned is that anything is possible if you focus all of your effort on it.

I was inspired to become a pilot by my Dad, who worked on jets as an engineer in the Air Force. He would take me to flight museums and air shows, where I was in absolute awe of the aircraft as they flew by performing daredevil stunts. My fascination with flight resulted in visions of breaking the sound barrier, taking off from aircraft carriers and flying at supersonic speed. YES! My passion was cemented. I knew I was destined to fly!

As I got older, my dream of becoming a pilot grew more ambitious. I not only wanted to fly through the clouds, but I also wanted to soar through the stars in space. I would spend countless hours sitting outside stargazing, observing meteor showers and lunar eclipses. On some occasions, I got to see rare comets with orbits that bring them into view from the earth every few thousand years. I was completely swept up in

this fascination with the cosmos, and I wanted to be there. I didn't just want to see space, I wanted to go there! I learned that I could make all of that happen by becoming an aircraft pilot with NASA, whereupon I could become a pilot for the space shuttle. Goal set. Seat belts strapped. Ready for liftoff. Except for the fact I was still in middle school!

While my mind was filled with the fantasy of intergalactic encounters during school, I remained grounded in reality, setting goals and focusing on learning. In the sixth grade, our school announced we would have the opportunity to actually observe a solar eclipse. We all ran outside after lunch and were told not to look directly into the eclipse as it would damage our eyes. I was stubborn and ignored these instructions. I looked directly into the sky, watching the solar eclipse with my own eyes, blinking and turning away every so often, because it was really bright. What a sight it was! But the next day something was wrong. I couldn't read the words on the chalkboard in class. My eyesight had deteriorated. Not by a lot, but enough that I now needed glasses. My dream was shattered. I was never going to be a pilot. But I could not accept this fate. I tried all sorts of remedies to return my eyesight to normal. I was even told that eating carrots would fix my sight, so I started eating lots of them. Sadly, nothing worked. While my need to wear glasses crushed my dream of being a military or NASA pilot, I learned that I could still get my private pilot's license.

I was crushed, but I still pursued a course that would get me as close to my dream as possible. As I progressed through high school and college, I was hearing more and more that my dream was really just that, a dream. I was told that I would never fly for the military or NASA, and I started to believe that my dream may not happen. Eventually, my dreams started to wane, and I thought maybe I should give up my dream of becoming any kind of pilot. I started to believe that there were other things I could do that could bring me just as much satisfaction as flying. I was wrong!

In college, I pursued many different degrees: history, business, Russian language, social science, and eventually I did find a passion for physics. A-ha—that's it! I could become a geophysicist and join a mission to study the geology of other moons or planets or become an

astrophysicist to help create new ways of getting into space. My life was becoming fun again!

As it turns out, my eyesight was good enough to be an aircraft navigator, but not a pilot. At least as a navigator, that would get me in the air, and I'd have the opportunity to go through pilot's training. I was elated, and I signed up with the U.S. Marines under a guaranteed pilot contract. However, since I signed the contract and had gone to training, I was now obligated to finish college by a specific date. My physics degree, however, did not allow me to graduate by the date the Marines required, so I was forced to change my major to something that would allow me to graduate faster—political science. I wasn't happy about it, but I didn't let that discourage me, because I was going to be flying! Ultimately that was my dream, so I did not care what my college major was. The next blow was a tough one though. I was told that there were no more flight slots available in the Marines. I would have to commission as an infantry officer. Wait...what? This is not what I wanted to do! I had a guaranteed pilot contract, and now I was not being guaranteed a chance to fly at all. Now I had the difficult decision of whether to withdraw from the Marines or commission as infantry. End of the line. I knew that being infantry wouldn't fulfill my dream of flight, so I withdrew.

Now what? Do I just give up? For a time, I tried to find something else that could replace my dream of flight. With a degree that didn't allow many opportunities for the world of flight, I interned with the Senate dealing with defense and aerospace and later returned to college to study project management. I even took a job working at an aerospace company so that I could at least work with airplanes. My mind, however, could not shake the overwhelming desire to be in the air, so I pressed forward down other paths to pursue my dream of flight.

Through my life's journey, I have acquired some incredible life lessons that have empowered me. It just takes a little perspective to see how the challenges I have faced have actually defined a roadmap for my future and a lifetime of success.

Lesson #1: Do Whatever It Takes

When one door shuts, find a window, chimney...anything! Just keep going, because if you stop too soon, you'll never get to the best part!

I could not be deterred from my dream of becoming a pilot. I had to fly! So I looked to join the Army and their pilot's program. I was told that I was too old at the time to enter this program, but I could still enlist, as enlisted soldiers were permitted to fall within a higher age-range and qualify for the aviation program. I had to decide whether to enlist in the Army. If I didn't enlist, my dream of being a military pilot dies. However, even if I do enlist, I still may not get to be a pilot. This was a tough choice, and it reminded me of what I went through with the Marine Corps., but this truly was the last opportunity that I saw to fulfill my dream of becoming a pilot. So I did it. I enlisted in the Army, and during the next five years, I dropped flight packet requests in an attempt to get into flight school. Each time, I was told that my requests were denied.

I was never shown the paperwork stating that I was denied, so I just kept at it until I was finally told to do it on my own without the help from the accessions officers. I remember going to the medical facility and asking for my "physical" papers to go through another flight physical. They came back with a manila envelope that was almost an inch thick. I asked what this was, and they indicated that it was my medical records from the Army. I opened it up, and I fully expected to see my denial into flight school, but what happened surprised me.

On the cover of that thick stack of papers was a black stamp about four inches square with writing in it with the phrase "Aeromedical Approved Waiver Granted." I took the pages back to the accessions office and asked what that stamp meant. I was told that it was the approval that was needed for me to enter flight school. Apparently, I had been approved for the last 3 years. He then asked me if I still wanted to fly. I said "yes!", and finally, I found myself on my way to flight school. After 32 years of striving to become a military pilot, my dream was back on track to becoming a reality.

After attending Warrant Officer Candidate School and passing that course I was pinned a Warrant Officer One and was off to flight school. It was hard work, studying and memorizing parts of the helicopters, becoming well-versed in how the systems operated and what the limits of the aircraft are so that proper action can be taken in the event of an emergency. Emergency procedures need to be memorized and repeated verbatim in class. Flights were tough, but fun. Flights under Visual Flight Rules (VFR) were always fun, and I looked forward to them. However, terrain navigation was difficult, and I must admit that we did get lost at times and had to figure out how to get back. Flights under Instrument Flight Rules (IFR) were a lot more demanding and I was usually drenched in sweat upon returning from them.

Incredibly, I was "pinned" an Army Aviator, having successfully completed all the courses, including learning to fly during the day, at night, in the clouds, and with night vision goggles. Can you imagine? Finally, after all of this time and work and disappointments and hope and tremendous work, my dream had now become a reality. Or at least half of it had. I now needed to become a pilot for NASA- no, I haven't given up on that, either. There was a really big problem with that- NASA had closed their space shuttle program. There was now literally no way left to become a pilot for NASA. But, my dream of going into space is still very alive. At 32 years old, despite seemingly insurmountable odds, I made my dream of becoming a military pilot a reality. Now at 37 years old, I am still working toward becoming a pilot for a spacecraft that will get me into space. Even if I am a navigator or other crew member, I want to fulfill my childhood dream of flying through the stars, and to cross that line that marks outer space and see the earth from the outside. My ultimate dream is to see the earth from the moon, and I am going to pursue my dream until it becomes a reality.

Lesson #2: Remember, success is about making things happen, you can't just wish for things

Since I became a pilot, there have been other dreams that I have wanted to reach. I wanted to own my own business—that's hard work, but I've got my own store. I'm learning different languages and traveling to places all over the world. I read a quote "give to the world the best you

have and the best will come back to you." Giving back is a huge priority in my life now, and I am looking for ways to help others, where I can provide service in a way that will lift others up and help them achieve their dreams.

I've come to a deep understanding that getting what you want is a combination of a lot of hard work, determination and never giving up. Just dreaming usually results in unfulfilled dreams. The most important things in life, the things that give you the most value, usually takes a lot of hard work—relationships, meaning, and fulfilling dreams. It may be uncomfortable, painful or scary at times, but when you break through those limiting barriers, that is where growth takes place.

Life doesn't just give us our dreams and desires just because we want it. Usually, there is planning and sacrifice to be had in order to see dreams become reality. First, we have to know what it is that we want, then we must put a plan together of what needs to be accomplished to get there. Once that plan is in place, we must take the necessary action to make the goal become reality. This may mean giving up on other things that you may want to do at that time. What is more important? Instant gratification now? Or the long-term realization that your dream was achieved by the sacrifices that were made.

Remember the old saying, "good things come to those who wait?" Be patient. It is easy to want something but harder to wait for it and sacrifice for it. There was this test where you tell a kid he can have one marshmallow now, or if he waits 5 minutes he can have two. Most of the kids will go ahead and eat the one because waiting is hard. That's how life works. Other temptations often distract us from reaching our goals. We see a shiny object and immediately turn to see what it is and lose track of our end goal, pushing it further and further away. Stay focused, learn to say no to those things that will deter you from where you want to be. If you pay close attention, you'll notice that there are all sorts of small things that can creep up and keep us from achieving our dreams. Be firm in what it is that you want to do, and don't let other things sidetrack you. It takes time to master any talent, to make new positive habits, so put forth the effort. Don't get distracted and give it

time. You'll soon find as you're working so hard, that you've actually reached your goals, and your dreams will become reality.

Lesson #3: Embrace being uncomfortable

Each of us at some point recognizes that we don't know what it is that we are doing. When we find ourselves trying something new, it can be challenging to make mistakes, feel lost or confused and maybe even a little discouraged. Our minds don't like the fact that it's hard, and often we hear this voice telling us to just give up and go back to what it is that we do know—it's comfortable there; we feel instantly successful and empowered. Learning new things, building new good habits, challenging ourselves is harder and uncomfortable, and those negative little voices can start nagging us. Please push through that. Tell that voice to be quiet and keep pushing yourself until you understand how to do the new task you are doing or build that new positive habit. Eventually, it becomes easier and you now have a new skill or routine, or whatever it may be that leads you towards achieving your goals. One statement I really like is: "We need to be willing to step into the darkness and let the light catch up." The darkness is that temporary uncomfortable spot, yet we push forward with confidence that eventually reaching that goal is imminent, and it is.

Relationships are also key to success. You never know who you're going to meet during the day and what they may teach you and how you can be a resource to each other. Remain humble and teachable. I have learned a lot about so many people I have met throughout my life. I use their stories as inspiration to help push me along and keep me on track with my goals. Go out of your way to listen to others and hear their stories, and you'll be surprised to find that, even though everyone has goals that are vastly different from your own, the struggles we all have in reaching those goals have big similarities. Lessons on how we overcome these obstacles can be shared. Take the time to learn from others, and know that every day there are opportunities where many can learn from you.

In the end, there are countless approaches to reaching your goals in life, and not anyone's approach is right or wrong. Remain open, driven, and inspired, and with hard, focused work, you'll get there.

Avoid negative talk and negative people. Don't let anybody tell you that you can't do anything. If you have the drive and the ambition to do something that you really want, then go do it. We can only limit ourselves; don't let others place limits on you. I have the mindset that nothing is impossible if you put your mind to it, so go out, reach for the stars, reach for whatever it is that you want to do, and put forth the effort to make it happens and you'll find out that as you do it, and as you continue to push yourself, you find ways across those barriers. You find ways to make those things happen, and then when it does happen, that taste of victory is so sweet. Then, savor the victory of fulfilling your dream, and prepare yourself for your next adventure.

Aaron Hills

began searching for his passion at a young age. As an imaginative child, he fell in love with flight and the freedom that comes with being amongst the clouds and stars. To further his understanding of the underlying technical aspects of flight and space travel, he obtained a degree in physics at Brigham Young University-Idaho. Here, his fascination with aviation and space exploration increased in intensity and purpose.

Aaron's passion for flight led him to join the Army, where he excelled as a military pilot. Not satisfied with being confined to the sky, Aaron continues to push the boundaries of his aviation career to new heights. Aaron is now seeking opportunities, including one with NASA, which will allow him to apply his mastery of aviation and fulfill his dream of piloting a spacecraft into outer space.

To learn more about Aaron, contact him at:

arhills@msn.com

What Have You **Forbes'd** Lately?

My name is Ann McIndoo, and I Forbes'd a career taking people's stories and turning them into books - now more than 1200 times! It's been a dream come true working with luminaries such as Tony Robbins, Mark Victor Hansen, Forbes Riley and so many more; guiding them to get their genius from their heads onto paper. As the Author's Coach, I have now Forbes'd online platforms to make this process available to everyone. There is such joy in actually holding YOUR book for the first time and I think everyone needs to "Forbes" that!

Our Stories Shape
OUR LIVES

By Ann McIndoo

My love for reading led me to write my first story at the age of 9, and publish my first book at 53 when I started my company, "So, You Want To Write", in 2005. Now, 14 years later, I have written four books of my own, two of which are Amazon Bestsellers, and have helped my author clients produce more than 1,630 manuscripts and books to assist them tell their story.

Most of my author clients include professionals, speakers, coaches, business owners, entrepreneurs, and celebrities as well as moms and dads. For a new author, a book can be a powerful tool to grow their business, widen their audience as well as develop their brand.

My professional book writing journey began with an amazing client. In 2003, I was invited to assist Tony Robbins as his Creative Assistant to help him organize the content of his book. It was an extraordinary experience – like going to a university in the "art of writing a book".

I loved it—the whole process of learning the various components used to build his book was fascinating. Working with Tony was truly extraordinary. He definitely walks his talk and I learned so much from him by just watching, listening and implementing his success strategies into my own life.

Soon after I finished working with Tony, others asked me if I would help them with their books, and after almost a dozen book projects, I decided to help others get their own message, wisdom and stories into the world and created my company, "So, You Want To Write". It has been a fun, inspiring, and wonderful journey.

There are so many benefits to having your own published book and that's why I encourage speakers, business owners, coaches, and entrepreneurs to have one. A book can be a powerful tool that creates credibility as well as makes you an authority on your topic. Notice the first 6 letters in authority? It's AUTHOR! Your book can also be a wonderful lead generator and marketing tool.

Many of my new authors ask: "What should I write about?" That is a GREAT question! Books can be focused on your business, your experience, and your wisdom. If you have a system for accomplishing a goal or achieving certain results, you definitely have the foundation for a book.

As an Author's Coach, I have enjoyed hearing people's stories and helping them create their books. I've learned how people have gone from surviving to thriving; getting through trauma and abuse; conquering cancer and being a parent to an autistic child; as well as the nitty-gritty details of finance, real estate, golf, sales, speaking on stage, overcoming fears, leadership, building self-esteem and confidence, building a team, building a company, building success, creating a successful mindset, the Holocaust, psychology, winning at gambling, the mafia, the internet and marketing online – the list goes on. It is incredible to see what the human soul can create, share and inspire.

I believe everyone has a book in them – yes, including YOU!

Here's what I have found every successful person has in their tool kit:

Lesson 1: Love what you do

To have a successful business it's absolutely critical that you love what you do. Being self-employed is not always balloons and cupcakes. Not only do you have the service you provide to think about, but there is

fulfillment, marketing, social media, website maintenance, speaking gigs, live events, product updates, creating new products, accounting, payroll, insurance and whole boatload of things to think about – in addition to leading, inspiring and motivating your team. You have to make decisions, follow-through and keep moving forward. I wouldn't have it any other way! Because I totally love it, it is never a chore or work, it is my passion to serve my authors.

Lesson 2: Cultivate Mentors / Keep on Learning

I have a few mentors I talk to about important decisions to help guide my steps and priorities. Having people you trust and respect whom you're able to reach and talk to is a key component to growing. Many of my colleagues have an advisory board that gives them guidance on critical decisions, which I think is a great idea. I also go to a seminar, workshop or online course at least once a month. This keeps me up to date and I get great ideas.

Lesson 3: Integrity, Honesty, and Authenticity

Integrity, honesty, and authenticity – these are a must. You must be relentless in the pursuit of being outstanding with yourself, with your clients, and your business. This is where trust is born, and trust will get your customers to buy from you. There are no shortcuts to establishing trust. I also know that living with these attributes makes life really sweet, because there's never, ever, anything to worry about.

One day as I was working with Sage Robbins, Tony Robbins' wife, someone called and asked her for a favor. I heard her say, "Yes." I was concerned that she didn't have the time to fulfill that favor, and I said, "I'll do it for you, you're very busy." Sage said to me, and I'll always remember this, "When you truly serve, abundance will come." And, I've learned that she was absolutely right. The pie of abundance is so big that there's plenty for everyone. Be open to sharing. It always comes back.

Here is Tony Robbins' Ultimate Success Formula:

Step 1: Know your outcome.

Step 2: Take massive action.

Step 3: Check your results.

Step 4: If you are getting the results you want, keep doing it.
If you're not getting the results you want, change your approach and take massive action.

This Success Formula works one thousand percent for EVERYTHING! Whether you're baking a cake, starting a business, planning an event, or writing a book—it works!

Ann McIndoo

is an author's coach who is committed to helping people tell their stories through books. Her company, "So, You Want To Write", has prepared over 1,600 manuscripts for speakers, coaches, entrepreneurs, and business professionals. Aside from working with industry heavyweights, such as Tony Robbins, Ann is the author of 2 best-selling books of her own, "So, You Want to Write" and "7 Easy Steps to write YOUR book".

Witnessing the lack of understanding of the book publishing process by her clients, Ann saw an opportunity to elevate her profession. She worked tirelessly to develop educational courses for writers to become more effective and efficient in getting their voice heard. Her work paid off, and she has designed several highly-sought-after courses, including: "Author's Boot Camp", "Author's Manuscript Grid", and "Author's Trigger Sentences".

Beyond assisting authors to write their book through her individual training and courses, Ann has worked relentlessly to expand the reach of her message to the masses as an established speaker and presenter. Ann is truly in a class of her own, with unmatched energy and passion for her work, and supreme dedication to her clients' success.

To learn more about Ann, contact her at:

Ann@SoYouWantToWrite.com

What Have You **Forbes'd** Lately?

My name is Ashonda Claxton, and I Forbes'd my way out of a pervasive trap called "poverty" and into a mindset and lifestyle of success. It's easy to believe you're just going to be a statistic, but I refused that message, and I never gave up on my dreams! I persevered even when, for most people, my dream might have seemed impossible. No! My dream, your dream—life is filled with possibilities. The only time anything becomes completely impossible is if you give up. Don't give up. Forbes your dreams!

The Greatest Show

ON EARTH

By Ashonda Claxton

My life has resembled one hell of a circus, complete with costumes, dancing, traveling and my fair share of tragic and entertaining sideshows. My mom, the "Urban Gypsy", led our family of 6, as we moved repeatedly across the country from place to place. Our family was close, and while we enjoyed life, we endured financial struggles, emotional despair, and physical pain together. While this adversity would show up unexpectedly throughout my childhood, I never succumbed to it. My ever present belief that I was somebody "special" prevented me from accepting this adversity as my fate. In fact, this adversity and my unconventional upbringing was the fuel I used to dream and inspire myself to create my own completely unique version of life, where I am the ringleader of my own circus of success.

As a young child, one of the most emotionally painful struggles I have dealt with was the fact that my stepfather was beating my mom. On some occasions so bad, that I'd hear her crying. One day, my mom told me, "If you hear me crying again, I want you to run out the door, and take everyone with you to a neighbor's house." She also said that if he ever does it again, we're leaving. Well, that day came. But because my stepfather was one of the "Good ole boys" from the Sheriff's department the incident was simply overlooked. The #Metoo movement still had a long way to go then.

One night, my mom had enough, and woke me out of deep sleep, and said, "Get your things, whatever you can grab quickly, and put it in the car. Gather all your brothers and sisters, get in the car, and let's go." And, we did. We drove all night. I had no idea where we going, but when we finally ended up somewhere we were in that battered women's shelter, tucked safely away, somewhere in Florida. There was a 30 day limit on our stay, which they extended because my mom had 6 children.

Eventually, we ended up in Philadelphia, PA, where we stayed at the Salvation Army. I remember being pulled to the side by my teacher in school, and asked what my home address was. I said, "Right now we're living in the Salvation Army." I didn't feel uncomfortable about it, because my mom was so strong—she held it all together, so it never occurred to me that there was anything awkward with the situation. From there, we moved to Ohio, and I remember going to elementary school and getting my first library card, but my name was misspelled. I asked the teacher to correct my name, but before I could get a corrected card, my mom moved us again. Eventually, though, we experienced some stability, and my mom was able to rent a house with the help of Section 8. We still never settled, though. After the years' lease was up, it was time to pack up again.

A year later, my ex-stepfather had found us. He showed up and took his kids for the summer. I stayed and watched my 4 youngest siblings ride off with their dad. It hurt a little inside, but I closed my eyes and said a little prayer for them. This made me think about meeting my own father one day, and how it would help me get a better sense of who I was, to fill that emptiness I had always felt. At that time, all I knew about him was that he was Nigerian, that my parents never married, and that he had a brother named Dirisu. When I was younger, I used to pray that I would meet him and my grandmother, as well. My mom told me she was a Nigerian queen in her village, which meant my dad was a prince, which by default, made me a princess!

I tried everything to find my Dad. I even wrote to Donahue and Montel Williams. I wrote to all of the shows and asked them to help me find my father. Nothing came from it. I felt that not knowing my father left a huge hole in my life and maybe even my identity. I knew that I didn't

want to use that as an excuse for not making a success of my life. But I always held on to hoping that one day, just one day, maybe, my prayers would be answered.

When I was 13 years old, and living in Youngstown, Ohio, I fell madly in love with a family friend, Terrence Cecil, who was always coming by the house. We went to the same church and lived walking distance away from each other. He always told me I was marriage material, not to let anyone turn me into a girlfriend, and that I deserved someone who deserved me. He was such a cool guy. It just felt good that someone trusted me with all their secrets. My mom got the itch to move and my ex-stepfather had found out where we lived, so we packed up once again. I missed Terrence and was so sad when we left Ohio for Georgia.

Crime was escalating and the death toll was rising fast for young black men in my old hometown in Ohio. Terrance's family felt it would be a life-saving move if he left Ohio completely. So he hopped on a Greyhound and came to Georgia. He promised my mom he was coming to get his life together and was not going to cause any problems. He needed a job in Georgia, but didn't have the necessary documents to apply for work, and instead of having them mailed to him, he returned to Ohio to get them. He never came back. Just a week after he left, my world caved in around me. Terrence had been shot. I was an introverted, overweight girl who didn't get a lot of attention, so I mostly kept to myself. He was the only one that made me feel special and meant it. R.I.P Trouble T-Fly. Nevertheless, into the dark tunnel I went. It took me a little while, but I found my way out by looking within. What could set me apart from this darkness? Seeking therapy wasn't common in the African American community in those days. I'm sure if I was diagnosed, I would have been labeled as depressed. With no guidance, I decided, I was going to come out of this state of mind, if for nothing else... I was a Claxton and the show must go on.

I was a junior in high school, and for the first time I had to think about my future. For once, thinking about my future wasn't about my family, my mom and all of my siblings, this was about me. I knew I wanted to go to college, and I wanted to go to F.A.M.U. Despite all of the chaos in my life and in my mind, I was very clear on this goal. The only thing

that I knew even more clearly than that is that I did not want to fall into poverty, and I thought college would be my ticket out of that.

My freshman year in college was spent keeping my head above water with my grades. I sang in the gospel choir, but deep down inside I really wanted to be a part of the "Shakers". They were a dance troupe that popped, locked and shaked (which would be called "Twerking" nowadays). Yes, I was always low key about the one talent I knew I had- dancing! Like Beyonce and Sasha Fierce, I also had a part of me that loved to dance especially when there was a contest. I'd take everyone by surprise. No one could challenge me on a street dancing battle. Who would expect this plump, shy, nerdy girl to come out the closet with all the latest dance moves? Music and dancing made me happy and provided me with a source of pride. I made it through my first year of college, went home for the summer and never returned back. I lost the drive to go and wasn't sure of what I wanted to do. So I took the following year off to just "try life" and see what opportunities would come about.

During this time, I sat down and thought of things that were important to me, almost like a self-analysis. My top 3 things on my list were uniform, not confined to one space, and travel. I decided that I wanted to be a flight attendant. All my life I was on the move, and there I was. I knew that the ordinary 9-5 life wasn't for me. I was cut out for anything other than the ordinary.

With a goal now in mind, it was time to set things in motion. I kind of felt like maybe it was going to be a bigger challenge for me because I was overweight, and you know all of the prejudices about that and the images of beautiful flight attendants in all of the magazines. I knew I didn't fit that image, but I had this determination that I was going to do it. So I prayed about it, applied and interviewed for it, and I kept getting rejected. It hurt a little but I kept at it because I had made the decision to. No matter what, I wouldn't let disappointment break me.

Then, one Sunday I was in church, the pastor stood up and said at the end of the service, "For those of you that are looking for a job, American Airlines is here at the church doing interviews." It was as if all of heaven had come down far enough for an angel to stand next to me and say …

"Now that we have gotten you polished up from all the rejections, you are ready. This is for you and you alone." There was nothing that anyone could have said to me at that moment that would have convinced me of anything other than the absolute divine fact that American Airlines had come to the church specifically for me, because of all of my prayers, and all I had gone through. I was determined to make this dream come true.

So, I walked into that interview with American Airlines with an open mind, full of hope and gratitude for this opportunity. I told them who I was. I turned on my personality and I gave it my all. The person that was interviewing me explained that there was a minority program, and they were especially looking for minority flight attendants. I was all about that! It was my time. It had finally arrived, and I was ready for it. After all of the interviews that I had done previously with other airlines, I had an idea of what to expect and what they wanted, and I knew I could deliver. It was as though I was had performed in multiple dress rehearsals, which culminated in that very moment of sitting in the interview with American Airlines. I had the outfit. I knew the hairstyle I needed. I knew how to best answer those questions. I was prepared. And best of all, I got the job!

From that point on, I have traveled the world as a flight attendant, and have grown fond of a little country called Trinidad. It became my stomping ground. I eventually bought a house in Conyers, GA, but in my heart was in Trinidad, which felt like home whenever I flew there. I fell in love with the country of Trinidad and Tobago. I loved the culture, the food and of course Carnival! I would always say " One day, I will live in Trinidad". As the story goes, one day I met a guy who "happened " to be from none else than… Trinidad. We met in Atlanta, but both agreed one day we would move back to Trinidad. By that time, I had been flying for quite a few years, and Trinidad became the route that I flew.

Carnival revived the dancer in me, and it energized my soul. No matter who you talk to, even to this day, they know how much I loved going to Carnival in Trinidad. I found the most authentic part of myself there, including my passion for dancing, being playful and taking on adventures. All of me was accepted there. It was more than anything

I could have ever imagined. I remember the first time that I went to Carnival, I didn't know anything about it. I didn't even know where I was going to stay. In fact, the day before I went, my mother asked, "So were you staying?". I literally had no idea, but I knew that Carnival was definitely for me, and I knew that when I get there I'm going to find somewhere to stay. Surely there are plenty of places to stay. Then, before I even landed in the country, I remembered I had spoken to someone months before, and they told me that if I ever got stuck in Trinidad "here's my number."

So, I landed, and I called their number. They answered the phone, and I said, "I don't know where I'm going. I don't know what I'm doing, but I know I'm coming for Carnival."

The voice on the other end said, "I'll pick you up. No worries."

The people in Trinidad have always been welcoming, loving and a big part of my life. But, I didn't really discover myself until after I got married. Remember my Trini-boyfriend earlier in the story? Well we got married, had kids, but we were currently going through a rough patch in our relationship. His aunt had invited me to come and stay with her in Trinidad, and after 13 years of not knowing how to get to Trinidad and how I could build a life there, I figured it out! I knew that's what I wanted, and I needed to let go of everything that had been holding me back and live my dream. Soon, I found a piece of land there, and I was determined to build a house on that land. I built a 12x12 room onto an in-law's house. I put a sink, a shower, a toilet, a makeshift closet, a bunk bed, and a ceiling fan. I hung some curtains and moved all our belongings in, that was home for 5 years.

With every paycheck I bought bricks and cement. Paycheck by paycheck and brick by brick, my house was being built. I did it mortgage-free because at that point my husband I had separated and eventually divorced. I was a single mom for the first time, and that responsibility of doing this all on my own was a heavy burden. I did not know how I was going to pull myself together. I had sunk into a deep depression. But Granny Myrtle always had a scripture or words of love to encourage me or remind me of how well I was doing. I didn't lose hope completely, because I have always believed that everything in life, even the greatest

challenges, is an opportunity to learn a lesson. Some things in life are teaching lessons, and some are tests. one piece of advice that has never left me, "When you change the way you look at things, the things you look at change." Wayne Dyer

No matter what life has thrown my way, I have refused to give up on the life I have been given.   Even though it took many, many years of repeating some lessons, I learned a little more each time, and I collected those little lessons until they finally culminated into all the tools I needed for success.   You have to be willing to sacrifice and dig deep enough to even find the lessons and solutions to experience more in life.

We only have one life to live, so wouldn't it be great if there were people around you who could help serve as your guide as you go through these different levels in your life and approach different challenges and learn various lessons? Well there are, and these are your mentors, teachers, coaches, and trainers.   I have become passionate about sharing my lessons, and now as a public speaker, I feel a responsibility to pass on my knowledge of the lessons I have learned to others, so they can accelerate their process of growth.

Lesson 1: The light at the end of the tunnel

I hold strong to the idea that I'm just in a tunnel when things get dark in life. It feels uncomfortable, gloomy and maybe even like there's no hope, but I know that all tunnels come to an end, and at the end there's light. When you hold firmly to that, don't ever let go of hope and push through to the end of whatever lessons you need to get through. At the end of the tunnel, you level up into the light.

Lesson 2: Commit to joy

I know that at all times I need to be the strongest person that I could be for my children. Just like my mother was to me, and the many single mothers before me. No matter how tough life gets, I must never lose sight of who I am and what I enjoy, because my kids will see that, and will learn from it. The happiness of my kids all begins with me. I'm their greatest leader and teacher in life, and I take that responsibility very seriously. I embrace joy, and others can feel it when they're around

me, and my children feel it and learn it from me. Joy is a gift and it's a commitment—one that we give to ourselves, our families and the world we live in.

Lesson 3: Deal with challenges quickly

Too often, we work too hard trying to avoid challenges in life because they're difficult and painful. Honestly, that's why so many people turn to crutches like alcohol and other drugs—they try to delay dealing with the pain of life's challenges by getting drunk or high, but in the end, that problem is still there. Just because you've ignored it, doesn't make the problem go away. More often than not, it just causes the problem to grow. Sometimes, out of one's control. It starts to infect other things in your life like your relationships, finances and even your mental health. I was determined that if a problem came in my life I wanted to recognize it for what it was and come up with the best resolution for it as quickly as possible, that way I could get past that level and move up to the next.

What I want people to know most is that everything you dream is possible. You have to start from the end, of course, which is the easiest way to plot out a course on a map. You start from the end—where it is that you want to go, and then you figure out your best route. Your dedication and energy will ensure you reach your goal. Sometimes you will come to forks in the road. Sometimes there will be stumbling blocks or boulders. You may even walk yourself into a cave or two. Those are times that you must remember your map is your vision.

Life makes sure doors to opportunity open at the right time, but it's your responsibility to be prepared to walk through them when that time comes. I love having the privilege to speak to those that have been in a similar situations as mine. By speaking the truth of my lessons learned in life, I am able to open that door just a bit for those in my audience.

Ashonda Claxton

has a unique pedigree by virtue of her unconventional upbringing in a family that includes a number of nationally recognized carnival performers. Because her family was capricious, often moving great distances across the country, she has developed the strength and resolve to adapt and overcome any adversity that she encounters.

The skills that Ashonda developed growing up have allowed her to maintain her calm and control in any circumstance. This has been especially important in her position as a flight attendant for the last 20 years. Ashonda thoroughly loves the opportunities that come with flying, including meeting new and interesting people, as well as visiting exotic locations.

Ashonda has continued to evolve herself and has become a strong role model for those in her family, as well as others. Finding success after divorce and strength while being a single parent, she continues to light the way for others. Ashonda has a passion for people, self-improvement and personal growth, which has inspired her to spread her message as a successful motivational speaker.

To learn more about Ashonda and her motivational speaking services, go to:

www.WorkWithAshonda.com/speaking

What Have You **Forbes'd** Lately?

My name is Bob Martinez, and I Forbes'd colleagues, consultants, mentors and friends to travel with on this journey of amplified success. Establishing, sustaining and growing your own business is tough work. But when you gather together great minds with experience, knowledge and dedication, everything great begins to happen. When you have a coach like Forbes Riley, challenging you to step up and never settle for anything but greatness, success is destined to be yours!

Business Disaster
RESTORATION

By Bob Martinez

Through my early life my financial destiny had been dictated by others. But my drive and passion to succeed as a businessman inspired me to take control of my success. I did not know exactly how I would achieve it, but my quest for a better quality of life sent me on a path filled with many obstacles, where I had to learn and evolve my mindset and business skills, while leveraging outside resources. I fought to blaze my own path to success, and it paid-off with a highly successful business and a life of my dreams.

My journey as an entrepreneur began in the auto body business. For 12 years I grinded, working on a commission basis. The amount of money I made was determined by how much work I could finish in a day. Unfortunately, the availability of that work was dependent on someone else, the salesmen/owner, which was frustrating because there were days we had nothing to do. As time went on, I started making less and less money. I saw the writing on the wall. It was time to make a career change.

I always considered myself a "clean freak". In fact, every 6 months I used to hire someone to come to my house and clean the carpeting and furniture. I knew I was onto something, and I was motivated, as I was having a difficult time paying my bills, and I was frustrated with

the banks telling me that I couldn't get a mortgage loan because my paychecks fluctuated too much. It was time to leave the auto body business. Head on into the business of carpet and upholstery cleaning I went.

Full of enthusiasm, I immersed myself into this new field of business. Not only did I take classes on carpet and upholstery cleaning, I got a job with a carpet cleaning company. This company lacked business ethics, and used "bait and switch" tactics on its clients to increase its bottom line. I clearly recall my instructor at the time teaching me their business model, which consisted of cleaning a client's carpet and furniture with only water, and then upselling them with cleaning pre-conditioner and deodorizer, as well as other services that they didn't want or need. While these unscrupulous tactics where inconsistent with my own strong sense of business ethics and belief in serving clients, I was able to acquire valuable insight into the fundamentals of the cleaning business, and in many instances the practices that I should NOT adopt in my own business. I learned incredibly valuable information, including where they sourced their equipment and cleaning chemicals, as well as business basics, such as how to formally establish my business and name, obtain a tax ID, open bank accounts, and acquire business insurance. What I was learning was great, but it was not putting money in my pocket, I was still working on a commission basis, where I only got a 50% commission for the cleaning jobs I completed. I needed out of this environment and grind. I was now armed with the knowledge needed to start my own cleaning business, so I left that job after a week or two.

I was filled with passion, energy and incredible dreams of success upon the launch of my own cleaning business. After about six months, I realized that this business wasn't as easy as I thought it would be. While I loved working with customers and performing the actual cleaning work, lining up a steady and consistent flow of cleaning jobs was incredibly tough. Again, I was not earning a consistent paycheck and I was having trouble paying my bills. I seemed to be stuck in this cycle in every job I had. It was a hard and painful realization that I was right back where I was when I was in the auto body business.

Desperate to change this cycle, I had to figure out how to turn things around, but I struggled to develop a strategy to execute. Not knowing what to do, I dropped my prices thinking I would corner the carpet and upholstery cleaning market. I quickly learned I was wasting my time. Sure, I got more work being the cheapest, but I was practically working for free. I reacted by pursuing another strategy. I would advertise in the Yellow Pages. But the same thing happened. I spent about $1,000 per month on advertising, but my sales of new cleaning jobs did not increase.

I learned a very hard lesson about the carpet and upholstery cleaning business. Even though I was personally willing to pay a good amount of money to have my carpeting and upholstery cleaned, not many people were willing to spend that kind of money. With this lesson learned, I applied my resourcefulness and adapted. I began a search for other business opportunities to get into that use the same cleaning equipment I currently had. I looked at everything, from commercial janitorial services, commercial window cleaning, commercial carpet cleaning, commercial construction, remodels, and disaster restoration. I decided that becoming a disaster restoration specialist was the "right" fit for me.

While I had accumulated a lot of business knowledge thus far in my career, I still needed to learn a lot more, including how to effectively market my business, as well all of the other nuances, such as taxes, insurance, and accounting. To this end, I hired a marketing consultant that cost me more per month than my business was currently making. But he had an immediate impact on my business by implementing a marketing strategy targeting higher-end clients. I stayed with him for a couple of years. And during this time, I took classes on water-damage, mold-damage, and fire-damage cleaning to enhance my skills-I wanted to be the best.

I first started marketing my services to the insurance industry, and landed my first client after about a month. The average cost for standard carpet cleaning at the time was $90 to $100. My first water damage job as a disaster restoration specialist was a $1,000! It didn't take me long to figure out that water, fire and mold mitigation services was a much better business to be in than carpet cleaning. But once again, work wasn't steady, and I wasn't sure how to fix the inconsistency.

I continued to travel around the country taking disaster restoration training classes every month. I was committed to learning the intricacies of water, fire, and mold mitigation. I did this while still working and performing sales duties for the business. I even hired my first employee during this time, who I was lucky enough to have stayed with me for 10 years. Together we built the business, but it still wasn't an easy road to success. There were many slow times, and I got dangerously close to going broke once or twice. But I never gave up. I kept trying to figure out what I could do to bring me work.

Then, I found a mentor who was very respected in the disaster restoration industry. He taught me processes and techniques that were more effective and efficient than what I had seen in use in the industry. He also taught me that I had to watch my financial numbers. I needed to figure out what my profit margin was on the services I was providing. When he went through my books, he explained to me that I was losing money on some services, and pointed out the services that I was making money on. So I dropped some services that were not making me any money. He showed me the margins for water mitigation, and that was definitely in the positive. He explained to me that I needed to learn more about water mitigation, a specialty within disaster restoration, and focus on that line of work over carpet cleaning because that is where my profits were being generated. That's when I learned about specialization.

I decided to shift my business and stopped being a jack of all trades and became a water damage specialist. From that point on, my water damage business started to grow. I marketed my services once again to the insurance industry, and we kept growing the business. But it wasn't growing at a fast enough pace, and finding employees was difficult because, once again I didn't know how to hire qualified employees.

My consultant changed my mindset from taking all these training classes on carpet cleaning, upholstery cleaning, spot removal and every other aspect of disaster restoration cleaning, and to start learning about marketing and sales. I started reading books on the topic, really trying to understand the roadmap for getting paying customers and developing relationships with them. The consultant helped me do some

postcard sales. He even had me doing cold calls daily, which was very difficult for me. I fixed cars in the auto body business in a shop alone, by myself, so clearly pitching my business to others was not a skill I had yet developed. I remember the first day he had me do cold calls, it was incredibly nerve-wracking. I would go to a prospect's place of business and stand at their door. Some of the prospects had a "no solicitors" sign posted, and I thought that meant I couldn't go in to talk to them. I had not yet formed the right mindset for sales. My consultant, said, "You're not a solicitor; you're here to help them with your service. Get in there! Just give them a card, introduce yourself, and then tell them what you're doing and how you can help them...that's it." With this lesson and my growing knowledge of proper marketing techniques, my mindset shifted, and my business started to grow... slowly, but it started to grow. Two of the most important things that I took away from that consultant was the power of sales and marketing. "No matter how good of a job you do," he told me, "it doesn't matter if you don't have customers."

I continued on the path toward specializing in water mitigation, and I started watching my numbers closely. I continued hiring consultants and taking every marketing class I could get my hands on, whether it was a book, a three-day event or any other resource. I learned to listen and connect with people's emotions, so I could give them what they want. I also joined a group of contractors from around the country. We would meet, and discuss our businesses. I met business owners that were doing anywhere from $2 to $10 million annually. Some of them were profitable and some were losing money. It was a broad spectrum of numbers from the group as some were making $2-$10 million, and others were making a $100,000-$150,000 a year. As we sat around the table, throwing around ideas, I was listening to some of these big players who were losing money with some of their subcontractors and other outsourcing. I suggested that they scale back or renegotiate to get their spending under control on these costs. Some listened, and when I checked in with them many months later, they were still in business. However, a couple of the larger companies that didn't listen to my advice ended up going broke even though they were doing $7-$10 million a year, due to their high costs and their low-profit margins. That was another learning point, that it's not about the top number or gross revenue. I don't care if I do two million dollars a year if I'm bringing

home the money I want. You could be bringing in $5 million dollars a year in gross revenue, and only net $50,000 a year in take-home profits.

In 2008 the economy changed. Houses were being foreclosed on, and people were entering into short sales. They would file insurance claims for damages incurred to their home, but the trend was for them to take the money and pocket it, without having any water mitigation work done. As a result, there was less work for us to do. Alternatively, if they had us do the work, they simply would not pay us. We didn't realize that some of our customers had their houses in foreclosure or were doing a short sale, so they didn't care about making repairs, as there was no investment for them to be interested in protecting. During this time, we lost money again, thousands of dollars, which required us to go back to the drawing board and change how our business operated.

Many of my friends went bankrupt during that time because they were running too heavy with high costs and low-profit margins. Fortunately, I was running lean. Most of my equipment was paid for, so I was able to weather the storm, and I learned to hire consultants and cultivate ideas from others. I implemented the business and marketing strategies I learned through classes, books, and consultants. I can't stress how incredibly valuable that has been. It has been clearly evident over my years in business that when I don't invest in my continuing education my business suffers, and when I do invest in myself my business grows.

Because of the incredible results my business has achieved from implementing what I've learned, I been able to better myself and the business. So, even after 21 years of being in business, I continue to improve and implement new strategies to meet the changes in my industry, so that I can continue growing and evolving my business.

Lesson #1: Learn and Adapt

One of the most important things I learned is that you can never stop learning, because the market is always changing, and you have to adjust to it. If you do not, you will die.

Lesson #2: Ask for help

You're always going to need some sort of outside help. I'm a big believer in hiring the best accountants, good lawyers, and good consultants. The best is never going to be the cheapest. I'd rather spend the money needed to access the top tier than the bottom. It's easier to do one job right the first time than to do it over ten times until you get it right. That translates to how I think of my own business as a specialist, too. I'd rather be an upper-tier business, such as Nordstroms, rather than play in the low-end, so I need to make sure my business is known for quality service, which keeps my brand valuable. Hiring the right people to support this effort makes all the difference.

Lesson #3: Help others

Mistakes in business and in life can really be costly, and I truly want to help others and to let people see that we all have similar troubles, which have real solutions. When it comes to business, it's not smooth sailing, but as long as you are continuously learning and applying what you've learned and help others to succeed then anything is possible.

Bob Martinez

is committed to helping others recover from devastating loss as the the result of natural disasters. As a disaster clean-up specialist since 1996, he has single-handedly helped thousands of businesses and homeowners recover from water damage and other disasters. Bob's experience has exposed him to many inefficiencies, misinformation, and lack of systemized strategies on managing a disaster scene that are pervasive in his industry. Armed with this knowledge, he developed his own industry leading best-practices for executing disaster clean-ups.

As a visionary, Bob knew his peers were in need of his expert knowledge, and that a higher-level of disaster clean-up training was necessary. To this end, Bob is currently developing a program to teach his best-practices to a certified network of disaster clean-up specialists. This will allow him to fulfill his goal of helping even more people who are struggling to recover from disasters in the most effective manner possible.

Bob's supreme skill in the disaster clean-up industry has resulted in his being recognized as the "King of Clean-Up". His ability to remain calm and in control as a disaster clean-up unfolds, while caring for his clients personal needs as they face devastating loss and uncertainty is unparalleled.

To learn more about growing your business or
expanding into the water remediation field, contact Bob at:

waterdamage96@gmail.com

Everything changes when you change!

- Jim Rohn

What Have You **Forbes'd** Lately?

My name is Chuck LaDouceur, and I Forbes'd my partner and dear friend, Forbes Riley. I found myself bouncing around in a variety of jobs and occupations, sometimes very successful but often feeling a little lost. Then, I met this magical person who has launched an actual movement to empower others, help them identify their dreams and give them the tools and support they need to go out and achieve their heart's desire. And she has invited me to join her, giving me life to my purpose, and I'm so grateful.

A *Father's Heart*

OF GIVING

By Chuck LaDouceur

L ife is a complete unknown. You simply never know what is going to happen next. You cannot figure it out. It is impossible. One minute you are amazed by your accomplishments, and the next minute you are neck deep in your own self-loathing, contemplating what all went wrong. I have learned that the key is to never stay "stuck" in any one "place", no matter how good or how bad, always keep moving forward and growing. The only constant in life is "change" and your ability to evolve will ultimately determine how successful you will be in life.

There was always pressure to decide what it was you wanted to do with your life by the time you graduated from high school. It was stressful to say the least. We didn't have counselors back then to help decide or point you in any direction. So being my pragmatic self, I knew that no matter what happened around me, everyone needed to eat, so the cooking industry was a career path I was going to conquer.

When I graduated from high school, I immediately left Omak, Washington and moved to Spokane to begin my education at culinary arts school. I spent the next 3 years learning all aspects of the restaurant industry, from waiting tables to cooking, along with the importance of the financial side of running a business. I thoroughly enjoyed culinary

arts, it really resonated with me and allowed me to express my creative side.

Upon graduation, I got a job at a Denny's restaurant in Spokane working the graveyard shift. I cooked for all the bar crowds, it was certainly interesting, but it definitely was not my "dream" job. I wanted more, so I moved to a small town in Southern California by the name of Borrego Springs. Here I worked at two different private country clubs for a period of 10 years. This was a wonderful time because I had the opportunity to express my creativity through cooking. In fact, there really wasn't a budget to be limited by. Everyone who was a member of the private country clubs came there because they wanted something that they could not get anywhere else, and I was able to provide that! It was awesome, and I was extremely passionate about my job. Unfortunately, the effort and energy I put into that job to perform at my highest level of execution did not match the level of compensation I received. I was disillusioned, as it seemed that this was a systemic problem in the cooking industry.

I was ready for more, so I reinvented myself, and moved out of Borrego Springs to a town just outside of San Diego, California. There I went in a completely different direction from culinary arts - I went to school to get my Series 7 broker license. Yes, I was going to be a stockbroker!

For a period of 6 years, I worked at two different brokerage firms helping people realize their dreams through investing in both short-term and long-term Investments. I found my true passion doing quick short-term investments for people. It was an adrenaline rush of pure excitement dealing with such large amounts of money every day. I also did venture capital investments, where I had a small group of investors that would invest large sums of money into short-term projects to get a company started. This would yield a great return for the investors, however, there was great risk as well.

My investment team soon found our niche doing short-term investments for casinos around the world, from Caracas, Venezuela to Cripple Creek, Colorado, where we funded the opening of smaller casinos. We had attorneys that would file all the paperwork for us, and towards the end of my 6 year stint of being a stockbroker one of the attorneys had

failed to file paperwork needed to sell these securities in the casinos. As a result, we were charged with selling unregistered securities, which ended my stockbroker career. I was devastated, but not down and out!

I had a little money saved up, so I didn't need to rush into anything right away, but I found myself trying to figure out what to do with my life. Although I wasn't cooking anymore, and I couldn't help people with their investments, I still had a passion for helping people. I just needed to figure out how.

Over the next 10 years, I found myself working at myriad jobs, from Dreyer's Ice Cream, Lasting Impressions siding and windows, Sears siding windows and fencing, to a variety of different sales companies.

While I was a stockbroker I got married and had 2 kids. And because I was at a crossroads in my life and I did not know what direction I wanted to go with my career, I decided that I would move back to Washington to be closer to my family. So I moved to Seattle where I worked for Dreyer's Ice Cream. During this time, I realized I was no closer to my family living in Seattle than when I was in California. I wanted to raise my kids in a small town, so I figured why not the small town where I grew up. So I packed everything up and moved back to Omak, Washington.

Again I recreated myself, and jumped right back into the cooking industry where I worked for a sole proprietor at a very small restaurant in Omak. This was very short-lived because I quickly found out that working at a private country club with a limitless budget versus working for a sole proprietor at the small restaurant were totally different. I did not enjoy working at the small restaurant as it had a very tight budget and absolutely no room for my own imagination, so I left.

I then went to work for a company, called Lincare, they provided in-home respiratory care to individuals. I found myself absolutely in love with this job because it allowed me to reach out and really help people in serious need, and it was so gratifying. It allowed me to enter into people's homes, and help them on a very personal level during one of their biggest times of need. I was responsible for providing them with all their respiratory care needs right before the end of life. Again, the

only problem was that my compensation didn't seem to be equal to the responsibilities that were demanded of me on a day-to-day basis, so again I started looking for something more.

I ended up back in sales where I worked for a liquor and wine company by the name of Southern Wine and Spirits. I loved the job because I didn't have to answer to a boss every day and I was able to be creative when it came to selling liquor and wine to stores.

Looking back at my life, it seemed like I bounced around a lot from job to job not really knowing what my true passion in life was. But having gone through that journey I had the chance to find my true passion and purpose. It was at Lincare, where I found that helping other people and making other people feel better about themselves is what fulfills me and makes me whole.

I eventually stopped working for Southern Wine and Spirits, and joined a number of different multi-level marketing companies mainly focusing in the health and wellness industry. I knew that was one way that I could reach out to other people and make them feel better about themselves. The first multi-level marketing company that I was in was a company that focused on healthy chocolates. This was a company that I thought would take off because everyone likes chocolates, and if people could eat chocolate and feel better and be healthier, then that seemed like the perfect match. I quickly grew that company for myself to well over 500 people in my downline. Then one day, to my dismay, I woke up to find that this company I had been so successful with no longer existed. The owner got tired of running it and shut the doors, and my paycheck got cut off instantly! I would not be deterred, and I quickly found another multi-level marketing company in the area that created a health-based shake.

Soon after I joined this company, I had heard about this famous woman by the name of Forbes Riley who was creating an infomercial. Forbes was representing the company that I was working with to help grow my income, so I thought I'd better do what I can to meet her. I had to find out more about this lady, so I looked her up on Facebook and messaged her to see if I could get to know her better.

Within a few weeks we connected and she invited me out to her television Production Studio in St. Petersburg Florida to attend her Pitch Mastery class as a VIP. I told her that I could probably bring about 16 people with me, and she told me, if I did they would all be VIPs and be treated first class the entire time.

We all arrived at the studio and Forbes welcomed us all with open arms, as if we had known each other for years. During the class, she had started this "what do you want" exercise when she brought me up on stage and asked me "what do you want" and laid out the rules for me. You can't repeat the same answer twice and it forced me to get down to the heart of what I wanted. At that time I really wanted a better relationship with my kids and my new wife-that is what I wanted! It was at that moment I realized I had fallen in love with the message that Forbes delivered, and I knew I wanted to be a part of her world. I then realized this is how I could actually get out and help people in the way I truly wanted. I knew that if I could somehow team up with Forbes, and get her message out to help people become the best they could possibly be, then that is where I would truly flourish. Not only would I help other people grow, but it would help me grow to be a better person as well. This is where I found my true passion.

By the end of the event, I walked up to Forbes and looked her in the eyes and said "I don't know how and I don't know when but somehow you and I are going to work together." She looked back at me and said, "I know" as if she had known it all along.

From there, I just kept showing up at her different events, volunteering to help her in any way possible. I knew that this was the one way that I would be able to work alongside her. It was at a Zoic convention that she finally pulled me aside and suggested that we work together on a full-time basis. I probably didn't show it at the time, but I was jumping up and down and screaming on the inside with excitement and anticipation of what the future had in store for me.

A few months later I flew to Tampa Bay, FL from Spokane, WA and began working with her and putting together what is now known as Forbes Factor Live.

I think one of the most gratifying feelings I get is when I first see everyone come into Forbes Riley's TV studio on the first day knowing how different they're going to be when they leave. I get as much out of each event as everyone else does each and every time that I'm there. My life has been an incredible journey, with many twists, but this has been, and continues to be, the most gratifying thing I have done in my life!

P.S. As this book is going to print, I have one last note about the miracle of Forbe'sing something. I just Forbes'd listing my house on the market in Washington State, remarkably sold it in one day, packed everything up and moved to St. Petersburg to join the Forbes Factor Team. Within 2 weeks I purchased a new house and had it completely set up ready to move in a few weeks later. As long as you stay focused on your task and don't let anything pull you away, you can accomplish anything no matter what others say or do.

Chuck LaDouceur

is a member of the executive team of Forbes Riley Enterprises. As a former chef, stockbroker and real estate agent, he brings a unique perspective and a vast knowledge of sales and leadership to the table. Throughout his life, Chuck has reinvented himself many times over. This has allowed him to find that his true mission is to help people seek personal growth and to assist them in finding the real version of themselves.

His caring and thoughtful nature serve as a critical asset when supporting those who embark on the difficult journey of self-improvement. Chuck's attentiveness to each and every client to ensure they are acquiring the skills needed to make their mission of personal growth a success is second to none. Never content, Chuck continues to grow his skill set in the personal-growth arena and is committed to finding even more ways to assist others on their journey to becoming the best that they can be.

To learn more about Chuck, go to:

www.ChuckL360.com
Chuck@ForbesFactor.com

What Have You **Forbes'd** Lately?

My name is Cindi Mirkamali, and I Forbes'd living in truth, even when there's a cost, because the real reward is my freedom from other's dark secrets. Every day is a gift, and to live a full, happy life requires a decision and action that includes work, dedication, and discipline. The work for happiness is not painful—it's simply a shift in mindset. When we keep smiling continuously and keep the joy flowing, fulfillment comes into our lives. Tomorrow is not promised to anybody, and in that, we find grace. I must practice and remind myself that happiness is a choice, and the choices we make are the key to success.

Daddy's Little
SECRET

By Cindy Mirkamali

***W**hat is your secret?*

We all have a secret, don't we? Maybe your secret is something that has happened to you, or maybe you did something you are hiding, like cheating on a spouse or living a double life? Maybe you're hiding something that you did when you were young, like shoplifting or cheating on a test? Your secret might even be much more painful. Maybe someone abused you or mistreated you, and you never told anyone about it. No matter your secrets, some of us have been hiding a secret for a long time, and these secrets often affect us deeply and can even influence how we behave and the choices we make.

I had a secret that I was holding onto for over 20 years, and this was daddy's little secret that I felt obligated to hold onto, because of the bond that we shared. I grew up as daddy's little girl, and he was my world! He taught me how to play baseball and soccer, as well as many life lessons. I loved my dad.

This was in sharp contrast to my relationship with my mom—she and I were never close. My mom was very unhappy, overweight, angry, and generally, she was just a miserable person. She would take great effort to find things to yell about, often losing her temper. My brother and I would do our chores around the house, and she never missed an opportunity

to rant about how we did them. For instance, my mom would check our clothes drawers, and if something seemed out of place, she'd dump all the clothes onto the floor and would make us put everything back, neatly folded. Mom made it very difficult to get close to her—in fact, it was uncomfortable at best.

When I was growing up and entering puberty, I had many questions, but I was afraid of asking my mom, as I was afraid she was going to yell at me or make me feel stupid for asking questions, so I asked my dad instead. Dad decided at one point to show me some "things" rather than tell me. I would be in my room getting ready for bed, and he would call me to his room. He would tell me this is "our little secret." I soon learned that I didn't want to go to his room—I hated it. I didn't know what to do, and I felt so disgusted and ashamed.

My mom worked nights at a clothing store, so she was not home when these encounters happened. I remember that my dad always said "this is our little secret," and he would wash me up afterward. I hated him for this. He destroyed my self-worth, and I was so ashamed of myself. My self-confidence was so damaged, I couldn't even walk in front of popular kids in school without feeling worthless. I felt like everyone was staring at me all the time, like I was a freak. Once I actually understood what was happening to me in my dad's room, I didn't go to his room anymore. I just tried to bury that "little secret."

Then, one day, 20 years later, something broke inside me, and I learned that my step-daughter was molested by her aunt. Seeing, or maybe it was actually knowing, what my step-daughter was going through really disturbed me, and I felt that this was the time to finally expose "daddy's little secret."

It was during Thanksgiving, when we all came together as a family that I shared the horror of daddy's "little secret" with everybody—I just couldn't hold it in any longer. I felt it eating away at me. My family did not believe me. My dad sat in shock that I exposed his little secret, and he completely denied what he did to me. My family believed him—they would not accept that my dad could have abused me. I was heartbroken, devastated. Not only did I have to live with the shame and guilt of this experience all of these years, but now my family did not believe me. I

was rejected. My family basically disowned me after that, refusing to believe the truth. It's hard to wrap my head around the damage that caused. In fact, the only person who did eventually, believe me, was my mom, but that wasn't as helpful as it might seem.

Months later, my mom came to me and asked why I didn't tell her when this was happening. I told her that my dad said it was our little secret, and I felt too ashamed and guilty to say anything. My mom believed me, but the damage was already done. My relationship with my family was never the same, but I guess that was okay with me. At least I was free from the secret and living in truth. I learned first-hand that pain can go deep, but living through the pain anyway is what makes you a strong person. I do blame my dad for what he did to me, and in a way, I've learned to thank him for making me the strong person I am today.

Lesson 1: Secrets keep your authentic self-locked away

One of the life lessons I learned is that secrets can keep you bound in this little box where the real "you" can't come out. You live in shame, and you feel worthless, but once you break free from the secret and push yourself out of the box and expose that secret, you will experience victory and freedom.

You'll be amazed at how great you will feel once you are released from the secret. You will not be bound to the shame that is not yours to carry. Some secrets you keep can determine who you are and where you will go in life. When you decide in your mind to break free from your secret and your limiting beliefs, you will not live in the shadow of your little secret anymore. You will have the freedom to achieve greatness, and your ties to your secrets will not keep you bound.

Only when you break free can you live a life of self-worth, being proud of the man or woman you have become. There will always be challenges in your life, but you only learn of your own resolve and resiliency once you unchain yourself from the lies and secrets that bind you. You must release your secrets so that you can be set free emotionally, physically, and mentally in order to be a great, amazing person you are meant to be.

The second life lesson I've learned is that life does not happen to you, it happens for you. I've been knocked down so many times, but I keep getting back up, and I never quit or give up.

In 2015, I lost my 24-year-old son and his girlfriend to a tragic motorcycle accident where they both died. They actually have a marriage made in Heaven, literally. My son went to his girlfriend's mom two days before the accident to ask for her hand in marriage. The mother said, "Well, we are Christians, and we need to know where you stand with God? We want our daughter to marry a Christian man."

My son said, "I'm angry at God, and I'm mad at God. He doesn't answer prayers, and He's not real."

So she took her time to minister to my son, and at the end, she asked him if he wanted to accept Jesus Christ back into his heart.

My son said, "Yes!", and he accepted Jesus back into his heart that night. So, my son and his girlfriend literally have a marriage made in Heaven.

I could have been destroyed after losing my son two years ago, and I'm a little surprised that I wasn't. But for God!! He is my rock and allowed me to call upon His name to give me the strength to speak at my son's funeral. But let me take you back quite a few years ago when I was 23 years old when I lost my first husband to cancer. I saw this healthy man 6'2" 200 pounds waste away to nothing, skin, and bones, and then die. Then, years later my mom was dealing with diabetes and was on dialysis. She did not take care of her health, and then one day she developed a bed sore on her back that grew into this really large sore that looked like a shark bite. She had no other option but to have another surgery and then be on her stomach for a minimum of a year.

She said, "No thank you. I am not going to do another surgery and then be on my stomach for a year." So, she stopped all of her medications and her dialysis, and she let her body fill up with fluids. A week later she took her last breath, and she passed away.

Then, my dad got colon cancer, and he passed away. A few years later, my brother committed suicide while I was helping him move from one house to another while having $30,000 of cash on hand. Imagine that, I never understood why my brother committed suicide.

About two years after that, my son passed away on October 2, 2015. This was the hardest time of my life, losing my son. But I want to tell you this, it doesn't matter how many times you get knocked down; what matters is that you get back up and press forward each time. You have an option, and you have a choice to make. You can stay in a downward spiral where you're going deeper and deeper into a pit of depression and anguish, maybe even not wanting to live anymore. Or you can change it to spiral upward into a cyclone, becoming greater and greater and greater, stronger and stronger, and living your life with purpose every day.

The choice is yours to make, and just as I had to make a choice to move forward and to be thankful that I'm alive. Every day is a conscious decision to choose gratitude and purpose. Now, when I think of my son, I ponder on all the good memories we had and the fact that I want to make him proud of me. I cherish the 24 years I had with my son more than I can describe. In turn, I encourage you to live your life to the fullest every day, and that's the third lesson that I've learned from life.

Lesson #3: Happiness and fulfillment is a decision

Every day is a gift, and to live a full, happy life requires a decision and action that includes work, dedication, and discipline. The work for happiness is not painful—it is simply a shift in mindset. When we keep smiling continuously and keep the joy flowing every day, fulfillment comes into our lives that we cannot explain. As we live every day as if it is our last day, since tomorrow is not promised to anybody, we find grace. This is the hardest lesson I'm learning myself. I must practice and remind myself of this each and every day; that happiness is a choice, and the choices we make are the key to success. You gotta keep that joy... you gotta keep that smile... you gotta keep that love... in your heart. Because if you don't, you can easily become depressed and lose all forward momentum, often getting stuck in place, and you can sink fast.

You must know that you have the power and life-force to pull yourself up and live an exceptional life, but it requires you to make that choice and do the work.

When you become aware of all of this, it's as if someone lifted a curtain where you can see the inner-workings of what makes people truly different—those who succumb to the pain of life and those who use their pain as a source of power. Then, you can start changing your mindset, and positive, powerful things just start to happen. When you think positively, speak positively and behave positively, doors start to open for you that allow you to achieve victory. So, smile in joy, and encourage someone else every day.

Enjoy your life, and pass it forward by making a difference in someone else's life. We all live life every single day, and we each die once. Make sure you make that dash count... You know, there's that line on someone's headstone that marks the day they were born and then the day they died, and there is a dash in the middle. You have the dash that symbolizes your entire life, and you determine what you make of the dash. So, live without regrets that you left important things and dreams and experiences undone, and live with fulfillment, gratitude, and joy. Maybe you desire to leave a legacy or you want to make a difference in someone's life. Whatever you choose, live with intention and make that dash count. Believe it so you can achieve it, because if you believe that you can achieve greatness, then you will.

Cindy Mirkamali

has demonstrated adept skill in overcoming obstacles in her personal life. She has operated a successful insurance agency for years, but her true calling is to see others succeed and become more in their lives. She applies her skills as an inspirational coach and mentors to help others escape what is holding them back in life. She is passionate about helping people get out of their mediocre lifestyle so that they can live life to the fullest physically, financially, and spiritually.

To learn more about Cindy and how she can help you, go to:

www.cmbiz.vcardinfo.com

What Have You **Forbes'd** Lately?

My name is Cody Iverson, and I Forbes'd being a successful entrepreneur. One of the most important lessons of being a successful entrepreneur is to be honest about what you do well and what you do not so well. If you're in a position where you can outsource a job, or can partner with someone who excels in that area where you're weak, this is almost always the better option, compared to just failing at the whole business because you're trying to do it all yourself. Partner up!

Entrepreneur at
HEART

By Codey Iverson

I always knew that I wanted to be an entrepreneur. Becoming a businessman in control of his own destiny was my obsession. I did not want to waste my precious time in school daydreaming of running an incredibly successful business. I wanted to live that dream-now! My vision for my future was vivid and clear. While I have been successful, the lessons I have learned in overcoming the many obstacles in my journey, and the mentors I have acquired along the way have put me in a position to make those daydreams I had in school a reality!

I was a triple major in Business Management, Marketing, and Studio Art in college. I didn't get my first job until I was a fifth-year senior. That job came as a surprise, and it was a result of me being curious and interested in people. In addition to being curious about others, I have found that it's important to be interesting as well, as it attracts people to you. This understanding of attraction landed me a tremendous opportunity, one that would usually take people several years of experience to attain. Once I started the job, it came easy to me, and I loved every moment of it. I really enjoyed working, so much so that I worked a lot of overtime.

Unfortunately, this job did not benefit me much in terms of monetary compensation, but I did gain tremendous amounts of experience. My boss gave me a lot of leeway, and I was able to make a lot of hard decisions and learned how to manage people. However, he was doing a poor job

of motivating and compensating me for my work. In actuality, he was taking advantage of me. There had been lots of empty promises, and I was essentially working for free since I was rarely paid. In my mind, I rationalized the job experience over the money, and I undervalued myself, which was a big mistake many of us are guilty of.

I needed someone who actually cared, and who was going to mentor me to the next level. It was during that time that I read my first book, Dale Carnegie's "How to Win Friends and Influence People." During school, I had never spent much time reading books. I had always skimmed over them, looking for just the answers I needed. This was the first book that I read cover-to-cover, and it taught me how to approach each situation with people with their best interests in mind. It explained the importance of starting a conversation with something positive and how that opens a person up to be accepting and willing to enroll themselves in what you have to say.

At my next job, I was fortunate to have a "good" boss who was there for me, and a mentor. His name was Mike Friday, and he treated me like a son. He cared and took his time to build a relationship with me to understand what I really valued. Not only did he care about me personally, but he challenged me directly. In Kim Scott's lessons, Mike would be considered a "Radical Candor", and he was my first mentor! He pushed me to get better and provided suggestions and solutions when pointing out where I needed to improve. He was not mean, but he was clear, and he wanted me to reach for higher goals and to become my ideal-self.

However, I didn't quite return the favor to him. During the time I was working with Mike, I wasn't fully committed, and I didn't put in much effort. I was able to work from home, and it's pretty obvious when you don't put in enough effort. When this happens and you're working for someone else, you end up disappointing them and yourself- it's not a great feeling.

It was during that time that I was trying to start my own business, and I had always known this is where I belonged. Although working for other people was great, it wasn't what I had wanted to do with the rest of my life. I ended up getting fired from that job with Mike, and it

was a completely mutual understanding. I told him, "I understand. I wasn't giving you what you needed, so I accept this." It was a humbling experience, but I've remained close friends with Mike ever since, and he actually became one of my customers later on.

In setting up my own business, I didn't do any market research. I didn't even know how to actually market online. In short, I was in way over my head. But I didn't let that stop me from building kick-ass branding and a great product! Despite this, sales were not coming in like a McDonald's drive-through—far from it! Without marketing knowledge, the future of my company relied heavily on cold calling. I hated cold calling, and my poor mindset at the time caused me to abandon this business because of it. I have learned that you need to work at your weakness until you are the best at it. Then you will likely love it, or at least not dread doing it every day. You can also subcontract parts of the job that you are not the best at to those who do those jobs well, and add to your success—like cold calling, marketing, etc.

Lesson #1: Outsource your weaknesses

If you're in a position where you can outsource a job, or if you can partner with someone who does excel in that area where you are weak, this is almost always a better option than just failing at the whole business because you're trying to do it all yourself. That is, if you can pay someone else to complete the job right now the way it needs to be done, you should get someone who can do it—this will speed up the process and get you the results you need. In fact, as a business owner, you should only focus on 3 key aspects of your job that contribute to the top 80% of your business success.

In my next entrepreneurial venture, I started a clothing company. However, the margins weren't high enough, and I didn't really know what I was doing yet. I thought that because everyone wears clothes it should be easy. Yeah, that didn't matter, even if they liked the shirt, it didn't bring them as much joy as their cell phone or watching a movie did. I realized that people buy for two reasons. First, because it makes them feel better about themselves, and second because it reminds them of themselves and tells others who they are.

After a few more businesses down the road, I eventually started growing my team, putting as much effort, time, and money as I could to give them the tools and resources that they need to perform at their absolute best. I learned that when you make your team better, you also make yourself better because it allows you to focus on the things that contribute to the top 80% of your business success. I found that the other 20% of my efforts didn't count for much, and were just mostly a waste of my time. Those are the areas and tasks that need to be delegated to your team. Wasted time is never made up, so consistently work with your team and invest in them to figure out more efficient ways to boost quality, productivity and efficiency. It's critical to achieve faster results, fail faster and find a solution that works faster. You're going to fail, so fail fast, and next time fail better till you find success!

If you're slow, and there's no direction, then you're likely not going to see these results, and it'll lead to a failure. With a growing team, I learned the importance of being a leader. Being a leader isn't about always being heard or being the one who gives orders. A leader is the one that listens, and it's important to say less and let your team come to the realization of what needs to happen to come to a resolution. It's more important to ask questions than to tell them, because people don't like being told things, and people are more likely to follow a plan that they devised themselves. This builds in ownership and accountability.

It can be hard for teams to accept at first, so it might seem more complicated than just barking out orders, but it's the right way to do it emotionally and intelligently in order to get consistent positive results, while empowering your team and letting them have a buy-in to their own success. The correct way to lead is to use emotional intelligence and guide them to their own answers by asking them questions. I learned this from books such as "The Coaching Habit" by Michael Bungay Stanier, "Primal Leadership" by Daniel Goleman, and "The Opposable Mind" by Roger Martin. Being a leader really comes down to the ability to plan, create relationships and realize results.

Lesson #2: Be a blue ocean

So, as I moved forward into my other companies, I made a transition into something that I did enjoy, and that was selling online. It was great,

and I was able to avoid cold calling, and I knew that I would be able to sell a little more quickly. So, in these companies I learned about the importance of creating a blue ocean in a world of many, many red oceans.

A red ocean is a market that is saturated with big sharks who feed on small fish, and as a result there are bloody waters to enter into as a new business. In order to really stand out, you have to create a blue ocean, for more information on this read the book called "Blue Ocean Strategy," by Renée Mauborgne and W. Chan Kim.

It had been almost two full years since I had my first job and read my first book, and I was on the right path, but not really getting anywhere significant in my life. I had not continued to improve myself. I wasn't reading, and I wasn't taking the time to reinforce daily habits that would help me succeed. I wasn't even improving my physical health and mental health, or my value. Once I did start to read again, and took the time to take care of myself, my life started to improve. It became obvious that if you want your life to improve, you need to work at it, and you need to be dedicated to it every day. It needs to be ingrained into who you are, because if you're not moving yourself forward, the progression stops, and you lose momentum and stagnate.

I finally created a blue ocean strategy for one of my companies, but I didn't know how to use Facebook for marketing. This time, I did look for someone who had these skills, and I bought their course on Facebook marketing. One of my mentors Ben Malol taught me that it is the tiny hinges that swing the big door. The ability to learn directly from Ben, from someone who has already succeeded, and to get his weekly input, was a massive experience that truly opened my eyes to a new way of thinking and operating.

This gave me the ability to really cut-out all of the nonsense that I went through trying to figure things out on my own. I was able to get the answers to what worked. More importantly, if you have a mentor, you're able to speak with them about real-life situations that they can help you overcome. When you don't have the answers and you don't have a mentor, you're going to have a very long and bumpy road to success, learning each lesson the hardest way possible, repeating mistake after

mistake and mending wounds. Alternatively, you can learn from someone who has already been there and done it, someone that can tell you what your next move should be. You'll still make mistakes, but you'll recover more quickly with better results much, much faster!

During this time, I also realized that I had too many problems with people from my past who were infiltrating into my present, current life. Your friends and family, they may be there for you, but they're not always there for you in the right way. Too often, they want to tell you what you can't do and what you shouldn't do, because they're afraid you might get hurt. Or they might believe that they can do it themselves, so they'll impose their limiting belief on you. A majority of my friends always wanted to have fun, and focus on doing things that don't matter, like playing frisbee golf or hanging out and drinking all the time.

I literally told them, "I'm going to spend a lot less time with you guys. I'm going to focus on making myself better and achieving my dreams."

A couple of them stuck around to support me, and a couple of them told me, "You know, there's a bunch of time to do that, and you should just hang out."

I quickly discovered that those are the people that don't really progress forward, and they don't really have a place in my life. It was pretty hard to say goodbye to some of my friends, but at the end of the day, a year later, it doesn't bother me at all, because they're still trying to do the same things and wishing for different results. All I could really do is tell them what I'm doing to get results, which could help them move forward, but ultimately, it's up to them. If they are not helping themselves, they will end up hurting you if you stick around them. Negativity and stagnation are contagious, and so is progress.

Lesson #3: Good habits lead to realized goals

In the beginning, it's important to have strict schedules in order to create habits and see results. Once good habits have been formed and results are achieved, you can allow yourself and your team more freedom and independence. I didn't quite get the difference between a goal and a

target at first, but knowing that difference is very important to ensure you apply the right formulas to success in achieving each. The difference is that a target is something that you'll achieve within the next day or week, and the goal is more of long-term outcome and an over-arching success.

Because goals are long-term and often have several corresponding parts to achieve them, it's really important for you to write down goals in the morning when you first wake up and then before you go to bed. That's because the last thought that you have before you go to sleep is the first thought you have when you wake up, and it helps to drive your subconscious to keep your focus. This goes for the feelings you want to keep hold of as well.

Many people will tell themselves, "You know, I need eight hours of sleep," when it's really not always necessarily true. Thus, if you get in the mindset that you need eight hours of sleep, and you're looking at your your clock, and you say, "Oh no! I only have 5 hours to sleep," you're already telling your subconscious that, "Man, I'm going to be tired and not perform very well," and you're going to wake up feeling tired, with low energy. But, if you're able to tell yourself before you go to bed, "Man, I'm going to feel great in the morning. I have this five hours of sleep, and that's great, so tomorrow's going to be a great day! I got this…" You will wake up feeling a lot better—energized, positive and ready to go. So, before you go to bed tonight, you need to set your mood for the morning. For me, it has been very important to map out my next day completely. In fact, I've mapped out a week-in-advance/content-for-every-minute, because if it's not written down, I don't have the ability to keep track of it.

In fact, writing down all of your thoughts and tasks is crucial in closing any open-loops in your brain. An open-loop is anything that is not complete or hasn't been written down, it's just a thought in your mind. Open loops take away subconscious energy that will potentially drain you. If you have too many open loops, you won't be able to perform at a high level, because your brain will keep trying to work on these unsolved things, and it will keep you distracted.

The other reason it's important to have your week fully-planned-out is that when things get added or if you fall behind, you don't feel like you can just push them off to the next day because your days are already full, and there's no room for it. That helped me create stricter deadlines and stay on track, which is critical to being able to produce at the highest level. The biggest mistake and cause of failure is underestimating how much time something is going to take to complete. Once you can estimate how long something will take to complete, you'll be able to see results and meet deadlines much more easily.

I certainly learned a lot through my various companies before finally finding success in a new business I had two business partners, and a small team of associates. In this business, I was dependent on a product that I didn't necessarily want associated with my name. So, at times it was difficult to really be happy with myself, and although I was making money to the tune of $130,000+, I was needed something more, something that I could put my face next to. I wanted to build a respectable brand with repeat customers. The importance of having lifetime customer value was something that this new company was lacking.

I came to discover that a business will die with a product that is only viral, and only has a short excitement period. So, with the success of this company, I was able to attend my first business seminar in Singapore, called the eCommerce World Summit. I realized that I had a long, long way to go, and although we were having some good success, and made some money, these other people that I surrounded myself with during this event were doing much, much more, and they had been in the game for a lot longer. It was the first time that I had felt like, "This is where I belong." These are the types of people that I want to spend my time with and learn from, to be inspired by, and share ideas with.

It was really great to be around a lot of people who are like-minded and have similar problems. It was refreshing, and I came back having learned so many new things. Prior to that trip, I thought we were doing great, and it showed me that I can never rest on my achievements, because you can never see what's around the corner. Businesses are living, breathing things. The person looking to steal your market and your money will work harder to take it than you will to protect it. So, you must treat your

business like it's your child or your puppy, and you have to feed it, train it, and give it the right knowledge. What you know has gotten you this far, but it isn't enough to get you to where you want to be. In order to get to where you want, you must continuously keep getting better, stronger and smarter, which comes back to your daily self-improvement, your reading, and your habits.

It was during this time that I read a book that has contributed to a majority of my success in terms of mindset, and that was "10X" by Grant Cardone. I learned so many really incredible things that weren't necessarily so obvious, but they are—once you see them, you can't unsee them, and you see them everywhere! I wasn't dreaming big enough. I wasn't thinking big enough, and in order to get to the level of the top 2%, I was going to have to dream and think a lot bigger.

To reach your highest potential, you're going to have to tell yourself that, "You deserve things that you never even thought of before." You're going to have to set goals like you already have them, so when you're writing your goals in the morning or at night, you would write them in the sense that you've already reached them. So, if you have a money goal, then you would say, "I have a net worth of a hundred million. Always 10X your original goal, so that way if you come up short on that large goal, you've already exceeded your original much smaller goal.

I also learned how to really sell myself, and the importance of being able to approach someone properly- always getting a "Yes" at the beginning of the conversation and agreeing with someone on the situation, as people don't like to feel that their ideas are bad, and they don't like to hear the word, "No." So it's important that you always agree with someone, and then state your opinion.

The most important thing that I learned from this book was that people who are negative are to be treated like they're toxic. Conversely, the power of positivity is something that's greatly overlooked. Something that I did with my team is positivity challenges, or the "no-negativity-challenge" where we'd set a clock timer for 24 hours, and we'd have to get through the whole 24-hour period without saying anything negative. It was definitely not the easiest thing, but it was really, really important for the environment and the culture of our team to keep progressing with

a positive attitude and finding ways to speak about a negative situation in a more positive, productive light, which would elicit solutions, rather than remaining stuck on a problem.

Always reach up, never down—the more that I reach up and the more that I surround myself with high-level players such as Facebook Guru Ben Malol and Forbes Riley. I met Forbes in Miami when I heard her speak from stage in front of 10,000 people. She moved, inspired me and more importantly, she taught me how to pitch myself, plus how I should always be enrolling people into my vision. The most important thing I learned from Forbes is that you have to be willing to break through your limiting beliefs, and that you must realize that you are enough to have all you want. This is the true blueprint to success. All you can do is improve on what already is inside of you, and there is magic there—true power!

I realized that I needed to keep reading, improving, building a team of experts and mentors, and connecting with like-minded people who are successful and who are ultimately reaching up. I know I would be much further along in my journey had I found a community that had all of these different types of mentors joined together as a team. I now realize that every decision I make impacts the bigger picture of my life.

It's a simple equation where spending an extra few minutes in bed in the morning could be the reason your car gets hit on the way to work. Had you gotten up and out of the house those few minutes earlier, you would not have been in that exact spot at that very time. So, set your goals far ahead, and get out of that reactionary state most people are in. Get as clear as possible on who you want to be 5 years from now, and reverse engineer what it's going to take each year to get there. Then break your action items down by month and follow it day by day until positive habits form. You will then be headed straight towards achieving your goals.

I wasted a year or more finding a formula that leads to success. For me, this formula has been a steady stream of work towards self-improvement, surrounding myself with successful people and building a team of experts in multiple fields so that I have access to answers to

help me achieve success in business and in life. Reach up, and work with those who are better than you, and support those on a similar positive path.

My current project is called "Massive Action", and it is all about igniting the fire inside of you, connecting you with like-minded people and the expertise you need to expedite your path to success. The simple fact is, to be successful in life, it is imperative to surround yourself with people who can open your eyes to what it takes.

Cody Iverson

has a passion for executing his vision in business. As an astute Internet entrepreneur, digital marketer and CEO, he has achieved much success. Cody gains tremendous satisfaction through helping others, and this is reflected in his commitment to providing his customers with products that improve their lives.

Cody is not content with becoming complacent with his success and is committed to constant improvement in both his mindset and technical abilities. He is a student of life and has a relentless passion for unlocking not only his own potential but the potential of others. Cody continues to expand his business empire, and actively spreads his message of personal growth and his blueprint for business success to others through his various initiatives, including his "Massive Action" project.

To learn more about Cody, contact him at:

www.ItsMassiveAction.com

A Friend loves you the way you are, Forbes Riley loves you WAY too much to leave you that way!

- Forbes Riley

What Have You **Forbes'd** Lately?

My name is Dr. Emily Letran, and I've Forbes'd countless opportunities. I've learned through experience that we can, and we must, create our own future. As I was growing up and going through extreme challenges, I didn't know that I was creating my own future by the efforts that I put in and by the intentions that I set. With my training and associations with people like Forbes Riley, Sharon Lechter, and many of the trail blazers in different industries, I've come to realize that I can create my own future and that I can just "Forbes" things as I need them.

Don't Just Survive...

THRIVE!

By Dr. Emily Letran

I was born in Vietnam in the late 1960's to a nurturing family, which included my mom, dad, an older brother, two younger siblings, as well as our extended family. It was a happy and loving environment inside of our home, but it was a stark contrast to the horrors we watched every night on TV—the Vietnam War. Terrifying images surrounded us, from bombings, dead bodies, and people fleeing villages in sheer terror. This was not your typical childhood for sure, but it's the only childhood I had. It was my "normal."

In 1975 Communists took over Vietnam, ushering in an era of darkness across the country. Not only were we frightened, but we were also hungry. There was not enough food and other essential items to go around. As a little girl, I used to stand in line for my family to buy whatever the government was willing to sell to us. It could be moldy noodles, old rice, or stale bread. I did not realize how challenging that task was for such a little kid, because that was just our way of life at some point, and we all had to do our part just to survive.

Then, the horror hit even closer to home. One year after the Communists took over our country, my mother passed away from cancer. I was eight years old. My mom, who was my rock, and my role model was stolen from me, and the trauma from that ran deep. I was so young and in

total shock but I did not have time to mourn or grieve. Instead, I had to learn how to take care of myself, quickly. The choice seemed simple to me as a little girl— survive or die! I wasn't alone—I still had my dad, brothers, cousins, and although I was a child, I was determined that we would not end here!

Three years later, in 1981, the Vietnamese communists were going to war with China in the North and Cambodia in the West, and they were drafting all the young men. My aunt decided that she was going to flee the country with her kids, determined not to lose her children to war. My dad thought it would be safest for me to go with them, and he explained to me that I needed to help her. It was a painful decision for all of us, but at the age of 13, I left my country and my dad. I headed out on a boat to America, and I never saw my dad again.

Many people in the United States have heard or read about the Vietnamese "boat people". I was one of them, and I lived through the nightmare of that treacherous journey. It was a fishing boat, about 50 feet in length with 60 people crammed together like sardines. The first two days we had some food, but during the last five days, we just shared sips of water. I remembered as we pulled away from the shore, shots rang out by the Vietnamese Coast Guard warning us not to leave, but they didn't stop there. They actually approached our boat, stopped us, came on board and robbed us of the meager items we had taken to survive.

That was the first time I witnessed first-hand the horrific spoils of war, and what my aunt and dad were so afraid of and were trying to protect me from. These were men who were supposed to protect us but they just rifled through our belongings, then at gunpoint stole whatever they wanted from us. It was humiliating, degrading and terrifying, but it did not stop us. In fear, we kept going with the knowledge that staying would be worse.

Seven days later, we landed at a Malaysian refugee camp. It was not quite the nirvana we had dreamed of—it was actually a deserted island the United Nations created with makeshift shelters, limited food, water, and electricity.

I think that because I was still a kid, I could find joy even in the worst situations, like this one. Rather than focusing on what we didn't have, we learned and practiced our English, and went swimming. I actually learned how to swim at that refugee camp. Imagine what it was like, being on that boat in the ocean for seven days, and not knowing how to swim!

Then, there were the stories told by the other refugees. These aren't the types of stories most children heard around a campfire, I'd imagine. These campfire stories would be etched in my soul forever. I learned at a very young age that sometimes when you think You have it bad, just start listening to others. In the glow of the fire, in the quiet of the night, I heard horrific tales of rape and torture, where people witnessed their loved ones being murdered right in front of them, their homes burned to the ground, and having all of their belongings wiped away.

Through all of this, I have arrived at an understanding that life happens "for you," not "to you". Maybe I have been guided by the memory of my mom, but I chose not to let the overwhelming human suffering I had witnessed and endured drag me under. It was in this remote refugee camp that I was tested the most, and I learned how incredibly strong I could be.

My mom was dead, and my dad was so far away. It hurt my heart deeply. I was still so young and my family, my parents, my protectors, and the ones who loved and cared for me the most were not there.

I remember walking on the beach every day looking West and I promised myself that if I survived all of this, I would create my legacy and build a family of my own one day!

When I came to the United States, I had no luggage. Hope and faith were all I had to bring to this new land. My aunt found us a place to stay and we all started school. I couldn't speak the language and we had very little money, but I was determined to make it through school. I started doing everything I could to stay ahead despite all of the challenges. I would stay up almost every night translating every single word of my homework from English to Vietnamese so I could understand what I was learning. I would wake up every morning at 5 a.m. for many years

to deliver newspapers, rain or shine because that was the one thing I could do to help my aunt add a little bit of income to the family.

My childhood was gone. I missed out on all of the activities and fun things in my new high school, as I didn't understand this new Western culture, and because I didn't have any money to join numerous school activities and functions. This was also a very painful time because I always felt like an outcast. But what got me through this was my mindset. I thought, "I'm just going to focus on what's most important to me, and I'm going to make the best out of everything given to me in life."

So, I did. I went from being a lost immigrant girl at 13 to graduating as Valedictorian of my high school class and receiving scholarships and grants to attend the University of California, Riverside. When I was at the university, I kept that same mentality. It was about focus. It was about knowing what I wanted and only concentrating on achieving my goals. I completed my undergraduate degree in three years, was in the honor society of Phi Beta Kappa, and graduated magna cum laude. Then, I went on to UCLA for dental school because I wanted to help people and I was interested in the healthcare field.

Over the next four years, I finished my dental degree plus a master's degree, which typically takes most people six or seven years to complete. The key to my achievements is that I'm always focused on the task at hand and how to get to my goals. Plus, I'm very specific about my goals—I write them down, and each day I remind myself how important my goals are to me. Regardless of whatever else is going on around me, I stay focused.

Understanding how to accept help from others is also extremely important in achieving your goals and so is gratitude. In this particular journey, I had so much help and I'm so grateful for it. We received help from the government so we could have free lunch at school. We were living in a housing segment where the rent was subsidized by the government. When I went to college, I received scholarships and grant money because of the financial status of my family. I was always keenly aware of how much help I had along the way that allowed me opportunities to reach my goals, and I maintained a firm commitment

that when I became able to, I would give back to my community and help others reach their dreams, too.

The commitments that I've made to myself throughout my life have helped shape the person I am today. When I finished dental school, I got a job and got married. I built a wonderful family with three beautiful children. I always think about my commitment to give back- I give back to my patients with abundant gifts and by taking care of them. I give back to the community, and every month we have a free dentistry day where we do free basic dentistry for our veterans and families with disadvantaged backgrounds. I always give my time to help organizations fundraise for various causes. I always say "yes" to helping people, whether it's connecting people who should meet to collaborate or share a hotel room at a conference to help people have better access to opportunities. Giving has become a part of the fabric that makes me who I am. It is part of appreciating what I have, all I've been given, all I've lost, and making the most of what I have, then give back when I can.

Yet, my journey has not ended. I've now transitioned from being a dentist to a speaker and a high-performance trainer and there is no difference to the method I use to achieve success. Being a successful speaker and a coach requires focus, determination, hard work, gratitude, community and giving back. In all things that are worthwhile, there's lots of learning and determination needed to push through the barriers, learning curves, and other difficulties. When I chose to transition my career from the healthcare profession to speaker and high-performance coach, I chose to help business owners and entrepreneurs maximize their potential, bringing out the best human superpower in them, and coach them to streamline their business to increase profit. My mission today is to help as many small business owners and entrepreneurs as possible, and I dedicate my focus, time, effort, and money to master this field and invest in growing my business to help others reach their goals.

I'm investing in learning how to build my skills as an effective speaker. Not only do I invest in mentors and coaches of my own, but I also sponsor speaking engagements so I can share the stage with big-name speakers to only accelerate my knowledge and career, as well as leverage

value for my audience. I do this because I understand that together we are far more powerful in creating the future we want in our world.

You also have to create your own opportunities. Not everything gets handed to you, and to experience real success, it has much more to do with your diligent work and ingenuity than luck, chance, or what others do for you. People will help you, but most of your success will be derived from the effort you put forth. I create my own stage and I put on my own events. I have superstar speakers come and support me because I understand the power of leverage. I understand that one person can only do so much, but together as a group we can create a great impact and help many more people than we can separately.

My goal today is to grow my speaking and high-performance coaching business to touch as many lives as possible. In my speaking engagements, I'm known for helping people come to understand that they are accountable to and responsible for themselves and their own success. Harnessing the power of personal responsibility and applying that to your goals is one of the most empowering stances you can take as an entrepreneur or business person. I help people discover that we each have a unique set of super powers already, and we just need to set those powers free and rise up to meet our potential. Plus, every one of us has a story—a powerful story that can break a heart, build up, and inspire everyone around us. If we collect all of these skills, focus them into creating the best, strongest versions of ourselves, we will uncover the strategy to accomplish everything we want.

Mentors, coaches, and trainers are invaluable in life and the journey towards success. The quickest way to identify where we're going and to have less distraction is to have a coach or a mentor guide you down that path. That's how I have reached so many of my goals with great success. My clients quickly experience this power, too. I have learned and continue to learn from so many talented, dedicated, and wildly successful mentors throughout my life and I eagerly pass this knowledge on in the world.

I am honored to count Forbes Riley among my most esteemed mentors. She has that big dream, too, to help people rise up and become the best version of themselves. Her dynamic character and tireless energy,

charisma, and knowledge are palpable when you're around her. She never holds anything back, and she shares all of the strategies that she uses to help people really unleash their potential in her events and coaching. What's astounding is her level of authenticity and vulnerability when she teaches others—because more than following a methodical curriculum, Forbes is far more intuitive, taking in the needs of the individuals in the room, and customizing each lesson she teaches to them. She helps so many people just by being herself and sharing her knowledge and wisdom to challenge each individual to reach their next level in business and life. I truly appreciate the opportunity to know Forbes and I feel so blessed to be able to carry on my mission side by side with her.

As a professional dentist for more than 25 years now, a speaker and high-performance trainer, I help people unleash the superhuman potential that is already within them and maximize that to more fully succeed in their business and life. I help people through this journey using my program, ACTION To Win, an engaging combination of high-performance habits and business strategies developed through my own journey, training and business experience.

Life Lesson #1: Strive to have clarity

To know what you want and how to get what you want is critical for success. I realized that throughout my life, I typically have a crystal clear vision of what I want. I was very focused when I was in that refugee camp. I knew I had to stay safe; I knew I had to learn English; and, I knew those were the important things for me to survive in the camp.

When I came to this country and started in high school, I knew I had to get ahead. Because I'm starting from the very bottom, there's only one way to go-up! But how fast could I go up? That was my challenge, to succeed as quickly as possible.

To do this, I stayed up late every night to learn English. When I was in school, I took multiple classes so I could graduate faster and be able to make money to help my family. My drive included a sense of urgency because my family needed me, and I learned that to accelerate success, clarity was paramount. In fact, it required clarity from multiple

directions: clarity on goals, on a plan of action and on sacrifices needed in the short-term to realize long-term achievement.

Life Lesson #2: Bring joy to life

Every one of us has challenges. How we perceive those challenges and what we do with them is what allows us to either grow or fall apart. For me, I always find joy and positive things in life, especially when that seems to be the most difficult task. In the refugee camp, my joy was learning English and going to the beach. And that's how I talked about the camp experience when I was in high school. My other joy was to be able to excel and to show my family, especially my aunt, that I'm doing well in school. I was able to show her that I'm doing my best and it brought me so much joy to be able to make her proud.

Today, when it comes to working with current clients, my greatest joy is to serve them. They trust me to lead them out of a place where they are not happy, where they may be stressed and challenged, to a place where they can look back and say: "I overcame that with the help of Dr. Emily." This journey for me is always about bringing joy to other people and helping others discover their joy in life.

Life Lesson #3: Commitment

Life isn't always very kind, and often it throws lemons at us. We need to be able to take those lemons and make lemonade. Okay, well, everyone knows that, right? Yes, but there's a deeper lesson to be learned in that allegory. Those lemons in life are not just good for lemonade; you can also take the seeds of those lemon and go grow your own lemon plantation. You can think bigger. Whatever life throws at you is a task for you to overcome and grow. Take your lemons, signifying hardship, challenges and even devastating blows, and make that into something positive, and nurture that into something even bigger. Think about how you can create a great impact on whatever life delivers.

For example, if you've overcome challenges and found success in your journey, you can help other people overcome their challenges. That's the big picture where giving back helps us all. Or, you can just say to yourself, "OK, I overcame that, I was good." You can keep your success

strategies to yourself, but I think the transformation and journey I've completed so far isn't just something to benefit me, alone. I embody a commitment. From my time as a little girl, having endured what I did, I've learned and thrived. I now can lead others to discover their greatness to push themselves beyond their current comfort zones. I now realize how much they can achieve with my help and I am very grateful to share my gifts with the world.

What have YOU Forbes'd lately?

I have Forbes'd opportunities for myself, and I've learned through experience that we can and we must create our own future. As I was growing up and going through those challenges, I didn't know that I was creating my own future by the efforts that I put in and by the intentions that I set. With my training and associations with people like Forbes, Sharon Lechter, and many of the trail blazers in different industries, I have come to realize that I can create my own future and that I can just "Forbes" things as I need them. I'm going to India for a week in September to speak, and then I'm going back there a second time with a follow-up event. I have also booked a speaking engagement at a women's conference, The Will Forum, and I have decided that I'm going to put on my own event while I am there to leverage my presence and help even more people along the way.

So the one thing that I will "Forbes" is going to be Dr. Emily's, "ACTION to Win" event that I'm hosting in Mumbai, India in December.

When I attended Forbes Factor Live with Forbes Riley, it was a unique experience—something far more personal and more deeply transformative than anything I've experienced at any other seminar. Forbes Factor Live is an experience. Sharing your story touches the lives of others and in turn, helps you grow. I think that's part of the genius that Forbes Riley possesses. She connects with people intuitively and gives them the opportunity to reach down to the core of their deepest barriers whether in business and life. One of the big lessons I took away from the event is that while everyone has a story, what you do with that story is your choice; she preaches, "Life happens for you, not to you!" We each tend to keep throwing the pity party about our stories, making tragedy a part of our identity versus something that simply happened

to us. "This happened to me 10 years ago... This happened to me 20 years ago," and so on. This negativity can prevent us from doing things like believing in ourselves, daring to dream bigger or experiencing joy. At Forbes Factor, I experienced miracles. Her unique training allowed people to break the chains of their past and reimagine their future. They shattered limiting beliefs that they had held for decades and the most amazing part was that they did it in minutes, not years on a therapist couch. This is a unique type of hope that I'm excited to share with anyone who has experienced serious trauma and wants to move forward in their life. I'm so grateful that something like this exists.

I know what you're thinking, because if I hadn't experienced it myself, I'd probably think the same thing, "This is too good to be true, right? In fact, this strategy of using our toughest stories to empower us is what I learned to do to survive and thrive through my own circumstances, even as a kid. Before I even learned all of these concepts in high-performance training, I learned to leverage my story to support my goals and push through hardship. In my high-performance training, I've learned to observe and pay close attention to the individuals in the room, and I've learned to encourage people and empower them to take ACTION for themselves, taking their lives to the next level of fulfillment and their business to the next milestone of success.

Dr. Emily Letran

has persevered in spite of seemingly insurmountable obstacles. The adversity she met growing up only strengthened her resolve to help others in life. To this end, Emily graduated with her D.D.S. and M.S. with honors from UCLA Dental School. For many years Emily has been a successful dentist, with her talents being featured in numerous publications, including Dental Town.

She has been a champion for those with disadvantaged backgrounds, providing dental services to those in need for free. Her compassion toward others, along with her business acumen, have been recognized in publications, including Global Women Magazine and See Beyond Magazine, as well as with various awards, including the Asian Woman Entrepreneur of the Year Award, and the Women in Red Award.

Emily continues to become a louder voice for those facing life struggles, and has expanded the reach of her message for personal growth. To this end, she has become a certified high performance life coach, as part of the High Performance Academy, where she provides coaching services to her growing following of loyal clients. Emily knows what it takes to overcome obstacles in life, and is committed to strategically applying that knowledge to help her clients take their success to the next level.

To learn more about Emily and how her coaching services can help you, go to:

www.exceptionalleverage.com/businessreport

What Have You **Forbes'd** Lately?

My name is Forbes Riley, and I Forbes'd THIS BOOK. I've had the honor and privilege to be surrounded by so many inspiring people who have touched me during my Forbes Factor Training with their candor, bravery, heart and drive that this book was born. Together we have manifested a legacy and a platform for these amazing leaders and dreamers to share and inspire the world so we may all benefit from their stories.

You Get What You
TOLERATE

By Forbes Riley

I began life as an actress, dancer, and dreamer. Along the way, I wrot books, gave great speeches and sold a lot of products on TV… over $2.5 Billion dollars worth! I've hosted Premieres at Hollywood Comedy Club, the Laugh Factory and introduced superstars like Ellen DeGeneres, Jerry Seinfeld, and Robin Williams. In a completely unrelated career turn, I co-hosted the original X-games with Stuart Scott on ESPN and became one of the most recognized faces in the world of infomercials. I hosted 180 of them, appeared globally and sold a billion dollars' worth of juicers around the world with the fitness legend Jack LaLanne.

They say…

You are the sum of the obstacles you overcome. When I first heard that motto, it was the first time my life made sense. It was the first time, the tragedies and trauma I had endured throughout my life, that are NOT mentioned when people read my bio, accolades, and awards, would turn around and become the fuel that would fire my future.

We all have childhood stories filled with memories: broken nose, frizzy hair, crooked teeth, braces for 8 years and overweight. I was bullied, lonely, and isolated.

My mom was 260 pounds – she was an only child from an oppressive religious and cultural background. My dad was a machinist, inventor, magician, and printing operator. He tinkered and had an otherworldly gaze like Willy Wonka meets the Nutty Professor.

And so, while my self-esteem and confidence were non-existent in school, I was smart and I was a dreamer. Addicted to movies and tv (such a blessing the internet had not yet been invented!!). I was a loner who had mad ideas about life, but kept them all to myself and just quietly DREAMED. I had to, just to survive. I was smart. Really smart. 2nd grade, I'm hanging with Principal Kilroy talking about schematics, building a computerized thinker-blinker and debating history and linguistics... I was only 8 years old. They put me in genius classes and while intellectually I could hold my own... I was the only girl and the only one without a pocket protector in my shirt.

I had no friends, played no sports, avoided gym class and ran from any sport that had a ball. Actually I didn't run... born premature, I suffered from lung issues and running made me cough and cramp. That mixed with my awkward eye-hand coordination just layered on the reasons the bullies had a field day with me.

In high school, I found a love for theater, dance and roller skating. And though I never got a lead role and often got stuck in the back as the Chorus or Townsperson #3, I never stopped dreaming I could be more. All of this, oddly enough, led me to a leading role on Broadway, opposite Christopher Reeve, a 30-year career on tv as an actress and host, and to being CEO of my own fitness company. The many other stories related to this won't fit in just this chapter— so I'll save some stories slated for the upcoming movie!

At 14, my dad was in an industrial accident in a printing press mishap, slicing off the front of his palm and fingers. It would take the next 3 years and 15 operations to get his fingers working and allow him to have limited mobility in his left hand. Financially and emotionally, it broke our family. And, at some point during his recovery, my mom got held up at gunpoint in our home. For two hours, two armed men went through our house and took everything of value that we owned, terrifying my mom.

Imagine coming home from school seing police everywhere and hearing sirens while thinking for a moment that your mom might be dead. I honestly reflect back and have no idea how we all survived the trauma, but we did.

For me, I think I survived because I had a dream. I dreamed that I could be more and make my life matter so my parents would be proud, have an anchor and perhaps get to enjoy their life again.

I started to perform just to see them beam with pride and smile. There was always so much hurt and frustration that I worked relentlessly to enjoy this life. I vowed to take them on a vacation, and made promises of more and more, and I did!

Lesson #1: He or she who dies with the most... does not win.

Life, as I reflect back on it, is a game made up of wins, losses, hills and valleys, tears and joys, and nothing else—it's a collection of memories in a book that only YOU get to choose.

In the beginning, you are told a lot of rules about how the game is played by people who have been playing it—and often not playing it very well. If they are happy, joyful people, that rubs off on you. If they are angry, frustrated people that rubs off on you too. But, ultimately it's always your choice what to focus on.

lesson #2: Life happens for you not to you

When you adopt this philosophy, you really do stop sweating the small stuff. Bad things do happen to good people—they happen to all people and there is true happiness when you turn everything into a lesson. I learned in my early 20s to start telling stories and find lessons in each of them.

I helped raise Dexter Ridout, a beautiful little boy from South Central LA as a black kid from a single mother. He came to us at 8, already programmed with a limiting set of beliefs about life and the world around him. It was my greatest joy to help shatter what he believed to be true about life, money, education and more. He talked with us, spent time staying in our home, and even served as best man at our wedding.

I loved him like I would my son. He would share stories about local friends, gang members, the shooting death of several of his friends, and I would hold him tight and promise him, HIS life was different because I was in it, because I believed in him and we had mapped out a plan for his future.

He never got there. His future was stolen from him on July 21, 2003, six months after I had given birth to my twins.

On a Sunday morning, my boy was walking, coming back from a haircut, heading to church, when a gang banger jumped out of a car. Dexter was wearing blue and that was the random target color. He walked up behind Dexter, shot him and unfathomable 10 times in the back and left him to die alone on the sidewalk. For no reason. He did nothing wrong. He didn't deserve to die. He deserves to play with my babies, grow up to have kids of his own and enjoy the gift of life so many take for granted.

So, life happens for you not to you, and I continue to pull these lessons out of the sky. I teach, preach and work hard to inspire others.

For me, some days are harder than others. Just writing this, I'm in tears even though this happened 16 years ago. I miss him and it hurts but life goes on.

Lesson #3: Find what makes you happy—that's all there is

For me, having my children, Ryker and Makenna, have been the blessing of my life and at times my salvation. I've poured all of my hopes, dreams, and lessons into these little guys, and they have emerged to be amazing teenagers, and I pray daily that one day I get to meet my grandchildren.

I love that I get to act in movies, perform in theaters and speak on stages with a drive to motivate and inspire others. I'm not sure the point of all of this — but I wouldn't have missed it for the world. May we all walk with faith, not sight and uplift those around us as often as we can.

Forbes Riley

is the ultimate renaissance woman! She shines brightly as one of today's most accomplished entrepreneurs, a highly sought-after product spokesperson, motivational keynote speaker, author and CEO of a fitness empire based around her signature product, *Spin*Gym.

She's hosted 180+ infomercials, co-host the original ESPN X-Games, hosted 2 National talk shows and 25+ years Guest Hosting on home shopping channels (QVC, HSN) worldwide.

Crowned as the $2.5 Billion-Dollar TV Host for outstanding and record-breaking record she now teaches what she knows and loves. Pitch Mastery teaches business leaders, sales teams and inventors, the power of the Perfect Pitch. Forbes Factor Live is her signature and is heart-centric training designed to help entrepreneurs unlock the limiting beliefs they have been holding them back so they can easily reach their highest potential.

Her mantra: Dream It, Believe It. Achieve It.

To connect with me go to:
www.ForbesRiley.tv

To attend a Forbes Factor in person go to:
www.ForbesFactorLive.com

What Have You **Forbes'd** Lately?

My name is Jerid Fenderson, and I've Forbes'd moving to St. Pete. The single most powerful force isn't thought, but action. Thinking in and of itself isn't even the first step, taking the first step is. When you can turn your thoughts into actions, you can turn your dreams into a reality. The "Forbe'sing" moment for me was getting my rundown, grandpa model, coolant sipping, oil eating, gas guzzling pick-up truck down to St. Pete with the intention of working for Forbes Riley.

Through The Cracks of
IMPERFECTION

By Jerid R Fenderson

*"It's through the cracks of imperfection where
the light of life shines brightest."*

I wrote that quote, I wrote two books; The Lost Art of Communication and The Best Dollar You'll Ever Spend.

I'll be honest with you, I'm a 22-year-old, black, bald man who isn't all that tall. Even though this is an accurate description of me, it doesn't define me.

I was raised by a single mother who worked her ass off to provide for us. She's a strong woman, but she taught me and, in some instances, showed me what it's like to feel weak and how to handle it accordingly.

From a young age, she always allowed me to express my thoughts and feelings openly, freely, without judgment. And, in return, I listened. When my mother spoke to me, I knew that she was speaking from her highest level of truth and that she genuinely wanted the best for me. So I took her words, watched her actions, did my research, and expanded my thinking.

I can say without a reasonable doubt that if my mother wasn't the person that she is, you wouldn't be reading this chapter.

I loved movies as a child, but I can't remember most of them for the life of me; however, the most quotable moment from my favorite childhood movie, The Iron Giant, is "You are who you choose to be."

Even though I'm not well known, yet, I'll never be "nothing."

I can't be "nothing" because I'll never choose to be nothing. When I have nothing, I'll have love; if not from others, then from myself.

The single most important person that you'll ever love is yourself. If you can't do that, then nothing else matters. No amount of growth, happiness, or pleasurable experiences will ever fill the void; only you can do that.

The truth: You do not find love, you create it.

Once you create love, you find peace. When you have peace, you gain the ability to realize that almost all circumstances that life presents to you are neither good nor bad: You gain the ability to define what they mean to you.

The best thing about being my height is that I'm always looking up. Not a day goes by where I don't have my head to the sky at least once.

The thing about being black is that I always see color. It's not through the absence of color, but through the acceptance of all the different colors, will there be peace.

The thing about being bald is that I'm always clean-shaven. In all honesty, I can grow hair, I just prefer not to.

Stop asking.

Now onto the story:

I lived a tale of a thousand tales. I've done more in my lifetime than most people would do in 10. I have a beautiful girlfriend, a few fantastic children, and a legacy that will echo throughout history.

I've made a fair amount of money, yes, with being a billionaire and all, but that's not what I'm most proud of...

What brings a smile to my face. Every. Single. Time, is the day where I was visiting a country that I helped modernize, just as a tourist this trip, and I had a child approach me on the street. All they said was, "thank you."

That's all they needed to say. I saw the whole story in their eyes. I cried.

I gave that child an opportunity that they otherwise would've never had. I created opportunities for the less fortunate that otherwise wouldn't have ever existed. I changed someone's life. I've changed many lives.

With the personal lessons that I've learned from my mother and the life and business lessons that I've learned from my mentor, Forbes Riley, I created an empire.

I never wanted for much, and I still don't. I don't own a home, but my company owns quite a few. I still drive my ol' 73 Chevy C10 every now and again. The only truly extravagant activity that I partake in is flying private.

Every cent of free cash flow after all the expenses was spent on "teaching people how to fish." Because of this, the U.S and the world economy is booming. No free country is without a noticeable spike in economic development.

There's also a significant increase in the global wellness and global peace index.

We're so close to a "perfect word", that the world I'm writing this in right now seems as if it's the story.

-- Here lies simultaneously, the beginning and the end of my story; a future story of my past life, watch it all come true.

Lesson #1: Once is a Mistake, Twice is a Decision

Life happens, wisdom doesn't.

It's not through the experience that you gain wisdom, but through the lessons that you learn from it. A mistake made twice isn't a mistake, it's a conscious choice to put yourself through the same pain that you've been through the last time you committed to that action or lack thereof.

Things happen, you give it a reason. Let that reason teach you the lesson that keeps you from making that same mistake repeatedly. Let that reason give you the opportunity to grow into something more beautiful than you ever imagined.

We've all heard it before, this new definition of insanity. I'm not here to tell you that I'm the sanest man on the planet, as I've made more than my fair share of dumb decisions, I'm here to remind you of what I need to remind myself of often too; mistakes happen, just don't make the same one twice.

Don't drive yourself insane, life's too short for that.

Lesson #2: "What if I Die Tomorrow?"

Often I get asked by my peers, "Hey Jerid, I know that you want to be really wealthy and successful one day, but what if you die tomorrow?"

I lived today.

Life is like a comic book, and we're our own main character. More often than not, we get caught so far up into our own story that we think that everyone else's story is like, or should be like ours.

The truth is, no two stories are the same, nor should they desire to be. It's not the individual physical characteristics that make us unique, such as being 5'2", black, and bald. It's not even the personality traits that you don't see, such as my charmingly awkward charismatic way of talking to large crowds, that makes me special. It's all of the above. And below. And inside of me.

What makes you unique isn't just a portion of you, it's how all those portions come together to make a whole serving you.

The specific ingredients that makeup who you are can be found in varying quantities in a whole lot of other people. But you as a whole, you're the dish that grandma whipped up right before her passing, cooked with that she recipe never wrote down. The way you're made is gone forever. You can add a little sugar and spice, but the best pie is your beautiful life pie.

Going back to the comic analogy, I want to hear your story, not live it. You can tell me what you're made of, that's also fine. But I'll keep my story exactly the way I want it, mine.

What makes me sweet might make you bitter. It matters not much what the flavor is as much as it does if you like how it tastes or not. Season to personal preference.

Stay true to you. Live a life that you're proud of, and when you die, that question will need no answer.

Lesson #3: It's Not About Me

The single biggest turning point for my life is when I confronted the truth; you're going to die one day and there's nothing you can do about it.

Working backward from my inevitable demise, I decided to create a mindmap of what I wanted my life to look like on my final day of reflection. I'm not particularly religious, but the man upstairs isn't the only one that's going to be judging you when you pass.

Imagine that you're 90 years old, you feel your days counting down, you feel that force that you call life fading away; what are your final thoughts?

Like most things in life, there are few objective right or wrong answers. As long as you're not an ax murderer, you can live however you want. Maybe you want fast cars, fancy clothes, a big house, and a trophy wife. Maybe you want lots of friends, a loving family, a caring support network, and a job that doesn't make you want to beat your head on a desk daily.

Want to hear something cool?

You can have both.

Who made those statements into opposites? I've seen happy rich folks, miserable poor folks, and everything in between. Life does require sacrifice. As a great man, Ray Dalio, once said, you can have anything you want in life, but not everything.

If you're willing to put the sweat equity in, you can have more than you ever thought possible.

In my opinion, the best people are the ones who have lots of cash, lots of love, and lots of drive. Those ingredients in that combination change the world more often than not.

You are your story, how will other's tell it when you're no longer around? Your life has an end date, but your story doesn't. If you want to live forever, live through the words of others. If you want people to tell your story, tell theirs. If you want people to love you, love them. If you want people to care, care. Decide to live a beautiful life today, and through that decision, you'll encourage others to do the same.

Happiness is only real when shared. - Christopher McCandless

Share.

Jerid R Fenderson

is a recent Air Force Veteran, entrepreneur, author, and business mogul. He works directly with Forbes Riley, as both an employee and a mentee. In his free time, he can be found working on his 1973 Chevrolet C10, reading a good book, or writing his next one. He's young, he's ambitious, and he's on a path of greatness, paving the way so that others may follow.

He credits his mom with providing him with the foundation and support of one of the strongest forces in the universe; unconditional love. To find out what that meant for him and how you can manifest this within yourself and everyone around you, read his latest book, *The Lost Art of Communication*.

To learn more about Jerid, find him on

Instagram and Facebook: @jeridfenderson

Find his latest work on Amazon and Kindle:

The Lost Art of Communication &
The Best Dollar You'll Ever Spend

What Have You **Forbes'd** Lately?

My name is Jim Cassidy, and I Forbes'd life! For all it's worth, I probably shouldn't be here right now, though I'm immeasurably grateful that I am. Against all odds, I've survived, and I'm prepared to make the most out of each and every day!

Do Life Bigger with

GRATITUDE, MINDSET, AND FAITH

By Jim Cassidy

There I was, hanging off the edge of a sandstone cliff. I could feel the sun beating on my already sunburned forehead. The sweat was starting to drip into my eyes and the salt starting to sting them. I could feel the wind blowing through my hair as I hung there. I had been trying to climb to the top of a canyon wall with some friends at Lake Powell, part of the Colorado River, and I thought it would be a good idea to do this in slip-on tennis shoes with no socks, which even made my next moves scarier and more difficult.

I was the last of 7 friends hiking and they were all ahead of me. I wasn't paying attention to them as much as I was to the majesty of the scenery around me… until, suddenly, I found myself hanging on the edge of that cliff. All alone. As I looked down there was about a 50-foot drop to a rocky floor with little pools of lake water, nothing down there was going to break my fall, for sure. My only choice was to go up, straight up the cliff. I had that fear in my belly that I might not make it out of there without getting badly hurt. My only choice was to try and rise to the occasion, put my fear aside and climb up.

But, wait. Let's back up… Let me tell you a little about who I am before we get to all that. My name is Jim Cassidy. I am a seeker of serenity. I am

an encourager for the discouraged. I can achieve what I believe. I live by faith, grace, and mercy.

My story actually started when I was a young boy growing up in sunny Seal Beach, California. My earliest memories were good. I lived in a safe neighborhood where we played until mom called us in or the street lights came on. Some memories were not so good, though. I have a very young memory of having a fever seizure around five or six years old. My parents thought I might have eaten some bug or varmint paste that they had put out in the yard. Luckily, I had not, but I was rushed to the hospital for a good old-fashioned stomach pumping. I then went through my elementary school years enduring normal fun and hardships of childhood. The only difference was I needed glasses around the third grade, and I didn't want to wear them out of embarrassment. I endured years of allergy testing and was told I was allergic to everything, airborne and milk. This meant no chocolate cake and ice cream at birthday parties. Those are some memories I had. Then I had to go to the hospital to put tubes in my ears because they didn't drain properly. I had surgery to have my tonsils removed. Then, I got braces on my teeth. That part was pretty normal as lots of kids had braces. Most kids, however, didn't have to wear something called "headgear" to draw their overbite back into alignment.

The headgear, I think, has been outlawed in most states today—I'm joking of course. If you're not familiar, a headgear is a device that had a metal piece that attached to your braces, came out of your mouth, and connected two rubber bands, one on each side, to a band of fabric that went around the back of your neck. Headgears made you look super handsome—again, I'm joking. There's a term they say, "chicks dig it-not."

Then came along a diagnosis of attention deficit disorder or today, ADD/ADHD, which back in those days meant you had something wrong with you. You couldn't sit still in class, couldn't pay attention or focus and often caused distractions. All of this was before I reached the sixth grade. I felt perpetually awkward, at best—maybe even more awkward than most 5th graders.

However, all of these obstacles or struggles in themselves were fairly normal, and not a big deal for most kids, but I had every single one of them, all of them, mostly all at once, and during my formidable years. Heck, I should've thrown in the towel and cashed it in right then and labeled myself a victim of extreme social awkwardness and withdrew from society.

Because of this diagnosis, I struggled through school, started playing music, and hung out with the party crowd, or what parents would call "the wrong crowd." Then in high school, I dropped out of school entirely, and I started my dream towards rock stardom.

I was going to be the lead singer of the biggest rock band in history. It would also be the beginning of starting and quitting things, including college. With all of this in my young life, though, there would be a silver lining and an amazing life that ended up coming out of it.

With long-suffering comes wisdom, the good book says. When I dropped out of High School, at the end of the eleventh grade, I had only one class left to complete. I still remember that teacher telling me, "If you show up every day and finish this class, I'll give you a D, which is a passing grade." I thought "you know what, I'm going to do that". Then, I took the GED or the California diploma equivalency test a year later and I passed it on the first try, so I guess that at least I had gained enough skills to graduate at a 12th-grade level. That was the first of many accomplishments that began to build my confidence and self-esteem. I've had a lot of things in my life that I've done that I've been successful at that I never thought that I would be successful doing.

One of those many successes was taking a test to become a real estate agent in 2005. I took a course, a quick crash course, and I passed. I've also been the lead singer of many successful rock bands and learned over the years to play piano, guitar, bass, and drums. Though I've had a lot of things that I wasn't able to finish, I have realized that through big faith you can achieve what you believe.

The important part of that is that you must have unwavering faith and you must believe. I had learned enough in high school to pass an equivalency test and receive a diploma, but I wasn't ready to go right

to college. From there, it took four years of working in dead-end jobs before I realized I probably should go to college and try and learn some new skills.

I attended college, many colleges in fact. I went to National University. There again, the cycle started over so I tried to do accounting and finance because I knew everybody needed bean counters, and I knew I would always have a job. My thought was that accountants make pretty good money, but again, I wasn't able to finish. That wasn't a good fit for my diverse brain; it wasn't my interest after all. I still went and got many jobs doing accounting for companies, but I wasn't very successful at that. I got fired or I quit because it wasn't a job I wanted. It was too boring, and I knew there had to be more for me. I think there's a pattern developing here.

So, here I was, playing in successful rock bands all through the 80's, singing in stinky stale-beer-smelling clubs all over the place, and it was a blast. In 1990 I landed a position at my cousin's hat factory in San Diego and was making the move down to San Diego from Orange County, California for a life change. I was going to be leading the operations department, which included cutting fabrics and accessories for headwear. We were sewing them, putting buttons on top and manufacturing baseball caps and other kinds of headwear. I thought "this is awesome, I finally made it". My cousin always said "this is your company too" which was quite smart because I felt the pride of ownership, and not just like an employee. I started to do sales to help grow the company. I became very successful at sales, and I found that, surprisingly, people really liked me.

I worked for them for 10 years, creating an atmosphere as though it was my business, even though it truly wasn't. I was "Forbes'ing it" before I knew what that was, and it was life-changing for me. It made me feel like I was more than an employee for the first time in my life. I took that and ran with it for a great 10-year career with them.

I decided to move back to Orange County, California in 2000 because I was commuting weekends to visit my girlfriend who ultimately became my wife. Because I was going to move back to Orange County, I created my own business called Cassidy's Originals. I wanted to find something

that would be fun, so I went out and found a pattern maker and created a pattern and found a supplier for fabric and started manufacturing Hawaiian shirts. This went on for four years, but it gave me my own business. I was finally a business owner. I was finally taking charge of my life, and I was no longer working for somebody else. I made a deal with my cousin that he would do the hats for us and that if they ever needed any apparel or Hawaiian shirts, I could supply them.

We did embroidery and screen print and promotional products, and it was a blast. It's tough to run an apparel business on a shoestring budget as I've found, and I slowly worked myself into debt. Luckily, it was debt with my parents, but it was still debt, and in 2004 I was invited by a friend to try my hand at credit card processing sales.

We are tops in the credit card processing industry in helping business' keep profits. Credit card processing to me wasn't a super honest industry; the banks took a lot of money from me over the years, and I thought "how can I make money in that?" I went for it anyway, and I couldn't keep up with both companies, so in 2005 I closed Cassidy's Originals. This was a new change for me, but I was super successful at it, and I was really enjoying the boss and the company I worked for. I was good at getting people to like me, and I was good at selling. I also started seeing some patterns in my life that I had changed. I had changed from being somebody who had a bunch of problems and a diagnosis to a person that was utilizing my best to create a life that I wanted to live.

When 2008 came and the housing and mortgage industry came crashing down, I hit rock bottom again as I had many times in my life. This time, however, I knew there was more. This time I realized it wouldn't affect me like the past. It's funny and ironic, I thought, because I was in an industry that was helping companies reduce a fee they had, and we were really saving companies a lot of money. I figured I'm giving companies money back for free, how could it hurt me? But what ended up happening was all those real estate and mortgage people were looking for jobs, and they crashed right into our industry because our industry was the only one hiring. I had literally gone from being one of the tops in sales in the company and making lots of money, earning trips to Cabo San Lucas, Hawaii, Las Vegas and more, to barely making any money, even though I was working harder than ever.

I quickly went from the top to the bottom, and all those old memories of failure started creeping back in. My claim to fame up to this point was earning a trip to Hawaii at the very last minute of the contest on a Friday at 5:00 as the contest was ending. Because of my mindset and because of my tenacity, I was able to earn the trip to Hawaii with one deal. I turned the paperwork in at 5 o'clock, the last day of the contest. It was spread around the company and used as a recruiting tool by the boss, and I was on top of the world. See, I had told him when I first came to work there that one of the goals I had was to earn a trip to Hawaii to take my wife within the first five years of us getting married. We both wanted to go there and we hadn't been anywhere like that. And I did it. I was the poster child for success at U.S.M.S. and it was my story that the boss told to every single sales rep that came through the doors.

That story and many other stories stuck with me in my life, and they have been an encouragement for me to step out of my comfort zone and to continue through challenges and struggles that I had in my life. But, we were still stuck in 2008, and there was still a problem. I was only making $500 a week. I wasn't being the provider that my family needed for money, and I quickly hated working in the environment that was changing around me. There were a lot of things that were happening in my life, and I was down. I felt like I couldn't sell water to fish, and the harder I tried to accomplish my goals, the worse it got.

Business owners didn't want to take phone calls from salespeople, especially credit card processing salespeople. There were thousands of us calling. So, I went from making 35 calls a day with high success to making 100's of calls weekly and having no success. I started to get frustrated, and I decided as some of my associates had that I was going to go on my own and start my own business. I had been successful at this before when I left the hat factory and started my clothing apparel business, with the exception of the little debt, and I knew that this had no overhead. All I needed was a computer and a phone and some leads.

There was no product to buy, no advertising dollars or anything else needed to get started. I knew I could be successful at this. I used everything I had, and I started calling all my old customers. All of them wanted to work with me, so I was able to make enough money to start my business the first year and have now been in business since 2012. It's

awesome. I now net a residual income of $8,000 to $10,000 a month, whether I work or not, and its growing. It's enabled me to start other businesses and coach folks and help other people learn how they can also do life bigger and live the life of their dreams.

I want to step back just a minute, now, and go back to that 2008 housing crash and the economic landslide. I call "hit rock bottom," because that was a very important time for me. I realized there had to be something more, and in talking to some of my associates, I learned that highly successful leaders read, and if you don't read, you're blowing it. One of my early inspirations was the writing of Og Mandino. He wrote "The Greatest Salesman In the World," and it was a life and business game-changer for me. The book focuses on the metaphors for success, and it has 10 affirmation-based scrolls.

You read each scroll for a month, 3 times daily, reading out loud, and it was such a blessing to see how my thought patterns changed with this simple exercise. Plus, it sent me on a path to learn more and improve myself through the teachings of others like Napoleon Hill's, "Think and Grow Rich," Zig Ziglar's, "See you at the Top," and Wallace D Wattles' "Science of Getting Rich," and more.

Ultimately, through my search, I found that I could be a creative salesman instead of a competitive one. It made all the difference in my life-being creative, rather than cutthroat, attracts abundance. I learned that if I visualize, meditate, write down and set goals and carry them around with me in my heart and my pocket, that I can achieve anything I want.

Lesson #1: Gratitude

I have huge faith in the power of gratitude and kindness. If we are grateful for opportunities and happy and kind to others, wealth and abundance will come back to us many times over. Now I'm not talking about just money here. I'm talking about something way bigger and more fulfilling. I'm speaking of fulfilling wealth and abundance in relationships, spirituality and health, and of course money. Some call it the law of attraction.

Gratitude creates joy. What gratitude does is pull us out of the doldrums and reminds us of scenarios where we think we're enough. It reminds us of situations when good things happened and reminders of our awesomeness to move forward. Gratitude also reminds us of things that we can be thankful for because no matter what, every breath I get, every new morning I have, there's something that I could be grateful for. No matter what circumstances are, no matter what the weather is, no matter what problems are going on in the world, no matter what people are saying there's always something to be grateful for.

So, one of the things that I want to share is that I started a gratitude journal. My gratitude journal is something I write in every day. I write three things in the morning that I'm grateful for. When I wake up at night and when I go to bed, I write three things I'm grateful for that happened to me that day. I also have a money journal, and I write down everything I get in money- maybe a free dinner, maybe somebody invites me to go to a movie and pays for it, and that helps me to realize all of the abundances that come to me.

I have those two journals. The gratitude journal has been something very special in my life and everybody I've shared it with has seen amazing results in their life. The gratitude journal has been a life-changing experience because I can go back a year from now and look at my gratitude journal and I can see what I was grateful for. Often a problem in life is that we all have a negative story going on inside of our head. We tell ourselves so many things that just aren't true, and they are merely a perception from our childhood. Many things that happen to us before we had enough life experience to assimilate them properly can still seem frightening or damaging, and we still give those memories that amount of power, even though any threat from those occurrences are long gone in our adult lives.

Lesson #2: Mindset Matters Above All

Mindset controls our well-being. Our mindset, good or bad, determines how we are going to view life. Mindset can control whether we are depressed or sad or are in contentment or if we have a peace of mind. The problem is, sometimes we allow our mindset to be controlled by

our lack of gratitude or other negative influences like the stories we constantly tell ourselves or other people's negativity. This can lead us to live in a victim mindset. If you find yourself saying things like "why does this always happen to me", "my job sucks and I hate it", "nobody treats me very nice", etc. this is often a product of a negative mindset that may be manifesting a negative reality. Too often we look towards outside factors, things we have little to no control over, and we blame those circumstances for controlling our state of mind. There are so many tricks and strategies to overcome this mentality, allowing you to live in a joyful, grateful mindset, but it's not always easy.

I like to think of the brain as a muscle. In fact, it actually contains a little muscle, although it's not a muscle in and of itself. I say this because sometimes you have to do things and think of things, like life, differently over and over to make real change—much like a workout. In other words, it's not always easy, it takes work and consistency like going to the gym, but it's always worth the change. If practiced, change will always happen, and positive changes will always be for your own good and put you in an awesome, joyful and peaceful state of mind. That's a mindset in a nutshell.

One of the greatest things I learned about was mastermind groups. Mastermind groups are an amazing way to get business ideas and network to grow your business and also build friendships with like-minded people. It's similar to a "think tank," but these are used for general business growth.

I took my many years of business and life experience and sales records, and I thought that I could make a grand difference in people's lives, helping them to create and grow their businesses and show them how to stop leaving money on the table. I set out on a new journey of service towards others. I started on a new journey to educate people about the power behind dreaming and believing and achieving. I'm sharing with them ways that they can take control of their own life. They can create the life of their dreams with less work and more thought and visualization than anybody ever thought possible, and I've been living that dream now for many years.

The 3rd part to my trinity is Faith. I believe faith may be one of the hardest things to have and especially to practice. There are so many definitions for faith depending on where you derive your faith. For example, if your faith comes from the universe, then it might be that you have a belief that something good happens for you if you think about it enough.

Webster's dictionary describes faith like this: "a firm belief in something for which there is no proof."

The Bible describes faith like this: "Faith is the confidence that what we hope for will actually happen; it gives us assurance about things we cannot see." I like that one better for myself. I want my faith to mean something, and I want to believe that things unseen are possible.

The reason is that lots of times in my life when I was to receive something by faith, it was often a lot better and more amazing than I could have ever possibly imagined. Faith lived out wholeheartedly, without any doubt of its truth, is super powerful. The reason I put them together in this order is, I believe with gratitude your mindset can improve and change rapidly, and if you stir in a little faith to that recipe your life can change and improve rapidly, and you will be on your way to do life bigger.

If we believe we can achieve, we understand that we are born with what we need to change lives and the world. We need to encourage and serve others to influence our world and make it a brighter place for all. There are just too many discouraged, sad, angry and disillusioned people out in the world today. There's no place for it that's healthy. It doesn't work. It doesn't fit. It's the wrong puzzle piece. I believe God made us all with what we need. The question is, do we use it? Do we find it? Do we keep searching for it or do we give up? We throw in the towel every time we cry- Why me?

Remember that story I was telling you at the beginning of the chapter about hanging on the edge of the sandstone cliff? Well, I told myself, I have no other choice but to go up. I couldn't go back, and I couldn't go

down. With every fiber of my being, I mustered my courage, prayed to my creator to fight the fear of failure, and I started climbing, straight up the cliff. One hand grip and one foothold at a time until I made it to the top. I finished! I achieved my goal against what seemed like insurmountable odds and succeeded. Funny thing was, all my friends had no idea what I had been through, and as soon as I got to the top they simply said, "Okay, let's move on." I just lay there in reflection and contemplation of what I had accomplished and what I could do with the rest of my life with gratitude, mindset, and faith.

James Michael Cassidy

is an experienced entrepreneur, business owner, musician and author, who has grown Alliance Card Group, a credit card processing company, to six-figures. In addition to his primary job functions, James has been recognized by his clients for his extraordinary vision and commitment to serving others. He is active in his church and family, enjoys playing music live, being in nature, participating in sports, as well as hanging out with friends and family.

To learn more about James, go to:

www.DoLifeBiggerProject.com

Just do it

- Nike

What Have You **Forbes'd** Lately?

We are John & Doris Vallee, and we Forbes'd doing things even when they're uncomfortable. When we met Forbes, we knew that she was amazing! We were touched emotionally by Forbes and decided to go to her Forbes Factor Live in September, 2018. There, we learned how to pitch at Pitch Mastery. Then, at Forbes Factor, we learned about ourselves, things in our past holding us back, how to let the past events go; what positive characteristics were learned from the past experiences, and how to move on.

WE FORBES'D IT

By John and Doris Vallee

O nce upon a time, there was a boy and girl named John Vallee and Doris Robidoux, that were born in the mid-1960s in a small town named Southbridge, in Southern Worcester County in Massachusetts.

John talks about Doris

Doris grew up the youngest of three children, and the only girl. The daughter of a truck driver and volunteer fireman. Her mother was a stay at home mom that wanted Doris to help with the cleaning. When drying the dishes, Doris' mother would sing old songs like Jimmy crack corn and downtown, but never really talked to Doris or spent much time with her. Doris liked hanging around her father when he was home. She would help him with yard work, painting the house, and enjoyed activities, such as going fishing, or riding bikes with him.

When she was younger, all the kids played in her yard. But as time went on, there weren't many kids her age, only younger ones and 3 kids next door that picked on her. Her brothers didn't want her around much, they would rather be with their own friends. Her brother, who was closer to her in age would pick on her, hit her and tell her mother she hit herself, and incredibly Doris' mother would believe him! The older

brother joked around and teased her, and the younger of the two when playing basketball, told her the only way she would get the ball was to get under the basket. And when she did, he would hit her with the ball!

In 6th grade, Doris's parents fought over the fact that her father bought her a 5-speed bike. Her parents later separated, which she thought, after hearing the fight, was her fault. They got back together months later, but it did not last, and they got divorced a year later. Shortly thereafter, her father got remarried to someone who caused a rift between Doris and her father. Her older brothers continued to get bossy, while her mother wanted Doris to do laundry and cooking, as well as cleaning. Because her mother was at work, there was not much time for Doris to fight with her, but the fighting between Doris and her brothers intensified. In response to the frustration Doris felt, she resorted to "acting out" by rocking out as a singer and musician in her bedroom. She used music as her outlet for being picked on at school, and having to cope with a quarrelsome home life.

Doris talks about John

In 7th grade, I met John Vallee when he showed up with my cousin and a friend at my house. My cousin invited me to go to a church festival with them. At the festival, my cousin and friend disappeared and left me with John. As John and I talked, I found out that my friend had been dating John, but had broken it off. John believed this ex-girlfriend felt guilty and need to set him up with someone else. After that, John and I continued talking, and on the way back to my house, I asked John if I could see him again. He said yes, and we continued seeing each other from then on.

John grew up as the youngest of five children. He was raised with strong family values. The three oldest kids kept to themselves. His father died when he was three. John's sister and grandmother babysat him while his mother worked. By the time John was around eight, his mother remarried, and the three older kids moved out. This left John and his last older brother home together to live with this new family. John was an altar server for his church from age 8 till he graduated from high school. He and his brother shared a bedroom and grew close until the older brother started to hang out with his friends more.

John had a quiet upbringing, and he enjoyed spending time with his stepdad. He met a girl in the early part of 7th grade, and they dated a few months, until one day she broke up with him to go back to her other boyfriend. In the passing weeks, she would keep asking John if he was ok, she had a guilty conscience he guessed. On the day of the church festival, John's ex-girlfriend and another girl came up to him and asked if he was seeing anyone. He said "no", and they brought him over to meet someone, and that's how John met Doris. They dated throughout high school.

John talks about Doris

During the summer between Doris's junior and senior year in high school she got a temporary job. She was excited to tell her mother she was going to work overtime, only to come home and find her mother on the floor. Doris was glad that her brother had come into the house with her, as they found that their mother had a stroke. She took care of her mother for many years. The house they lived in was given to all 3 of the kids, which caused many arguments, even now. She spent a year unemployed. Doris worked 2nd shift, which helped avoid her brother, who was drinking and doing drugs.

Doris talks about John

In the summer of 1985, John asked me to marry him. Before I answered, I asked John if he could see past working at McDonald's? He said "no", so I declined his proposal. I didn't think it was the right time for marriage, given my need to get away from my own mother's control, along with John's grandmother not liking me because I was a tomboy, and John not showing any ambition to support us. I also felt that I was not yet mature enough, and that I needed the freedom to discover myself. I suggested that John and I remain friends, but after that, I didn't see John again, until 2003, even though we went to the same church and lived in the same town.

During that time apart I met a friend at work. In fact, I was the maid of honor at her wedding. Unfortunately, she and her husband later divorced. To help my friend, I assisted her in raising her 3 children. I worked as a material handler, but kept getting laid off from the factory

I worked at. I was also having a hard time at work because my boss harassed me all the time, as he believed women should stay home barefoot and pregnant. My friend suggested maybe going back to school. I often talked about how much I enjoyed working with computers with regard to production and labeling.

John talks about Doris

Doris decided to go to Quinsigamond Community College for the study of Management Information Systems. During her time there, her and her brother decided to put their mother in a nursing home because she kept falling. Years later she died. In 1995, at the age 30, Doris stopped living with her brother and moved upstairs in the same house. Later she changed jobs and went into order entry. And when her job changed systems, she assisted the other order entry and customer service employees in learning the system.

Doris had to take a pay cut from the factory, so she started working at a nearby lumber company. Staying in school was difficult financially, but she worked through it to get her Associates Degree. She started her new career working at a Y2K company as a programmer, before joining a financial company.

Doris talks about John

On September 11, 2001, I was working at the financial company when one of my co-workers came in talking about the first tower of the World Trade Center getting hit. We watched it on the Internet and saw a plane hit the second tower. A co-worker from the next department came over. He was physically shaken. He had been on the phone with a guy and his wife who were in the towers when they were hit by the planes. We all calmed him down. Then the manager came over telling us all to stay off the Internet and the phones, so they could download everything from the stock exchange. This was also the first day I was supposed to start Clark University for my bachelor's degree in computer science.

During that time John had tried to get in the Navy, but it did not work out, so he stayed living with his mom and found work. He never dated anyone after breaking up with me. He moved out on his own at 35. He

later let one of his older brothers move in with him to give him a place to stay, this helped John with the bills and gave him some company. Later on, his brother stopped helping with the bills. Then he ran into me out of the Blue at CVS in the summer of 2003. I asked him if he wanted to get together and talk. He said yes, and we began dating again.

John talks about Doris

In November 2003, I asked Doris to marry me. Again, she said "no" because she thought it was too soon, as they had only been dating a few months.

On February 14, 2004, at a restaurant in front of a fireplace I asked her again, and she said "yes". We then went to her father's and I asked him for her hand. Then went and told his mother.

Doris talks about John

On Memorial Day 2004, John moved in with me to be able to save money for the wedding.

On May 7, 2005, John and I got married. Unfortunately, on that day, our wedding photographer, who was a coworker of mine, told me they were laying people off in my department. In spite of the bad news, we went to Disney World in Florida for our honeymoon. The first day back to work I was congratulated on my marriage, but was also told that I would be laid off as of July 19.

In November 2004, I started a new job on a contract in Boston. However, with the commute that was required, I barely saw John, as I would leave at 5:30 am and not get home until 9 pm. They liked my work, and asked if I could be there every day, as a permanent employee. They decided to move to Mansfield, MA so I would be close to the train giving me a shorter commute.

John talks about Doris

Doris and I moved into a housing facility around Christmas. Shortly after settling in our new home, I got a job in Braintree, MA an hour away. Then, by summer we had someone tamper with our car and loosen lug

nuts. I did not realize it, and as I was driving to work the tire came off and rolled past me. I was still in shock when I called Doris to tell her the news with a very shaky voice. Doris was worried, but I was glad I was alright. We reported it to the police, but with no way of knowing who had done it, the investigation did not lead to any arrests. A month later, someone let the air out of one tire of the car, Doris noticed the cap missing. In September, someone tried to break in our house in an area of the wall above my head. Doris woke up, hearing someone prying at the window, and yelled. The yelling made the person leave. We reported the incident to the police and the housing complex, but they were unable to do much for us. At that point, we decided to look for another place to live. In the meantime, Doris slept very little, keeping a bat by the bed.

Doris talks about John

In October 2005, John and I moved into a condominium complex with 10 condos. There, we meet a family with an autistic son. We helped that family by watching him. Then, in July 2013, we moved to Attleboro to get a bigger place. The day we got the keys to the place in Attleboro, John lost his job, but later found another job. In the meantime, I kept going in and out of contracts in the same place where I worked.

I lost my job again in 2016 for 10 months. We then decided to try our hand at an eBay business. In January 2017, I lost my job again, and with not making much on eBay we decided to get involved with a company learning to sell on Amazon. We have our own store on Amazon called "Amazon Dragon's Keep".

In March 2018, we went to a business seminar and an ASD Marketplace in Las Vegas, where we met vendors to buy merchandise for our store. While there we met Forbes Riley. We were touched emotionally by Forbes, and decided to go to Forbes Factor Live in September 2018. There we learned about ourselves, things in our past holding us back, and how to let past events go. We also learned to take away the positive from negative past experiences, and how to move on. We learned that you are the sum of the 5 people you are closest to, and to do things even if they are uncomfortable, and strive to do better.

Most Important Life Lesson: We have support

We learned that we have friends and people who want to see us succeed. Thank you, Forbes!

John and Doris Vallee

have built a strong foundation of love and business passion during the course of their marriage. Frustrated with the ups and downs of working traditional jobs, they have together staked their claim in the world of eCommerce. Their company, DragonFire Ventures LLC, owns Dragon's Keep, an Amazon store, and Honey Bunny "N" Teddy Bear, an eBay store.

John and Doris have leveraged their technical abilities from their former job roles to enhance the success of their online ventures. In particular, John has applied his technical skills acquired from his work in plastic injection, while Doris has applied her computer knowledge attained from her Associate's Degree in Management Information Systems.

Outside of their work in eCommerce, both John and Doris are extremely caring and have a strong interest in helping children learn and grow, especially those with autism and special needs. They are extremely active in their church and in the community, and they take pride in making people that become their friends part of their extended family.

To learn more about John and Doris, contact them at:

Dragonfireventures@comcast.net
www.DragonsKeeps.com

It's in your moments of decision that your destiny is shaped

- Anthony Robbins

What Have You **Forbes'd** Lately?

My name is Jose Elizondo, and I Forbes'd the belief that I can achieve my dreams. Being born in a different country can be challenging and full of limiting beliefs. Since meeting Forbes, my outlook and my mindset has completely shifted and I believe that I've become a better father, husband, and more successful in business. Staying curious, staying hungry, and thinking outside of the box, have now become my new norm.

Playing Big Since
I WAS SMALL

By Jose Elizondo

I was born in a small town in Mexico, where my mom, who had 10 children, ran a convenience store. In fact, the town was so small that her store also acted as a telephone center, a payment center for electricity bills, and a post office. My mom always made sure our family's needs were met, even if it took working 24/7. Looking back now, I know we were just getting by, but mom made us feel like we had all we needed. She was the most hardworking, humble, and generous role model I knew. She was a firm believer in being the change that you wanted to see in the world. She would say that if you cannot help the person next to you, you will never be able to help the world!

And my mom always said, "I'm naming you Jose Jose because, my son you will live a live for both of my twins.

One of my fondest memories of my mom is when she let me sell my own product in her store. She took me into the city when she had to purchase products for the store, and she let me choose whatever product I wanted. This time I chose balloons that had a pull tab. It had a whole bunch of different types of balloons, big ones, long ones, stretchy ones, of all different colors. For 1 peso you get to pull a tab and if you got lucky, the pull tab would be attached to a real "cool" balloon.

My mom wanted to change the world, and she knew that if she committed to bringing out the best in everybody she came across, she could make the change in the world she wanted to see. She always told me that you don't need to have a lot of money to achieve the success you crave. By just starting with the small things that you have available to you, you will find that soon enough you will have made an impact in your community.

It wasn't just me and my siblings that my mom took care of. Our house was always full, we often hosted the Tarahumara people that would come down from the mountains. My mom would give them a place to stay as they weaved the baskets they sold in town. Before they left and went back up to the mountains she would have us run out to the orchard to pick some pears and apples to give to them. People were always coming into the store even when they didn't need to buy anything. They just wanted to talk to my mom, she was almost like the town's ear. She took the time to listen and get to know everybody. Anybody that came to the door in need would get helped. She would give them an orange, a bottle of water, anything. Sometimes she would give them the aluminum cans she picked up off the streets and tell them to take them, so they could get a little money. Because my father wasn't around, my mom served as an example of how to live life. I knew that the most important thing I could do in life would be to help people.

As a child, I dreamt of being an inventor, and I unknowingly added to my mother's ever-growing list of responsibilities, as I would take everything apart to figure out how it worked! She never complained though, even if I could not put it back together, instead she would encourage me. She inspired me to be ambitious and made me feel strong enough to move mountains. It amazes me how much of a difference one positive voice can make in a kid's life. When I was learning multiplication, she told me if I learned all of my multiplication from 1 to 10 I could have whatever chips and soda I wanted out of the store. Later I used this technique on my own daughters when they were learning their multiplication. I told them I would give them a prize, anything they wanted. My Daughter Bea chose to color her hair!

When I was about 14, I was very interested in computers. My older brother Jeff bought me my first computer on the condition that I would

learn everything I could about it. He said I would have to know it in and out before I even thought about getting the Internet. This was back when the Internet was still dial-up. I ended up taking the whole computer apart and putting it back together!

I looked up to my mom and it was my goal to make her proud. I knew I would have to do more if I wanted to make a big change in the world. When I talked to my mom, she reminded me of how big of a difference I could make if I just focused on inspiring one person to become a better person each passing day. That became my goal, I started asking myself every day, "Did I make someone's life easier today? Did I put a smile on someone's face?"

The value of hard work instilled in me as a child helped me to create a successful construction company. When I came to the United States I started working in construction for $40 a day. Then a friend invited me to work in Minnesota. So, I moved from Kansas City to Burnsville. Once in Burnsville, I was invited to join another friend's construction company. I helped the owner of this company get set up and organized digitally. I became part of the company and later I bought him out and it became my own.

My company was doing really well and growing quite large. I managed 15 crews that hung drywall. I had a little over 100 employees. I was getting ready to expand to North Dakota when the housing crisis of 2008 hit. The economic crash took me down with it, financially and emotionally. Looking back now, I realized it was a lack of education that limited me from pulling through the hard times. I fell into a small depression, I no longer wanted to leave my comfort zone. I didn't want to fail, I lost the drive to push for success. I stayed stagnant in my own little bubble.

I moved back down to Mexico. About 6 months into living in Mexico, my brother Jeff offered me a job in Palm Springs, California. We were expanding a casino and I had to live with the workers there in Palm Springs. It was really tough on our family to be apart. My wife was pregnant, and my daughter Bea was 2, then my second daughter Mica was born, and they stayed with my in-laws during that time. I would go visit them on weekends, and I started seeing that my father-in-law had

more of a bond with Mica than I did. When I got there, she was scared to see me, as she didn't know who I was. It struck me deep inside. I called up my brother and told him "I have to figure this out now. I need to get an apartment, I need to move my family together, and I need to have more work to make it happen." It really pushed me to work harder until I became a partner in his company. I kept working there until I was offered this opportunity in the oil field in West Texas.

I moved my family to Texas, and we went through a couple ups and down. Work wasn't as consistent as I thought it would be. I knew I needed to do something more. A friend of mine recommended I follow Tai Lopez's 67 Steps. I took it very seriously and it pushed me forward. I began to research various self-help gurus, and I was re-energized and began to invest in myself again. My curiosity was sparked, and I started taking course after course. I learned about self-drive, social presence, and marketing on social media.

My passion for helping people got a reboot as well. I thought that I could mix the 2 things I wanted to do the most, playing with computers and helping people. I was inspired to pursue this further. I kept challenging myself and eventually became a certified marketing strategist. I began helping mom and pop restaurants grow their clientele, it really brought me joy to see the impact I could have on someone. I had come so far but I still couldn't figure out what was missing. I knew I needed a mentor. I found myself attending the Internet Earners Summit in Los Angeles. I felt lucky enough to be there to meet some of my online mentors. At one point during the event I stepped outside to have a one-on-one conversation with Jaiden Gross, and by the time I had stepped back in I found out I completely missed Forbes Riley's speech. I didn't know what her speech was about or the significant impact she would later have in my life. I actually didn't even know who she was at the time. I continued on with the event and took many courses from many potential mentors, but something kept drawing me back to Forbes Riley. I finally thought "I'm going to take the time and find out who she is." Luckily, I did!

Forbes pushed me until I was finally able to break through the emotional baggage I had been carrying around since childhood. Things like not having a positive male role model, or the pain I felt from being

so different from the people in my town. I always felt like I needed to suck it up and keep moving on, but she showed me a new approach that helped me to finally break free from the pressure I was feeling. She worked with me in small steps, asking me questions to help me gain clarity. She taught me that I needed to stop explaining my life to myself and just tell my story. She then helped me understand why I did the things I did throughout my life. Knowing these things about myself helped me to let go of them. To no longer let my childhood trauma tell me how to live my life.

I felt renewed and I can't really explain how it feels. Everything I had set out to do just started working, and I began to achieve the success I had been craving. My commitment to myself has allowed me to learn more about myself every day. I've found all these hidden talents and strengths I hadn't been utilizing and I'm able to do more than I thought I could. In fact, I feel my internal drive and self-motivation has brought me back to just like when I was a little boy telling my mom how I wish to change the world.

My name is Jose Jose Elizondo, and I am only going up from here!

Jose Jose Elizondo

was born in Mexico, but his ambition to be a successful entrepreneur led him to the United States. His business focused mindset, and versatile outlook on life, kept him in constant pursuit of strategies for achieving business success. One of his earliest successes was growing and managing a thriving construction company. This triumph only fueled his quest to broaden his portfolio of entrepreneurial skills, particularly in the area of digital marketing.

Jose utilized his adept problem solving abilities and forward thinking to develop a strategy for launching affordable social media marketing campaigns for businesses. His campaign strategies dramatically expanded the marketing reach of small businesses. This success was a satisfying and profound accomplishment for him, and resulted in Jose pursuing other ventures, including one where he facilitated the expansion of a transportation company, which grew over 200% in under 6 months. Jose has also applied his business savvy and leveraged his relationship with this transportation company to grow his own rapidly expanding trucking business.

Jose's business experience and marketing expertise has made him a go-to resource for business strategy and development and his business IQ is unmatched. His ambition for incredible success never allows him to become complacent. Jose is always seeking new opportunities to apply and evolve his business skill set and is always open to new business challenges.

To learn more about Jose, contact him at:
www.Jose360.com

You can't build a reputation on what you're going to do

- Henry Ford

What Have You **Forbes'd** Lately?

My name is Joshua Self, and I Forbes'd the love of my life, Forbes Riley. I would never count myself as someone who was lucky with love, and I've only had a couple of relationships in my life. Meeting and falling in love with this extraordinary woman has put so many pieces of me together. It's given meaning to my achievements, talents, and goals beyond anything I could have ever imagined. I truly love you, Forbes Riley.

Portrait of a

CHAMPION

By Joshua Self

Alone... I was surrounded by thousands while I was on that stage, but I was still all alone... I had nothing to cling to at that moment other than the pain, the sacrifice and the passion I had poured into my pursuit of competing with myself. My body was literally "stripped" of everything tangible—there was nothing to hide. I knew this day would come, it was my destiny to confront the relentless scrutiny and judgment that came with being a world-class competitor. My mind, body and spirit were aligned, I was at one with my place in the universe on that stage. The mental toughness I possessed was forged through a lifetime of fighting for the life I wanted, and it would not let my body show the slightest hint of frailty. My mind and body centered on a singular focus and mission—winning! This quiet boy had now stepped into the spotlight reserved only for those with a championship state of mind. As I commanded each of my poses with mechanized precision, I beamed with strength, power, and personality in a way the judges could not deny. In one fleeting moment, I reflected on how the tumultuous events of my life pushed me to this pinnacle, this one defining moment on that stage. It was then I realized this was what I was meant to become—a champion—a two-time Arnold Classic Champion and a WFF World Champion in fact!

I believe that all of us have a history that shapes us. Sometimes that history can be used as fuel to propel us forward in life, or we can allow it to cling to us like a weight, which holds us back from our goals. It is our choice. My history began when my dad died in a car accident when I was only two years old. My mom got remarried to a man who had two kids of his own, so I had three brothers that were older than me. I was the youngest of the kids, and that kind of made me the last priority. My stepfather was more of a father to his own biological kids than to my brother. Eventually my mom divorced my stepfather, and remarried when I was in the first grade. He was the closest thing to a true "step-dad" that I had. He truly stepped in as my dad, coaching me in football and baseball, and helping me with athletics. Devastatingly, he died in a car accident my freshman year of high school.

As I grew up, I got made fun of a lot. I was kind of thin, funny-looking with big ears and hairy arms. I couldn't pronounce my "R's"—my best friend's name was Mark, and I called him "Mah'k." Kids made fun of me for all of that and more. The emptiness I felt from the loss of my biological dad and my step-dad, caused me to withdraw into isolation, and it kind of turned me into a mean kid with no direction or focus.

I was a loner in the small town of Washington Courthouse, OH, and this allowed me to focus on solitary activities like drawing. I love drawing—to this day, I can draw anything I see. I was also an athlete who loved sports. One of my favorite sports was wrestling, which I did for 10 years. It was my best sport because it just came naturally to me—I was undefeated for years.

During this time, there was a lawsuit over the semi-truck that hit my biological father and killed him, so we ended up with a lot of money. We moved to a nicer house in the same neighborhood, and my brother and I got cars. That didn't turn out so well for me—I was a stupid and naive kid—really irresponsible, and I wrecked that car when I was 17. I was just reckless, and it caused over $7,000 in damage.

Luckily, I walked away from that crash without injury, and went on to have the best year ever playing high school sports. I trained in track, basketball and wrestling. But I quit wrestling when Michael Jordan became my hero. From there, everything for me became about

basketball. I was obsessed with jumping as high as I could—I wanted to touch everything I saw. That lead me to become a high jumper, where I won a state championship my junior year. I also played center on the basketball team, although all of the other centers were taller than me, I could play that position because I could jump. Basketball really became my love, and that's all I wanted to do was play.

Art, especially drawing, also continued to be a constant part of my life. I was good at it, so good that I loved to show off and see what I could create if I pushed myself. But not everything in art came easy, there were some things that I struggled with. See, I couldn't draw what I visualized in my mind, I had to see it live. But like all things in my life, I persevered to improve my weaknesses.

My brother and I were different from other kids in school. He wore stylish and provocative clothes, and I wanted to do the same. Because we lived in a small town, most people dressed very conservatively, and my brother and I wanted to wear clothes that were more fun and interesting. We got made fun of about how we dressed. But we did not care. We would wear different shoes and clothes, not your typical blue jeans and t-shirts. You might say that we were a little more trendy than most of the other kids.

After high school, I went to college on a track scholarship. I was still all about basketball, but I had an amazing experience there that really opened up my perspective on the world. There was so much more to life than my small town had to offer, and beyond basketball and drawing. I realized I had a physical presence and "looks", so I became interested in modeling. After two years in college I realized it wasn't for me, and I decided to go out to Los Angeles and become a model.

Los Angeles was huge and it was little tough for me, having coming from such a small town. I was not prepared for LA, I mean my brother and I wearing clothes other than jeans and t-shirts was almost earth-shattering to others in my hometown in Ohio. So, now imagine me in LA, trying to navigate my way through the modeling industry. I felt lost and a little scared. I didn't have anyone on my side—I was doing this all on my own, so I'd go out to LA, stay for a month or so, then drive back

to Ohio. Then, I'd go back to LA, then back to Ohio. I did that like three times. I just couldn't figure it out. Maybe I just didn't want it as badly as I thought I did.

I was just there in LA by myself. Alone. I didn't know anybody, and to be honest, I wasn't willing to sacrifice myself because I quickly found out what it takes to make you "Hollywood", and I didn't want to sacrifice who I was in that way. So, I went back home, and I went back to college. I went to ITT Tech, in Dayton, Ohio and I was there with my girlfriend and a friend, Gary. I instantly had friends. Because of all of that support, I was able to stick to college and graduate with a degree in electronics. Honestly, I'm not sure why I chose that major: transistors, capacitors and all of these other things. Obviously, I hadn't yet learned to stick to doing things I really like, so that was a little detour in my life.

After a little fumbling around in my new-found electronics career, I moved to Albuquerque, NM where one of my mentors, Martin, a father-figure and photographer lived. Martin became a friend of mine in LA when my agent sent me to him to take some test shots, and he had a bunch of computers there and software that piqued my interest. He showed me Adobe Illustrator and Photoshop, and that got me interested in learning 3D graphics. I stayed with him for a couple of months until I ran out of money. I didn't know exactly what to do, so I went back home and I decided to join the Navy.

The military is a great place to go when you're feeling lost and without any direction in your life. The Navy gave me focus, it gave me something to do with purpose and passion. After the Navy, I moved to San Diego where I met my girlfriend, prior to moving to Ohio where we had our baby girl, Alexa.

After several odd jobs that didn't work out so well, and my girlfriend not loving my little hometown in Ohio, we moved to Las Vegas. I also went back to school again for three more years at the Art Institute with a specialty in divisional text motion graphics. I tried to find a job in Las Vegas only to realize that my line of work is pretty much only done in LA, New York and a few other spots where movies are made. My career wasn't going great, and I was working out all the time then, still

thinking about modeling, and working in 3D graphics, when one day while working out in the gym some guy came up to me and said, "Hey are you competing?" and

I said, "Competing in what?"

"You know, men's physique," he said.

Our conversation carried on like that for a bit, and I explained that I had never heard of these competitions. He showed me a picture of himself in a competition, and then he said Mr. Olympia is coming up, and there's some type of model search. It all certainly interested me, so looked into it, and tried it.

So, here I am at my first physique bodybuilding competition, and everyone thought I was going to win, but I lost. And that began my bodybuilding career. I even started doing some modeling and performing and got in with an agency. I also continued to work freelance in 3D graphics and I worked in film production. Now, the bodybuilding competitions started becoming a focus of mine. In the first competition in Las Vegas, I placed in the top five. My second competition was in LA, and I placed second. I placed in a few other competitions, then I won the Arnold Classic in 2015 and the Jay Cutler in Vegas, then the Arnold Classic again. That came with a contract from a supplement company.

My most recent competition was in Orlando, FL with the World Fitness Federation (WFF), which is based in Australia, and I was representing the USA. They have a sports model division, which I competed in. I ended up in 3rd place because they said I was too big. Next, I went to Ireland to compete in men's physique where they call it "beachbody", and I placed third again. I usually get sponsors to pay my way or most of my expenses for these competitions, and they are such great experiences. Most recently, the competition came back to the USE in Huntington Beach, CA. I won my division, and then I immediately got bumped up to the Pro division that competed right after my first win, and I placed second in the Pro division. Competing in the Pro division allows you to win prize money, so I won $500 for getting second place, which was the first time I ever made money doing this. There are other opportunities that can come from this, in the form of sponsorships and such. Also,

getting an agent who believes in you can make all the difference going forward.

The recipe to being a champion includes doing something you're good at; continuing to improve at it; and being competitive and wanting to win. Champions understand what it means to win—it feels great to win—it feels great to be on top. Winning is a great motivator, it helps you to keep pushing yourself and striving to do even better. I have a passion for working out and it lead me to weightlifting and eventually to my bodybuilding competition career. But, even if I wasn't competing as a bodybuilder, I would still lift weights, and I would still strive to be the best I could be.

Not only was my professional life as a bodybuilder taking off, my personal life hit new incredible highs. I met this beautiful woman, Forbes Riley, who is the love of my life, and we're now engaged. She won my heart. I've never had anyone in my life who believed in me so much and supported my dreams, just appreciating me for who I am. When I first met her, she was so energetic, kind and so incredibly happy. She just had this fire that I've never experienced with anybody else before. I reached out to her and started flirting and she flirted back. That led to us meeting again, where I really had to opportunity to learn who she was. Not only was she very successful and energetic, but I got to experience how she changed people's lives so that they can realize their dreams. So that makes Forbes a very special person, and that's the Forbes most people know. But, I have had the privilege to explore another side of Forbes, the one that is exposed when her guard is down, and the audience is gone—the more vulnerable, nurturing, loving side. There's a curious, funny little girl that lives deep inside. She's so innocent, so beautiful and she just seemed to lock that part of herself away. But she's allowed me to open up the door to her heart. And I love her for that.

Lesson #1: Know what it takes to get what you want

If you don't know what it takes, then you're going to fail. Most things take some form of sacrifice, some grit to get through, determination to challenge yourself and beat your last achievement to keep succeeding. In bodybuilding, I have to sacrifice eating fun and tasty foods. But, after

a while you get used to it, and you notice the difference it makes in your performance and the physical changes in your body. Over a course of years, those changes are enormous. My grandfather once gave me advice when I was helping him build a roadway, and I had to break up all of these rocks. He would tell me not to think about it and just focus on doing the job. So, when I eat, I don't think about what it tastes like or how unpleasurable it is, I just eat the healthy foods and get it done.

Lesson #2: There are no options but winning

I just don't entertain any option other than what I need to do to win. When I'm training for a competition, I wake up very early, and try to get in one extra workout. I don't think about how tired I might be, or if I feel like doing it. I just get up and put in the time and focus, because I know that putting in that extra time and energy might be the difference in getting a win at competition. It's the extra focus on the goal that gets me to put in the additional work to win, and I don't allow myself the time to think about what I feel like doing. The priority is winning and doing the work to win, not caring about how I might feel about it at any given time.

Lesson #3: Always believe

It's not easy, continuing to believe when everything seems to be going wrong, or you feel lost or without direction. But, belief in the fact that the journey is worth it, that the sacrifices are worth it, that the heartache is worth it—on the other side is winning the championship, earning the gig and getting the love of your life. Believing that it's just around the corner and putting in the work, makes it happen.

Joshua Self

has always aspired to greatness, and his success as a 2-time Arnold Classic bodybuilding champion and World Fitness Federation bodybuilding champion is no surprise. He has an unparalleled drive to be successful, which is reflected in his strict dedication and commitment to his training. Incredibly, Joshua is only beginning his journey on his path to world-wide acclaim, and is actively training to become the next Mr. Universe.

Aside from his passion for pushing himself to be the best, Joshua is a student of exercise physiology and biomechanics. His understanding of the precision movements of the body has allowed him to avoid injuries during his own bodybuilding training. However, Joshua enjoys teaching these techniques to his personal training clients, which allows them to train more efficiently, with less strain on their body, while achieving faster results.

Joshua expresses himself creatively as a 3D design and rendering artist, and has received his degree in this specialty from The Art Institute in Las Vegas, NV. He has also had the opportunity to work as a model and actor in a variety of nationally-recognized television and movie projects. Joshua's ambition is boundless, as he is currently developing a unique online physical fitness training program, which utilizes an animated 3D virtual avatar of himself to teach the correct biomechanical form for each exercise.

To learn more about Joshua, contact him at:

www.JoshuaSelf360.com

Nothing in the world
is IMPOSSIBLE -
even the word has I'M
Possible in it!

- Audrey Hepburn

What Have You **Forbes'd** Lately?

My name is Julianna Stark, and I Forbes'd a successful career while valuing what matters. Too many people think that's impossible to have balance. It's not. Have you ever watched someone die? I have. The absolute hardest thing I've ever had to do was watch my beautiful, young mother suffer through a battle with cancer. When you're on your deathbed, absolutely nothing else matters except for the time spent with your loved ones. Know what matters, and never lose sight of it—you're business can thrive at the same time, more or less, I promise.

6 Figures in
BOOTS & JEANS

By Julianna Stark

I don't really need an introduction. I'm a bold woman and always have been. I've never followed the guaranteed path, because I thrive on excitement and pushing the limits. Risky adventures, which excite my spirit have always been an essential part of my life. My destiny is to influence the world, and to have this impact I have learned that I need to live a life unconstrained by society.

Life is more interesting when you don't have all the answers. In September 2016, I decided to sell everything I own and start traveling around the United States. I just jumped right into this adventure, and still to this day I don't have all the answers. I saw an open road full of excitement, and I got behind the wheel. This has been one of the most freeing experiences of my life. You don't know freedom until everything you own fits into a vehicle, and you can bounce through the states without agendas.

I cannot stress to you enough about how freeing and peaceful this newfound life is. You really don't realize how much stress clutter puts on your subconscious until you get rid of everything that isn't a necessity. I have nothing weighing me down and nothing to worry over. By eliminating the unnecessary, I have found more money and less stress. Minimalism is not that you should own nothing, it's that nothing should

hold you. I naturally focus on what really matters now. It feels better to experience things than to have ideas. Word to the wise—concentrate on the stuff you really love and get rid of the rest!

Lesson #1: Stop being "normal" and be more "you"

To me, being normal is the same thing as being inauthentic. According to most, I am not normal because I chose a free ride over white picket fences. Surprising to many, I am not poor. I am not uneducated. I am, in fact, not homeless either. Just because I live a different life doesn't mean that I'm not normal. Really though, who's to say what normal is? Not me or you, so travel the path that is true to your soul. Maybe, in fact, one day I will settle down, but until then I move to seek other places, other souls, and different experiences. My mission is to die with no road untraveled.

Lesson #2: Live life on your own terms

Mark Cuban said, "It doesn't matter how you live. It doesn't matter what car you drive. It doesn't matter what kind of clothes you wear. The more you stress over bills, the more difficult it is to focus on your goals. The cheaper you can live, the greater your options."

Life is too short to always toil away, so figure out what your best life looks like, and live it on your own terms. Get off of the hamster wheel of waking up, working, and paying bills. There's so much more to life than being chained to your job so you can afford luxuries. You don't need to make everyone happy or impress anyone. You need to do things that make yourself happy even if people don't agree with it, and a lot of times they're not going to agree with it. By doing what makes your soul happy, and not conforming to society standards, you're being true to yourself, and that will cause you to have an exciting and fulfilling life because you listened to your own heart.

Lesson #3: Life is short—focus on what matters

Have you ever watched someone die? I have. The absolute hardest thing I have ever had to do was watch my beautiful, young mother suffer through a cancer battle. When you are on your deathbed, absolutely nothing else matters except for the time with loved ones. All I have left

of her are the memories that will forever be in my heart. Memories of her sending flowers to school every Valentine's Day. Memories of her shooting hoops or playing volleyball with us kids. Memories of her always being home when I got off the school bus. Memories of her loving and supporting her little wild child.

I get my adventurous spirit from my mother, and she always encouraged me to take risks and live life however I wanted to. Since I grew up with the mentality of "the greater the risk, the greater the reward" it was only natural for me to get into the most challenging industry in America- insurance sales. This career has been a blessing because it has allowed me the freedom to travel all over the United States while helping families and building new friendships along the way.

My mother's cancer battle opened my eyes to the financial devastation that unexpected illnesses can cause. She battled for a year and a half and was way too sick to work, but yet we had everyday bills to pay. It was extremely tough, and we had to receive help from our friends and church. The financial strain put a lot of added stress on her, and if only we would have had a cancer insurance policy that paid cash directly to us, then she could have focused on the fight and not the finances. I tell everyone I meet about what I do because I believe that every person needs this coverage, as 1 out of 2 men and 1 out of 3 women will get some type of cancer in their lifetime. Family history doesn't even matter because 90% of cancer is caused by our environment these days. Take a look around because it's everywhere: air, food, water… where we work and live. Cancer plays no favorites.

If cancer, heart disease, or an accident strikes today, is your backup plan to wipe out your savings and sell off everything that you worked so hard all your life to acquire? If you answered yes, then I encourage you to reach out to me for a free quote and to see how your premiums are refunded (less any claims paid) if you stay healthy.

Are you are stuck in a dead-end job and know that there's more to life, and are you ready to experience fun and freedom? Are you sick of corporate America and playing by their rules? If you answered yes, then I would love to share with you how you can make 6 figures in boots and jeans by joining my team at Stark Enterprise Group.

Julianna Stark

is ranked in the top 10% of insurance sales agents in the country and has set an extraordinary record of selling $24,000 in gross annual premiums in 90 minutes. These skills have allowed her to help people avoid financial devastation due to the result of life-changing events, such as car accidents and cancer.

She holds the #1 spot for the best week in sales in 2018 and her sights just keep getting bigger and bigger. Julianna is committed to retiring by the age of 40 and is eager to fulfill her dream of retiring and traveling the world with her significant other while embracing a life full of adventure, serenity, and abundance.

To learn more about Julianna, contact her at:

Juli_Stark@yahoo.com
@StarkEnterpriseGroup on Facebook

It's a funny thing about life - if you refuse to accept anything but the best, you very often get it!

- W. Somerset Maughan

What Have You **Forbes'd** Lately?

My name is Justin Holland, and I Forbes'd my renewed youthful drive and innovation thanks to Forbes Factor. I was feeling like my life was in a rut—not bad, but stuck. Meeting Forbes and following her teachings taught me to work through strategy, motivation and intention, and that it's better when you think in terms of team and partnerships. Creative work tends to be solitary, but business requires teammates, even if you're just there for motivation and support, but it gets even better when you don't just stop there.

My Future by

DESIGN

By Justin Holland

I was 14, and my mom didn't have much money. I just wanted to look cool, as I had just entered high school, where looks were everything. I went to a school which had 4,000 kids. Some people blended in, but I stood out. That became my thing. While the clothes that I wanted were not in the family budget, I was resourceful and came up with my own solution to the issue. I asked mom to teach me how to sew so I could make my own clothing. Mom pulled out the old sewing machine she had, put the thread in it and said, "there you go", and walked away. The lesson was over! This was daunting to me, but it made me even more determined since she was obviously not going to be of any help. Back then, the Internet did not exist, there was no way to YouTube it or to ask Google. I had to teach myself everything. My mindset was that someone was going to make these clothes, so why not me? The excitement I had of making something unique and cool that no one else had was hard to contain. My first completed garment was the result of finding some fabric laying around the house, cutting it out and sewing up a shirt from a pattern I made myself. That single project laid the foundation for my journey into the creative and exciting world of fashion design.

By senior year in high school, I was making my own shirts and thrift shopping suits. Everyone thought I was one of the rich kids because of

the way I dressed. I financed my fledgling enterprise with two other businesses I had started. The first business was selling cookies I had made to students in school. I wasn't supposed to, but I wasn't going to let a little thing like a stupid "rule" get in the way of my fortune. I had a cult following for the cookies (The first question out of everyone I have reacquainted within recent years is "Where are the cookies?"). The second business was a DJing company. I played homecomings, club parties, etc. I guess you could say I've been a serial entrepreneur since the beginning. I did not want to work for anyone else as an employee. What started out of necessity morphed into an attitude of "I can do whatever I want, so why do it for someone else!"

This pervasive feeling for job independence was cemented by watching my parents. My dad is a nurse, and he would come back from work talking about wiping up vomit and such, then getting screamed at by his boss. This did not sound appealing to me at all. Mom, by my senior year, was a salesperson for a slide house, which made slideshows. She didn't like it, but it paid the bills. During this time, she watched me grow as an entrepreneur. This gave her the "guts" to go back to school. She then became a government employee with her new education and worked for the EPA for 26 years. It was not quite an independent job, but at least she liked it. She was doing something she wanted to do rather than what she thought she had to do.

After high school, I applied to one college- I knew where I wanted to go and what I wanted to do. I was in the early college program at the School of the Art Institute (SAIC), and they offered a 20% scholarship to one lucky recipient from the program. That recipient was me! I actually had 9 college credits thanks to the program before I even started college. Since the School of the Art Institute of Chicago was local, and I could stay at home while going, it made sense. I would have loved to have gone to Parsons School of Design in New York, but that was cost-prohibitive, and besides, SAIC is just as good.

I definitely wanted to make clothes when I got there, as I was hooked on fashion design. The first year, you have to do all of your prerequisites. Then, you have to apply to get into the fashion department. I got into it, but I also have a major in surface design. I actually spent more time in the surface design department than the fashion department.

Money was always tight, but my parents helped me. So this created the need for me to explore more entrepreneurial options. I had a scholarship that helped out tremendously, and I got the Perry Ellis Scholarship while in school, but none of this came close to covering all of the costs. By junior year, I had a job, I was DJing 3 weddings a week, doing 18 credit hours, and had started a sewing production company making cummerbunds. Needless to say, sleep was optional.

One thing led to another, and by the time I graduated from school, I found myself promoting parties and DJing in clubs. During this time, I became more serious about clothing production. I had a crew that did the sewing, while I did patterns for local companies in the fashion and uniform industry.

From there, I started a line of clothing called "Tru Native". I sold to Native American casino stores and convenience stores on Native American reservations from Michigan to California. I almost broke into the uniform business, as I had several orders with a big casino in Wisconsin. But the great recession hit, and this opportunity evaporated. I was once again forced to be resourceful. So I recreated myself by restarting my pattern production company. While I still do patterns for companies, I have started an Amazon business, and am now making my mark in real estate investment.

There was a time, quite recently, when I felt as though I had become stagnant. I was fortunate to have met Forbes Riley and worked with her during Forbes Factor Live. That experience amplified my life. Working with Forbes has reminded me that there are no limits to what I can do. She has shaken me out of that complacent mode and kicked me into high gear. I have charged up my inner-drive, which served me well when I was younger. But now, I am doing it with much more experience, help and focus. Forbes has forced me to once again dream bigger and get out of my comfort zone. She has proven that things I thought were holding me back were all in my mind. She taught me that every day I need to first concentrate on a few action items, then do the tactical work that is needed to get paid. Her mentorship has dramatically shifted my mindset, and the results that I've achieved in my recent pursuits in life clearly reflect that. There is so much more left to create, build and manifest, and I'm excited to see what happens next.

Justin Holland

developed an eye for fashion design in high school. The excitement he received from seeing his vision come to life on his mother's sewing machine led him to obtain a Bachelor of Fine Arts degree at The School of the Art Institute of Chicago. Justin excelled at his craft and was awarded a number of prestigious accolades, including the Early College scholarship and the Perry Ellis Fashion Scholarship.

Throughout the years, Justin has created clothing designs ranging from streetwear to high-end couture. He is presently in the development of a couture streetwear line, merging high-end technical execution with a modern streetwear aesthetic. The goal of Justin's fashion designs is to express a sense of empowerment and youthful enthusiasm while making the wearer feel comfortable through precise and thoughtful tailoring.

Justin's abilities are not limited to fashion, as he has successfully leveraged his creative mindset and outside-of-the-box thinking to cross-over into other successful entrepreneurial endeavors, including a number of rapidly growing eCommerce businesses, and an expanding real estate investment portfolio.

To learn more about Justin, contact him at:
www.HollandClothing.com

*It's what you learn after
you think you know it
all that counts*

- John Wooden

What Have You **Forbes'd** Lately?

My name is Justin Yanagida, and I Forbes'd a support system for my fitness business and a healthier me. Growing up, I always taught that if I wanted to get something done right, I would have to do it myself. That unhealthy mindset threw me into horrible physical health, to the point where in my first few years in business, I had collapsed two times from anxiety attacks. I love fitness, but I realized that my business wasn't acting like a business. I was a solopreneur or a self-employed business owner, but doing everything on my own was literally killing me.

Aloha

ACTION!

By Justin Yanagida

I was born with a liver condition, was 40 pounds overweight as a teenager, was diagnosed with attention deficit hyperactivity disorder (ADHD), suffered from chronic asthma, was physically attacked, and subjected to daily bullying. I have lived a beautiful life! It may seem like an endless cycle of pain, abuse and turmoil to others, but all of these obstacles have given me my superpower-the incredible power to "choose". I always had it, but I never realized it until these obstacles forced me to confront my inner strength, and to become unafraid of wielding the immense power I possessed. The obstacles I faced pushed me to life's edge, literally, as I stood there on a bridge, up high over the tranquil beauty of the island of Maui. It was there where the pain and turmoil of my tumultuous life intersected with a gripping purpose. As if the hand of God was rescuing me from my life of anguish and placing me on a new path, a mission, a new way of thinking, while all of the negative experiences were being washed away by the soft breeze of the Hawaiian air. I pulled my leg back from the edge of the bridge, and stood uplifted, strong, and renewed. I had made the "choice" to never be a victim again, and made a commitment to myself of fulfilling my destiny of helping others.

Being a victim was something that seemed to easily cling to me throughout my life because I let it--out of fear. This pattern of victimization began

early in school, where I was ostracized as an overweight and awkward kid. I just did not fit in. It was incredibly rough because I desperately wanted to have a set of friends, but no one wanted to associate with me, let alone be a "friend". My parents were always there for me, and were as loving as any parents could be, but not even their immense shield of love could spare me from the pain I endured at the hands of others and their ridicule and bullying. While my own personal pain was deep and very real, the deepest hurt I experienced was from witnessing my parents being verbally assaulted with prejudicial remarks. I looked up to my parents with pride, I saw myself in them, and each time I heard them being verbally attacked with hurtful remarks, such as "go back to where they came from", or "to speak English" caused a little piece of my heart to be crushed. I was overwhelmed, all of my physical and emotional pain had manifested itself as depression, anger, and the worst of all, defeat. I could not find any stability or strength in my life, I was struggling each day to find something to cling to so that I would not be washed away by the relentless waves of my feelings of anguish and loneliness. I filled my time fantasizing how I would end my life to free myself from this hell, wondering if anyone would care.

The lines between fantasy and reality soon blurred, as I attempted to take my life on many occasions. On my last attempt, fate brought me to that bridge in Maui. I was waiting for something, anything other than this feeling of pain I had carried for so long. The feeling of death and its acceptance grew within me with each passing breath. My defining moment had arrived, as I stood high above the beautiful serenity of Maui. My vision and past memories slowed down as if in slow motion, and my thoughts started to come into clarity. I allowed all of the clutter in my mind to drift away, and my intense feeling of impending doom was replaced with a slow focus toward what meant the most to me in life, and what I held dear to my heart. My pain and despair with life led me to this moment, and it allowed me to see that I had a "choice". I had never felt that before. I was always a victim-a powerless victim. And now my desperation and my willingness to crumble, aroused an inner strength-a superpower. I made the choice right then that I wanted to contribute and leave something to the world one day, and that belief helped me hang on to a purpose greater than myself. I stepped away from that bridge shattering that hollow shell of a life, with a renewed

purpose, drive and determination. With my superpower revealed, I carried boundless inner strength and confidence that I could conquer any obstacle and reach any goal I ever wanted. I had crossed over a bridge to a new life.

The self-confidence I began to experience continued to grow stronger every day. And this new feeling of individual strength lead me to become involved in training Brazilian jiu-jitsu, and wrestling for the high school team. I had finally found a focus and a passion. One day while training, I was targeted by a bully. There were no coaches or anyone that could help me. I was being targeted as the victim again. My mind rapidly played back all those years of being victimized, bullied and being treated less-than. And in that moment, instead of submitting to the feeling of helplessness, as I had in the past, I chose to make a stand for myself and those that supported me-my family. My power radiated, and I subdued the bully within an instant of him attacking me. I had taken personal responsibility for my safety. For the first time, I would no longer allow myself to be victimized—I had the power to control my circumstances, and it felt incredible!

I continued to fall in love with the sport of wrestling and Brazilian jiu-jitsu. The sense of inner strength and confidence I had was infectious, and it made me want to challenge myself and compete against those at a higher skill level above me. I needed to improve my strength and conditioning, but the words "purpose" and "dedication" were words that did not really apply to my world in the past, and now they defined my new mindset. I began a rigorous and ambitious weight training regimen to increase my strength and ability. I became obsessed with my training, and I committed to learn from many different experts to become more efficient in my training efforts. I wanted to be the best I could be. My life was looking up!

During college I struggled to maintain the level of dedication to my physical training that I had when I was wrestling. I fell off my commitment to myself, the one I pledged on that bridge in Maui-to never be a victim again. I still had doubts about myself and my confidence, and I let myself slide to the point that I started hanging out with people that did not really care about me or themselves. The

gradual disregard I had for my own well-being eventually lead to all-out recklessness and partying, which was fueled by a combination of weed and alcohol. One Sunday afternoon, one like any other, I woke up in a malaise after a hard night of excess drinking. This was different though, something was "off". As I went to move, I felt a sharp pain ricochet through in my abdomen. The pain grew in intensity, to the point where it affected my ability to walk or move. I had the pain checked out by a doctor and discovered that I had a liver condition that I was born with. Combined with the excess partying, he told me that I was on track for liver cancer, and that I wouldn't live to see my 30th birthday. The only hope I had was to take a drug that was not fully FDA approved for my specific condition. In fact, the doctor wanted me to sign my life away in case it failed.

Almost immediately, my world felt like it was slipping through my fingers, and I descended into a deep depression, and I dropped out of college. I felt terrible about myself and for the worry I put on my family. This was a wakeup call in the truest sense. If I was going to fulfill my destiny of helping others, I had to reconnect with my pledge of not being victimized by my health setback. Recommitted, I rid myself of all things and influences that were not helping me grow physically, mentally and spiritually. In fact, it lead me to my current path in life, one as a fitness trainer and nutrition specialist. This profession is one like no other, as it has given me the incredible privilege of serving thousands of people. It has been personally gratifying to see my clients living happier and healthier lifestyles and enjoying their progress and success.

Lesson #1: Gratitude

Gratitude is highly underrated and one of the best medicines for our mind, body, and spirit. Research shows that when we are grateful our body produces endorphins— "feel good" hormones. Nothing is impossible, everything becomes a blessing and were able to see opportunities when presented when we have a heart full of gratitude.

Lesson #2: Commitment conquers all

What I realized, what my professor would always tell us about what is excellent was—it had everything to do with commitment. In my opinion, he worded it in little differently, but for me, excellence is a commitment to finish. That's what excellence is: commitment to finishing a task or a project with complete dedication. Learning how to apply commitment in my life was the single greatest game-changer I experienced. It changed my life. I started to improve our business, my education, I started to read interesting books, I started learning from the best people, and I eventually found my way to success.

Lesson #3: We can't do it alone

I learned that we can't do everything ourselves, and that's one of the hardest life lessons for me. Growing up, I always thought that if I wanted to get something done right, that I would have to do it myself. So, I'd do everything myself. This unhealthy mindset threw me into very bad health, to the point where my first few years in business caused me to collapse multiple times from anxiety attacks. Sure, I am promoting fitness being healthy: healthy body, healthy mind… But here I am collapsing from anxiety attacks! I got my blood tested and had physical examinations. The results showed that my cortisol, which is a stress hormone, was so high that it started eating my organs. I realized quickly that I needed to make big changes, immediately. I loved fitness, but I realized that my business wasn't being run like a business. I was a solopreneur or a self-employed business owner, but doing everything on my own was literally killing me.

I made a new commitment that day to train fitness leaders who are able to help me impact the state of Hawaii, the nation, and internationally to Japan. We are very blessed, and I have learned the power of delegation. My business now has seven incredible staff members, and we are still looking to add more people to our dynamic team.

By learning the art of delegation, I've been able to have a healthier balance in my life. Not just improved balance in my own body, but in relationships. Now I spend much more time with the people who

really need it and much more time with family and loved ones, as well as taking valuable time for myself.

Finally, I am looking forward to creating a "mastermind" program to impact the lives of the people in Hawaii. I want to help young adults succeed who don't fit into corporate America. This will be a realization of my life's purpose amplified, and the fulfillment of the purpose I have set for myself.

Justin Yanagida

has always been committed to pursuing the best version of himself. That passion and his quest for excellence has yielded a deep desire to excel as an elite health and fitness professional. Justin's commitment to his clients' success is reflected in his commitment to having a deep understanding of the science and research behind optimal fitness and health.

As a graduate from the National Personal Training Institute and a National Academy of Sports Medicine Personal Trainer and Nutrition Specialist, Justin knows how to formulate a customized strategy for a successful diet and training program. His skill and methodology for motivating and teaching his clients transcend the physical training industry as a whole, and has set a new benchmark for elite personal trainers.

Justin does not just want his clients to achieve exceptional health and fitness, he wants them to excel in all facets of their life, and is committed to spreading this message across Hawaii, including his beloved Maui.

To learn more about Justin, go to:

www.YanagidaFitness.com
@Justin_Yanagida on Instagram, Facebook,
and Snapchat

What Have You **Forbes'd** Lately?

My name is Kevin Cabriales, and I Forbes'd the development of my, hard- fought, technology/health business. Forbes shared her life story with us during an event in California. Through this story, she inspired us to achieve our dreams. She also invited us to attend her event in St. Petersburg, FL, the Forbes Factor Live and Launch Lab.While there, I learned how to overcome my fears, ask for help, and partnered with people who had the skills and resources I needed and lacked to get my business off the ground.

Health in

PARADISE

by Kevin Cabriales

I knew nothing about how I would reach those in need or how to start a business. In spite of my fear, I chose to push forward on my entrepreneurial journey. My passion for technology and improving the lives of others was ignited, and it led me to develop a solution that could be accessible to nearly everyone on the planet. This solution centered on incorporating modern technology with chiropractic medicine, which would provide valuable information through a health-related website and mobile application, or "app", for a smartphone that assists people with their health needs. For example, the app will provide important insight into the multitude of health focused products and services that are available, allowing users to make informed choices about how to improve their health and stay fit. The app will also help people connect with others that have similar health/fitness goals, as well as trainers and other professionals who can provide valuable information about any health topic.

During my business building quest, I got an invitation to attend an event in California hosted by Casey Adams, a well-known social media influencer. This event included many successful entrepreneurs. But it was Forbes Riley who took the stage and inspired me to unleash my passion for helping others, to improve their health, and to reach for my dreams. This event was life changing, and it altered how I viewed

the impact I could have on the lives of others beyond my chiropractic practice.

I had the opportunity to see Forbes again at another event, Forbes Factor Live, where I listened, transfixed to the experiences of the other entrepreneurs who shared how they overcame the challenges life threw at them by sheer determination. I also had the chance to meet with these individuals and gained an understanding of their mindset, and the extreme level of passion and determination that is required for making a business a success. They were self-starters who learned everything on their own, and then took appropriate action to build their businesses. I learned a wealth of information from these people, including business tactics and strategies, overcoming personal barriers and dealing with the stress of running a business. Most importantly, I've made personal connections, while leveraging the skills and expertise of others to increase my business IQ.

Forbes made me understand that being afraid won't take you anywhere. And unless I reach out to people, I will not know whether or not they are willing to help me. In fact, this mindset lead me to meet the CEO of a large company, whom I have asked for business help. If not for Forbes, I couldn't have done that.

I have devoted an incredible amount of time developing my health app and becoming business-minded, so that I can help people effectively achieve their fitness and wellness goals. While I am still on my journey to see the launch of the app, I've learned many lessons, and here are a few l want to share:

Lesson #1: Invest in Your Fitness

Don't overlook your fitness, and invest in yourself. You'll experience better health overall, less illness and more energy, which will help you focus on your goals and live your best life.

You can also learn from the health and fitness experiences of others, so you won't end up buying ineffective products/services. For instance, instead of buying energy drinks, you may find out that you should take

more vitamins to boost your energy and to maintain equal blood sugar levels throughout the day.

Lesson #2: Follow Your Dreams

If you believe in your dreams, doors will open for you. Even if the goal seems unrealistic, you should do everything you can to make your dreams a reality, and you'll find that nothing is impossible.

Some people taste success early, and others struggle. No matter how long the journey is for you, be careful not to let others tell you what you can or can't do. Often, you'll come across people, even close friends, and family who care for you, who try to convince you to let go of your dreams. They don't understand what's driving you—that your journey is bigger than your fears. Don't lose faith in your dreams if you want to become successful. Thank them for caring, but politely dismiss their negativity, and keep pushing through. That's where all success lives.

Lesson#3: Real Goals Take Time

There's no shortcut. You need to keep in mind that it takes determination and immense effort to achieve your goals. But nothing can stop you if you stay focused and determined. You should have a long-term vision and the will to achieve those goals.

Use mentors, books, seminars, and masterminds... surround yourself with people who are where you are striving to be. They will give you tips and resources to help you overcome challenges and avoid costly mistakes along the way. But, it is still not a substitute for hard work and effort.

Kevin Cabriales

is a chiropractor enriching lives through mind-body alignment and breathwork sessions. He is also writing instructional guides to reach others around the world on the Internet to deliver valuable health-related lessons and tools.

Kevin enjoys traveling throughout the state of Hawaii and beyond. He continues to grow his business IQ through mentorship from leading chiropractors, business leaders and entrepreneurs.

To learn more about Kevin, contact him at:
aligndakine@gmail.com

*Be someone that
makes you happy*

- Neil Strauss

What Have You **Forbes'd** Lately?

My name is Kinzey Ray, and I Forbes'd self-worth. It's so amazing what happens when you decide that you're worthy and you're just as good as the next person, because you are! That's where the magic happens: I learned that when you choose to love yourself and everything that comes with that, the flaws, the good, the bad, the ugly, and everything in between, because nobody's perfect, it's pure magic!

Beyond
BEAUTY

By Kinzey Ray

I have been a professional model for the past 10 years, and it has been an incredible journey. I've realized when people look at me, they must think "Oh man, life must just be so easy for her. She is tall, skinny and pretty, and she just gets paid to be beautiful." The industry itself, the people in the industry, the work and your inner-self are huge contributing factors in a modeling career, and you truly can't judge a book by its cover. You have to take time to open up the cover and really read the story, because truths are going to be a lot deeper than you could ever imagine based on a pretty cover.

I've done some incredible things in my modeling career. I've worked with big brands, like Maxim magazine, Yamaha and Jägermeister, just to name a few. In addition, I have been published in magazines and billboards across the nation and even won an international bikini contest. My success over the years has been incredible success, and often that's what people see when they look at me. They see this bright, bubbly ray of sunshine, and they think that's all there is to me.

When people see me, they think that's how it's always been in life, that it just must be so easy to be "her." Being in the vainest industry on the planet, I've learned that the stigma against models runs deep. You're expected to look perfect with no flaws, they expect that you'll be late all

of the time and lazy with no work ethic, no personality and no brains. "Don't you just stand there to have someone take a photo?", people ask.

People love models because they're pretty, and I understand that, but it's as though they don't realize that we're also whole people—it sounds a little crazy to say, but experiencing it is very tough. Even models, believe it or not, are complex humans. We are intelligent and professional, and we have a full range of talents, skills, emotions, and struggles, just like anyone else. Just because you can see us as a 2D image in a magazine or on TV doesn't mean that we aren't real people living our lives with all of the similar challenges life flings at everyone.

I've overheard people say that I'm just this airhead who can't think for myself, that I'm just pretty and entitled; and that I think "Oh, just give me whatever, because I'm pretty". Of course, I knew that I wasn't any of those things, and I have been bold enough to stand up for myself and break that stigma, one instance at a time. And that's always been my mission, since I decided to be a model—I didn't want to be thought of as that entitled pretty girl. I wanted to be a role model, somebody that girls can look up to and when they learn about me, they'd learn that I worked for my success. They would see that I chose to advance in my career by working my butt off, being professional, having a good work ethic, building professional relationships, caring about quality and my reputation. They would know that there are real people behind these images they see who take their career seriously, who want to inspire others and who are committed to achieving with dignity. But, I haven't always been this way. I haven't always been so confident and sure of who I am and what I want.

For so many years, I didn't think I was beautiful, and I certainly didn't think that I could be a model. A very painful part of my reality is that I struggled with self-harm as a teenager. I have scars all up and down my legs, and just that flaw alone made me believe that I could not be a successful model. You see, being a professional model was always a dream that I held, but it was one that I thought I would never be able to bring to life. I thought it would be ridiculous to even attempt to pursue this dream of mine due to my scars, and that was a deep blow, especially because I had done this to myself.

I believed for so long that because I wasn't perfect, I could not be successful; successful as a model or anything, really. I remember going to my second photo shoot and seeing this girl, she had the most beautifully sculpted legs. She must have played soccer or something, because her legs were so lean and toned. I remember watching her at that photoshoot, she was walking around in short shorts, dancing around the room in these high heels, and she looked so beautiful! I just remember looking at her perfect legs, and I was crushed. My heart broke knowing that I will never have perfect legs like her, and I told myself that story over and over in my head that I should just give up on my dream. It's stupid to pursue, because I'm not perfect—I mean, look at those legs!

I'd dream of being perfect, being a model, traveling the world and taking beautiful photos... Then, I'd remember the scars on my legs—those scars that now live on my skin forever to remind me of how stupid I was, and it's something I can't take back. I made a mistake once, and now that's who I am forever. I'd let that negativity sink in and poison my confidence, self-worth, and my dreams.

Hold on! What? That's crazy, right? I was just as pretty, tall, skinny, and just as capable as the next girl. Why am I letting some marks on my legs, something so small and so tiny, hold me back from pursuing my dreams? I needed to decide that I was worthy of achieving my goals before things could ever start really happening for me, but that took a little time to achieve. Until one day, I got it!

Lesson #1: You are worthy

It's so amazing what happens when you decide you are worthy and you are just as good as the next person, because you are! That's where the magic happened. I learned that when you choose to love yourself and everything that comes with that, the flaws, the good, the bad, the ugly, and everything in between, because nobody's perfect, that's pure magic!

I don't care if you're the most beautiful person on the planet or anyone else; we all wake up with bad breath in the morning, and we all have flaws. We are all equal, and you're just as capable as the next person, and once that really sinks into your identity, it's like fireworks start

exploding. That's when things will change, and that is when you truly are limitless and nobody can stop you.

Lesson #2: Believe it to manifest it

It was in that moment that I finally believed that I was just as good as the next girl, and I could do it just as well, if not better than anyone else. Once I started believing in myself, that is when everything changed, and that is when I started to manifest all of my dreams into reality. I look back at all of my accomplishments, and I'm still in awe-- how did I do that? Because if we are being real, I am in the most vain industry on the planet--modeling. You're supposed to look perfect-- that's expected. And realistically, the girl with scars all over her legs shouldn't be a bikini model, but I am. I won an international bikini contest!

Even more interesting, I get people who ask me all the time: Do pros in the industry care about your scars? Was that an issue with you being a model? Honestly, I don't know. Maybe they cared, maybe they didn't. Nobody ever said anything, because I soon learned to lead with inner strength and confidence when I walked in the room, and I knew I was worthy enough to be there, and I was good enough to get jobs and contracts. I didn't care about my scars anymore—I no longer let them define me. So, I didn't care, and apparently, they didn't care.

Lesson #3: Confidence wins

It's such an important concept to remember: the most confident person in the room will always win. If you think that something is an issue, and you let it get to you, they're going to think something is an issue too. But, if you don't let a potential issue get to you—if you don't let it define you—if you're so confident in who you are and what you're doing, that's what people are going to see. I no longer walk into a room and think "oh my gosh, what are they going to think?" No, I walk into a room so sure of myself, so confident, and that's what people see.

You have to believe in yourself more than anyone else. You have to believe in yourself first before anyone else will believe in you. The struggle doesn't end, either, it's a journey. Even though I had gained confidence in who I was and what I wanted, I still always viewed myself as an underdog. I always felt as if I had something to make up for, and I'd

think about those few minutes of extra photoshop they would have to do on my legs to airbrush my scars. I felt like I had to make up for that, so that people wouldn't notice or wouldn't care. I always made it a point to go above and beyond to break that model stigma: I was always early, because in the modeling industry and in life, if you're not early, you're late. I remember that lesson stuck with me from the beginning, and it has played a huge part in my success. I would always do my part to ask what I could do to be of service. Do you need help moving equipment? Do you need anything? How can I be of help? I would show up early. I would stay late. I would work harder than anybody else, and I take my career and professionalism seriously.

I've spent hours and hours and hours and hours and hours, Friday nights and Saturday nights in the studio, working on my craft, working on my skill set. When I walk into a room, I know I deserve to be there, because I've put in the work. I wasn't there just because I was pretty. I was there because I

was talented, skilled, and I knew what I was doing. The confident person that I eventually became radiated so bright it transcended the scars, because they love my kindness and my work ethic and just being around me.

So many people talk about models as having zero personality and being stuck up, but that stigma isn't even the norm, and it certainly wasn't me. I added value everywhere that I went. I truly believe that's what made me so successful, because hard work will beat talent when talent doesn't work hard. My hard work is going to kick your merely talented ass all day long. I truly believe that the time I put into the work was a huge factor in my success, plus just believing in myself.

I won so many contests that I technically shouldn't have won, and from sheer "votes," I almost always was behind. But, I came in first and won anyway. I won billboard contests and an international bikini contest against all odds, because in my heart and soul, I believed that I was going to do it. I don't know why, but I just knew that this is what I'm supposed to do. I am supposed to win this. I'm going to be on that billboard, and I'm going to win that international bikini contest. So, I did, and it's so cool!

There is a quote by Henry Ford, "Whether you think you can or you think you can't, you're right." Any time I doubt myself, that doubt fails me. Anytime I believe in myself, I win every single time. Only confidence wins, which is such an easy concept to forget: you will win when you believe you will win. I hope that out of all of what you read in this chapter this is your main takeaway: If you choose to love yourself exactly how you are and if you stop comparing yourself to the perfect girl on Instagram, because she's really not as perfect as you think, and you just love yourself and work on yourself, and are actively working on being the best you that you can be, and fall in love with who that person is, you will be able to do anything!

It's that love for everything that you are and everything that you aren't that creates some serious magic in your life. Realizing that you are a gift to this world will change your life, because there is no other you! People are so worried about being themselves, they even try to be somebody else at times—comparing themselves to others, competing with others, wishing they had someone else's life and so on. Success begins when you stop wishing to be someone else and start falling in love with your unique self. You have a special, unique gift that you were supposed to share with this world, and you cannot truly share it with somebody until you accept who you are and put an end to wishing you were somebody else. I wished to be other people for so long, and it wasn't until I was like, oh my gosh, Kinsey (me) is pretty cool. I want to be her. And, then I started developing Kinsey and started focusing on becoming the best me possible; that that's when my life transformed. Because I do have an amazing gift to share with the world, and it's unlike anyone or anything else. And you have a unique gift that the world is waiting to receive. Once I stopped trying to be perfect and thinking that being perfect would impress people, I realized that I could inspire others more by showing them how I embraced my imperfections and used them to build inner-strength and confidence.

Plus, being perfect isn't inspiring. People don't like "perfect" because it isn't attainable, and instead it's intimidating and elitist. Real power happens when you embrace your past and your flaws out loud so you can lead by example, then show others how they can do the same, because that's who you really are. All those imperfections are a part of

your experience, and it helps shape you and helps get you where you are today. Showing others how to harness that strength is a valuable gift!

Don't let your past and your flaws define you. That is only a part of your whole story, and it doesn't have the power to write your future. I don't have to be Kinsey with the scars. I can be Kinsey Ray, model, light, magician; I can be whoever I want, and I don't have to let these scars be who I am. I did let them define me for too long, but now they inspire me. I am inspired to help others through my personal experience. I realize my scars are just another piece of the puzzle that make up who I am. It's not who I am. This realization has been so phenomenal in terms of personal growth and how I've been able to give and be of service to others.

One of my greatest joys is to see the people who hear my story realize their mistakes, whether they were in prison or have something in their past that they feel defines them, then when they let that go and realize "that's not who I am! I can be whatever I want in the future."

I love teaching people that you can be absolutely anything you want, all you have to do is stop giving away your power to the events that occured in the past, and start focusing on what you want and who you are.

Kinzey Ray

is a successful model, who has won numerous awards in the U.S. and abroad. She has been featured in numerous high-profile publications, such as Maxim magazine. Kinzey has a passion for seeing people grow to their potential.

In addition to her success in front of the camera, she owns and operates her own nutritional business. Her mission in life is to make the world a more magical place, and to help others live a life full of health, wealth, love, happiness and magic.

To learn more about Kinzey, go to:
www.KinzeyRay.com

*Kill your excuses, or
they will kill you*

- David Wong

What Have You **Forbes'd** Lately?

My name is Kipling Solid, and I Forbes'd a path towards self-healing and improving my business. For too long, though I excelled at encouraging others, I was lacking in my own ability to cultivate a loving relationship with myself. My goal was perfection. Anger would turn me against myself and others close to me. I blew the whistle on self-criticisms before anyone else could. Demanding more self-imposed control backfired. I felt helpless inside. Eventually, I learned that what I was battling with was depression that I merely dismissed as anxiety. I've learned how to ask for help. That went a long way, so did finding other healthy ways to cope. Ultimately, I also learned that helping and caring for myself allowed me to help others just that much better.

"Solid"

SUCCESS

By Kipling Solid

You have ants in your pants." That is what my aunt Bessie used to say. I can see why. I talked too much in class. I was always tapping my pencil or jiggling my legs. I never got anywhere by simply walking, instead I jumped, hopped, skipped, cartwheeled, and bicycled everywhere I wanted to go. Now, looking back, I see that other adjectives assigned to me in childhood, such as tenacious, curious, and fearless still fit me today. What my aunt Bessie and others didn't see is that it wasn't "ants" that sent me into a state of perpetual motion, but something much more significant.

My life's story is still being written, but it is a tapestry of who I was and whom I was meant to become. Being tenacious, curious, and fearless paved a way towards a single-minded goal. That goal was to never, ever sit at a desk job!

My mom, a single parent, was in tune with my energetic side. On my 9th birthday, she gave me a pogo stick! This was not just any pogo stick- it was the Rolls Royce of all gifts! It had a built-in counter from zero to a thousand! I could actually track every jump. It would take 20 or 30 sessions with the pogo stick before mastering 1,000 consecutive jumps. I remember looking over the handles and hearing that wonderful "click" of the counter as it turned over and read 1,000. Mission accomplished!

I was "performing" for me. I did not need someone else to be my hero. I was my own hero. When I had accomplished that mission, I exclaimed a resounding, "YES", and uncoiled a powerful fist pump into the air, as I cried out like an Olympic champion!

My childhood became a blessing that drove me to become the motivating force I am today. I was tenacious--because it was not safe for me to be anything else but resolute in whatever I put my mind to. Unbeknownst to me, I had already begun my own motivational training for a future in personal training. I saw it as fun, not work, to push others beyond their own limitations to achieve their goals. What I knew early on was that serious work had to be fun. Today I am able to help people stick with an exercise routine because of my deep personal love of expression through movement. I figured out that transforming bodies was like performing magic or molding clay. I wanted to educate others about the power of distraction from their self-limiting beliefs. The personal-training space was the perfect environment in which to teach these concepts.

Perhaps I did not know how to mind my own business--or was I just curious? At 6 years old, I remember approaching an elderly stranger on the street. I was very concerned. My first thought was that he must be sad. He was a grandfather-like figure, and could not stand up straight, and appeared to be in pain. His appearance was that of a twisted and tangled vine. My optimistic nature suggested that he must have lost something if he's looking at the ground. Dropping my mom's hand, I marched confidently up to him asking loudly if I could help him find what he lost. He just chuckled and waved me on. I wondered what was so funny. I later learned that he had acquired a debilitating problem with his spine.

I remember being aghast at how painful his condition appeared. I had many questions. Why doesn't he get help? Where do you think his family is? Can they fix him? I find myself asking the same questions today. I am a problem solver. When it comes to bodies, each one is like a new canvas, and I have much appreciation for those stepping into my care. Call it desperation or hope, but I am usually the last resort for people when it comes to resolving physical pain.

Today, I am able to pick up on the tiniest nuance. I am acutely aware of unspoken ailments that leave individuals favoring one side of the body ever so slightly. I have seen those who, for years, have not been able to connect the pains in their body, mind, and hearts. The body has its own language and gives cues through subtle "hints". I am particularly aware of these hints and it allows me to be particularly effective in helping those in my care.

In my own life, I struggled for years with physical limitations and injuries, experiencing muscle pain and a lumbar disc problem. My joint pain began in college, and it became like a rhythmic drumbeat of "Military Taps." I didn't want a lifetime of "just getting by" with my physical issues, followed by regular doctor visits. What would healing look like if stillness settled down and my mind wasn't on hyper pain alert? I did not know then that "breathing" leads the crusade for healing and managing pain in an imploding body. Exploring how to yield and listening to my breathing pattern calms the "ants in my pants" that I've carried around for so long.

I approached my goals fearlessly when young. The older I got the more I realized there must be a tape looping in my head with the self-deprecating thoughts. "I'm not enough." When was the last time you got silly and played, jumped or danced in public while no one was watching? As kids, we "went for it!" In adulthood, manifesting a carefree spirit gets noticeably harder with the numerous stressors, traumas, and responsibilities one tends to take on.

As I digress towards a memory when life made it easier to pounce on what I wanted. My first official impromptu stage performance happened at Chicago's "Second City" Theater. As everyone began taking their seats for the show, a voice announced over a loudspeaker, "while the actors are getting ready, if anyone would like to take the stage you may do so now!" I looked around for any takers. My internal dialogue and a momentary internal argument ensued. Should I stay or should I go? I quickly decided to "go for it." I took advantage of an opportunity then, much as I do till this day! Climbing onto the stage I began my performance.

"Behold!" A vision of chaos! I launched into numerous cartwheels, giant leaps, twirls, and high kicks. Talk about "flying by the seat of my pants," to which I still hear till this day. My first choreography of ballet and gymnastic skills. Arms reaching, legs flailing, putting all of me on display was freeing. This chaotic display ended with multiple somersaults and a dizzying leap to standing. When I think back, I wonder, who does this? Is it the "only child" syndrome? As an adult, it would look like insanity unless we were Gilda Radner, as she always brought out a childlike thrill to the stage. Losing ourselves and exploring our imagination does not conform to a world where we just have to "grow up".

Returning to reality from this event was difficult and disorienting. As I returned to the controlled me, I felt a polarizing sense of shame and embarrassment for losing control. I quietly slithered back towards my seat. All I could hear was the pounding of my heart in my ears. I believed an alien just hijacked my physical and emotional well-being up there. For God Sakes what was I thinking? In retrospect, this moment was a right-of-passage for me. I was live in front of an audience and nobody hissed or booed! I booed me. Reflecting, I not only survived the event, but it was a rush, and I somewhat thrived on the excitement.

I soon enjoyed performing in ballet recitals and leading roles in plays. The more I put myself out on a limb, the more often I began to wonder, "was I really good enough?" This message would haunt me most of my life. The more I performed and the better I became at the things I tried, the more the self-judgment and my internal criticisms grew louder. New experiences were uncomfortable, difficult and less fun. Now I had truly become the actress I've always wanted to be. Live the lie with a smile while the pain went deep into denial. My relationships began to shape me into what I did not know about myself. I liked myself less and I began taking on the colors of a chameleon not knowing how to love me. But maybe someone else would?

My childhood experiences shaped my creativity and desire for reaching beyond personal limitations and boundaries. As an adult, if I could not control the environment around me, I would control me more. Experience showed me that life, marriage, and children will quickly point out our lack of control over anything in life. It's difficult to hold up

the mirror and ask "who are you?". When your world starts to crumble who do you run to? I reluctantly had to look inward.

When starting my personal training business, it was a perfect marriage for me to control the framework of our goals. It was natural to be the glue or foundation for others to lean on, cry on, praise on and hate on. My passion became more about serving others needs and limitations and less about noticing my own needs, lack of growth and emotional limitations. After all, I was busy, and had a baptism by fire acquiring clientele with seizure disorders, mastectomies, cancer, MS, Parkinson's, ALS and on and on. I became intimately attached and acquainted with other's pain. I sometimes watched helplessly while clients were frustrated, discouraged, or lost in their battle to their disease. With joy, there is a real hardship and physical frailty, which sometimes causes a broken canvas to be unable to be fixed. A reminder that ultimately we are not in control. Through the decades, I've walked alongside individuals wearing the same armor of control as I have.

Ultimately our body will surrender in this journey. It takes determination to live and determination to die.

What matters is that we were created with a fierce spirit for survival, hope and a purpose to value and help others in life. It is healing to my soul to witness the strength of the human spirit in my clients! I could not imagine another career quite as fulfilling.

Helping others is gratifying work. But if we go home at night and neglect ourselves, emotionally, physically and spiritually we will become hollow inside. Setting goals and expectation can be very gratifying but when things do not go our way it comes with a price.

I conditioned, rather beat my body into submission to gain power and strength. Imposing tough demands on myself became a shield for a lack of confidence and safety. Into adulthood, I began to wear my physical attributes as a badge to preserve the lie that I had some form of self-worth. Inside myself, lied anxiety and worries about being a failure, which haunted me. I could not and would not let myself fail. It seemed like fear was lurking around every corner whispering, "you are an imposter." By today's standards that might be called "a poser." It became

the perfect cocktail to launch me into self-imposed extremes. Feeling physical pain with extremes, whether by exercise or relationships became a way of managing my emotional pain inside my frail world. When I could not control the environment around me, I controlled "me", and it was not in self-love.

Where I excelled at encouraging others, I lacked in my ability to cope with a loving relationship with myself. My goal was perfection. Anger would turn me against myself and others close to me. I blew the whistle on self-criticisms before anyone else could. Demanding more self-imposed control from myself backfired. I felt helpless on the inside. Ultimately, I learned I was battling depression that I merely dismissed as anxiety. I have learned how to ask for help a long way, while finding coping mechanisms, strategies, and tools, such as a "self-activation system," to continue my healing and to help my clients along this life journey.

I was good at holding others at arm's length without looking obvious or needy. A broad smile from my days of theatre served me well. I could beat myself up quietly and walk onto the stage and take a bow so to speak. My struggle to heal wounds of the heart and settle my fears left me very guarded about whom I would allow into my world. I believed if anyone really knew "me" they would not like what they see including my deep flaws. My judgments about not being good enough looked like overgrown weeds by adulthood. I started to become introverted and wondered where my voice went. I felt silenced and too fearful to communicate what I truly

wanted to share with the world. I knew I had something to say but felt too insignificant, all the while still looking like the extrovert.

One way I continued to manage to function was through a personal faith in God. I focused on promises and good truths that were His and it did take root.

When I took my eyes off of my own circumstances, I was able to look around and see all of the blessings in my life. If we welcome positive individuals into my inner-circle we can learn about ourselves. I decided to trust God and see myself through His eyes and friends and family

that loved me, and maybe someday I would believe in "me", too. A great start for change is changing your state of mind.

The Fitness Field opened up tremendous possibilities for my future. As I became more confident in my abilities over the years, I found the fire and motivation to keep my finger on the pulse of an ever-changing industry. I was determined to keep up by learning from others. Always learning and growing!

I visualized my future the first moment I laid eyes on Jack LaLanne and was glued to his exercise show in the 1970's. He revolutionized the fitness industry into big business and helped pave a way for my career.

My DNA and genetics determined that I was going to be fascinated and mesmerized by the body and muscular system at a very young age! Jack LaLanne's gymnastics jumpsuit rocked his muscles, while his smile had me dreamy-eyed. He exuded a life of health, energy, joy and happiness. He seemed to reach through the picture tube, and gave you a piece of himself, which has impacted me to this day. From that day forward, I longed for a such a journey of my own.

By the late 70s early 80s, Jane Fonda's stick-like thighs were all the rage. It was a toss-up for me. Go for the flat butt and skinny legs, which I thought was a feminine look, or get some of Jack LaLanne's muscles.

It wasn't long before women's bodybuilding would be a more provocative door into the fitness world. I would soon catch the bodybuilding bug. I would pore over Joe and Betty Weider's, *Muscle and Fitness* magazine. This time I chose building my muscles over worrying about my thighs touching. I enjoyed idolizing shredded feminine muscles like Rachel McLeish, or a combo platter of looking like Cory Everson and Carla Dunlap. I chose a nice blend of feminine and masculine approach. No more skinny dreams for me! After educating my mind and body in bodybuilding, I trained for my first competition and emerged as a tan bodybuilding goddess.

The self-flogging theme continues to rear its ugly head as the "external" me was more confident than the "internal" me. I did get better at ignoring the "ants" in my brain. As an adult, I have learned that an

imprisoned mind limits optimal performance in the body and in business. For me, a lifetime of moving freely has fueled my energetic abilities, thus inspiring me deeply to feel to the core of my being. I can bravely speak from a place of managing anxiety and depression by moving from a passionate place deep in my core. It is a very real place when endorphins are released to bathe the mind in rest and recovery. I jokingly call exercise my "Prozac." By definition, endorphins are groups of hormones secreted in the brain which activate the body's opiate receptors, causing an analgesic effect. I can basically say that a lifetime of exercise has protected my psychological well-being, but not withholding meds if and when necessary.

Do you know I already determined I had won well before winning my first bodybuilding competition. What I did not know after 3 months of training is that I would become the first-place and overall winner. I swept 2 shows in one evening! I was in disbelief that by setting my intentions and doing the work were correct. It was my rockstar moment as I heard my name chanted from the audience. When I stepped off the stage, I felt like a champion inside and out, much like I did when punching the air after a thousand jumps on my pogo stick years before!

Lesson 1: Determination

Determination takes us beyond our own limitations. Expectation becomes a satisfactory outcome. I conditioned my body to gain power and strength, which appeared as confidence and safety. I wore my physical attributes as a badge to protect my self-worth. Extreme exercise becomes a way of managing my inside world when I could not control the environment around me.

Where I excelled at encouraging others, I lacked in my ability to cope with myself and my relationships. Eventually my anger turned inwards, and that was my form of remaining in control. Ultimately the struggle to heal wounds of the heart and settle my fears left me very guarded about whom I would let into my world. I felt if anyone really knew me they would see my flaws. My judgments about not being good enough took root by adulthood. I began a path towards being an introvert all the while still looking like the extravert.

Lesson #2: Follow trailblazers—the path to success

Whether it's jack LaLanne, Jane Fonda, Rachel McLeish, Cory Everson, Carla Dunlap or Joe and Betty Weider's "Muscle and Fitness" magazine—following the ones who paved ways and left large paths is always a good strategy to find success!

Lesson #3: Free your mind

Before a competition, it was important to know I was a winner even before winning. I was seen as disciplined and earned a level respect from others. The "external" me was far more confident in my younger years than the "internal" me.

My high school friend, Paul, insisted I should meet his friend Forbes Riley. It took me 3 years to reach out to her. Finally ready, I heard an internal voice saying "pack your bags and go serve and learn from her". With Paul at my side, we served as staff and support at the 4 percent conference where Forbes commanded the audience with her passionate words and fierce presence.

Meeting Forbes was like being given an opportunity to meet a reflection of my own childhood. Hearing Forbes say: "I am enough" reminded me of just that—Yes, I am enough! At her Forbes Factor Live event, I was invited on board as staff, and then I was informed that I was also to be a participant. As her event began, I quickly noticed Forbes was a master at reading everyone in the room. (Psst! even if her back is turned towards you.) Forbes understands the human condition and is acutely intuitive of human behavior. She has mastered her craft.

I could not have predicted Forbes would peel back my layers so easily. The sting of Forbes' awareness, was like a cold glass of water tossed into my face. I emerged from this event with a badge of courage that day.

*"Success is not final, failure is not fatal-it is the courage to continue that counts." --***Winston S. Churchill**

Forbes, thank you for believing in me—ants and all—from the day we met you have helped me believe in myself and inspire others to do the same.

Kipling Solid

pioneered one of the first in-home personal fitness companies in Chicago's gold coast over 25 years ago. She has developed cutting-edge innovations in both fitness and pilates in the areas of strength training, functional movement and injury prevention.

Her experience has led her to create the BungiGym Fitness System, a system used to align, redefine and heal painful movements in minutes.

If you would like to learn more about Kipling and how BungiGym can make massive changes to your body, go to:

www.cmbiz.vcardinfo.com

Leadership isn't a rank, nor a position, it's a choice, a decision

- Simon Sinek

What Have You **Forbes'd** Lately?

My name is Lari Thomas, and I Forbes'd trust and confidence when I thought those qualities might be lost forever in me. Trust can be frightening, but it's critical to life. Trust people, even if your trust is totally obliterated from past experiences. Keep trusting people, because eventually you will find people you can truly trust, and they will make your life so rich and beautiful just by being in it. You don't have to have a big circle of trust, but everyone needs a small circle of trust. Thank you, Forbes Riley. Through your compassion, insight and wisdom, you've given me a chance to get to know who I was meant to be.

Creating
CONFIDENCE

By Lari Thomas

I am not perfect. But, there is no question that I am enough. I am not the smartest. But, I am absolutely brilliant. I am not the prettiest. But, I am incredibly stunning. My value was defined the day I was born, and it is not negotiable. My life has been filled with pain, struggle and turmoil, but what many would say was insurmountable, I have now overcome. I alone define my own self-worth - no one else. The battles I have overcome have given me the virtue of an empathetic heart and an undying optimism for the future. My passion to inspire others to succeed who have suffered through emotional and physical abuse continues to this day.

Life had never seemed very fair. Rather cruel in fact. My earliest memories are filled with physical and emotional abuse inflicted on me by my mother, because in her opinion I was not perfect and she felt insulted by it. I cannot deny it, I am not perfect. In fact, I was born with crooked legs, which required many doctor appointments, hospital stays, and many procedures to straighten them. But all of the attention I received from this made my mom jealous. It is hard to even fathom, but my mother didn't like the fact that I was getting all the attention at that time. No matter how hard I wanted it, my mother and I never connected.

I still wear many of my scars, and they remind me of the physical struggles I have endured. I particularly remember that when I was about 4 years old, I was playing outside with my friends, as any little kid would, and my mom wanted me to come in to take a bath. Incensed because I wanted to continue to play, she grabbed me by the hair, dragged me to the bathroom, turned on the tub and held my foot under the stream of hot water, and then she forced my right hand under the water as well. Later that day I remember being on the couch and her telling me that just because I got "hurt" doesn't mean that I can just sit around and do nothing! I suffered permanent burns to my skin, and I wear the scars to this day.

You are probably wondering why I wasn't taken away from her? Well, she told everyone that I was trying to be helpful and didn't realize that I had to turn the cold water on as well. Perfectly reasonable? Of course, it is. My mom always masqueraded her lies as the "reason" I was injured. My role in my family was to be part of the clean-up crew. I was always told that I was to be "seen" but not "heard", and not to talk to anybody. I have been referred to as "Cinderella" many times. I did all the cleaning, from the house cleaning to the laundry, as well as the cooking, lawn maintenance, taking care of the animals and taking care of the trash. I did anything and everything that had to be done to make the house presentable at all times.

I recall one occasion, when my mom didn't want me going outside to have fun at a birthday party next door, and she made me scrub a spot of paint that had been there since the house had been built, just because all of the other chores had been done. Fortunately, the 100-year-old woman who the birthday party was for realized I wasn't there and insisted on holding the party up until I could attend! Although my mother was angry and fuming, she always liked to keep up appearance of a normal life, and she eventually allowed me to attend the party. My mother was the type that when people came over to the house, she would always say "Don't mind the house it's a mess" and they would say "what mess?" Then I would have to scrub the whole house from top to bottom since people came into the house.

I only remember having 2 birthdays before leaving that house. It was easy to cover up not celebrating my birthday since my littlest sister's birthday

was the following week. The thinking was "why have 2 parties?" The two I remember are my 5th birthday because I got a Minnie Mouse Ice cream cake from Carvel and my 15th birthday because my mother stood over me until I woke on my 15th birthday and told me to get a job because all you're getting is a roof and food. I am not paying for anything else for you. Of course, I'm the only 1 of the 6 kids she said this too, and as time went on I found out that my mother told my father that she didn't even want me or my older brother anymore. However, she still wanted the support for both of us included with the check she expected to get for my other 4 siblings.

Well, I did get a job, and because of that job and my second job, which was an almost full time, I paid for my Senior Trip in High School, which back then was very expensive. Incredibly, my mother and I worked at the same place at my 2nd job, and my boss was giving her my paycheck instead of me. She "lost" all of my paychecks, and I had to go back to the boss and ask for my money to be given directly to me, which my boss didn't want to do. He said that it's my fault that I couldn't keep track of my paychecks. I then replied that I thought it was against the law to give a paycheck to someone other than the worker named on the check even if they may be giving the checks to the worker's mother, especially without that worker's permissions. I lost that job soon after that confrontation.

When the day for taking the High School trip arrived, my mom decided that she didn't want me to go. I told her that since I had paid for the whole trip plus the clothing to wear on the trip I was going and that she could not stop me. I was going. In fact, I was so close to 18 years old, the police would have laughed at her, and escorted me to the airport.

Finally, when I couldn't take dealing with my mom anymore, I met this boy at a concert--one that I wasn't supposed to go to in the first place. It was Def Leppard, third row on the floor. What 16-year-old girl would say no to that opportunity? This boy was in college and was my "white knight." He showed me that there was more out in the world for me than what my mother was telling me was available. He gave me the courage to go to my senior prom and never go home.

Don't get me wrong, I love my mother. I'm just very sad about the way she is. I am long past forgiving her. But I did try and make up with her multiple times because I had been told "that's your mother, you should still be with your mother." The first time I tried, she told me that everything that was wrong with her life was my fault. So, I spent the first part of my life being very shy and quiet. I didn't know how to asked for help because every time I ask for help I was punished. Even my own family looked at me funny and treated me differently because my mother was very good at making it look like it was all in my head, and that I was just causing trouble to get attention.

When I started working in the bigger world and learned that I actually do have a voice and can take control of my life, I still heard my mother's voice in the back of my mind that I was useless, no good and wouldn't do anything good with my life. By the way, she actually had said that to me at a time that I was working a full-time job, as well as going to school full-time to become a court reporter, all while paying my rent and all my bills on time, on my own. After I graduated, I actually did both jobs at the same time for about 3 years.

Then came the day my grandfather died. He was the one who kept life bearable when I was a kid and who was a big influence on my life. I decided that Connecticut was no longer for me, so I moved south to Florida. My dad and stepmom lived in Naples. What a big change—Florida was a whole different world than the Northeast. The mixture of people is amazing. They are from all over and working in the courthouse as a court reporter really opened my eyes to the fact that everyone has a story. I lived with my dad and stepmother, but they were newly married and still doing the newlywed thing, and I felt like I was intruding, so I moved to Tallahassee, Florida.

After moving to Florida I realized that Tallahassee was too small of a town and that it was going to be difficult to be a court reporter there, and I was really tired of waiting for attorneys to pay me, so I started working as a temp through an agency to find out what else I might like to do.

I was working all of these jobs as a receptionist, which I was way overqualified for, but not knowing anyone, it was a great way to meet

different people and get a feel for the area since I was new and alone. It was also an exercise in futility. I never stayed at any one assignment more than a few weeks. Let's just say that there are only two good things I got out of being a temp worker- I met my husband, and I stumbled into the health insurance field.

At first, I wasn't so impressed. I was still a temp, initially, but the manager I worked for turned out to be a gentleman who believed in giving people a chance to go outside of their designated job assignment, and I was getting bored of being a receptionist and assistant. I was told there was a need for people with health insurance experience. However, the people out on the floor have health insurance experience but they don't have my computer skills. My then manager knew that I updated and made the court reports better, and I got all of the other the departments are on the same page, so that they could see everything quickly. I knew I could do health insurance, easily!

I was finally hired in the health insurance industry, and I had found my niche. I loved it. I was helping people who needed it, and it was more of education than anything else. I started as an assistant, and I progressed up to sales, which is where I really shined, because not only was I helping people with their problems, but I got to solve them too. I found my voice doing sales for BlueCross BlueShield of Florida.

Now at the time, I had a little dog named Petey who was black & white, and he had a black eye, and I had my two little kids. BlueCross BlueShield monitored our calls to see if their sales scripts were being used, who was more successful selling their products, and how we describe their products. I used their scripts, but I'd put my spin on them. One day, we had a big team meeting and they were going through the roster. Then they called my name, and as I stood up they said, "Lari Thomas, wait a minute, you're the Petey Lady. We've been listening to the stories of your little dog all these months. It's nice to finally meet you!"

I was amazed because my co-workers were so sick of these stories that they used to tease me, but I didn't think anything of it. Then there was this one gentleman whose child was home sick from school and kept bothering him. I said, "Is he bored?" Yeah, because now that he's home he's feeling better. So, I actually asked this gentleman to get a bucket of

warm water with some soap and a toothbrush. He said OK. I then said, tell him if he's so bored he can go clean his bathroom and hand him the bucket and the toothbrush. It's something my grandfather would do to us kids when we said we had nothing to do. Well, this gentleman did it, and the kid went and found something to do and didn't bother us for the rest of the call.

Of course, this is the one call that is reviewed for my weekly training call for that week. The rep for BlueCross BlueShield said I cannot believe you told a potential customer how to handle their child and that they did it with a smile and we still got the contract. That is the funniest story we'd ever heard. This was my first try at sales. I had no previous training. I knew the business. I knew the product. I knew how to use the software and I just went for it.

Then there was my husband who I met in Tallahassee before moving to Orlando just prior to our wedding. Throughout my trials and tribulations, he was there. He liked to cook and shop and take care of the kids. He would let me sleep in late on the weekends so he could take the kids to work with him. He always encouraged me to go back to school, to try new things and to go out with my friends. Then, while I was working for Blue Cross Blue Shield, things changed, and my husband got sick. It started simply enough. He had a simple slip and fall, which turned out to be a pinched nerve, which turned out to be ALS also known as Lou Gehrig's disease. Then, my life quickly became: get up, get the kids to daycare, drive to work for a full shift, drive back home 40 minutes to pick up the kids and drive back 40 minutes to the hospital or the nursing home that my husband was in every day, so the kids could see him, and then drive another 40 minutes back home, then dinner and bed. That was the routine, just to have it start all over the next day!

I did this for over a year. I was no longer able to work for Blue Cross Blue Shield, which was rather sad because I did enjoy it. I did find out later that my name had been up for Rookie of the Year, and the prize was a full expense paid week-long train ride from Florida to Ontario, Canada. Since I had to leave, I was no longer eligible, but I thought "that's not bad for my first try in sales", and I was proud of that. Less than a week after leaving the company, my husband passed away.

After my husband passed away, I moved back to Connecticut. I tried once again to reconcile with my family. As soon as I got back up there, I realized it wasn't my best decision. I finally realized how toxic my mother was for me and my kids. She started telling everybody how I was dating other men already. It wasn't true, of course. The truth is, I was basically in bed for the next year, grieving. I was only getting up long enough to get the kids off to school, clean the house a bit, and sleep until the kids would get home from school. I would make them dinner and get them ready for the next day. I stayed up long enough so that they could do their homework, play, and then I would sleep until the next morning. I was depressed and mourning. This went on for almost a year and a half.

I finally woke up one day, because my husband and I made an agreement to each other before he'd gotten sick, that if anything happened to either one of us the other one would continue on with their life. We've got so much to offer people, I don't want you wallowing in just being a parent. I will always miss him. He was an absolute gentleman. He was a wonderful man and my kids will also always miss him.

I also finally figured out that somehow I was in a competition with my mother. All these years I grew up with a narcissist, always putting the heat on me and siblings to take the heat, so that she could be seen as the Mother of the Year. The biggest discovery was when my brother told me that my mom didn't like that I was a widow. The lightbulb went off in my head. She was Roman Catholic and in her mind, I was the Big W (widow) which is a respected position in the Church as opposed to the Big D (divorced) like she was and I purposely had a husband who died just to show her up. Like I wanted any of this to happen! Actually, between you and me, the Pope actually dissolved my parent's marriage thru a Papal Bull.

I got back to Florida, and I have a gentleman friend. We've been together for seven years. My kids are now in high school, and they're both getting excellent grades. My daughter who is 15 already has a scholarship for two years of college, and she's on the road to early graduation. She wants to be emancipated per her request. She called me the other day and told me that she found her first job by herself for the summer, however,

she's upset because she has to wait until she is 16. I then reflected on all of this from where I came from, and I said to myself "You know, I may have been put down when I was a kid, but boy I turned out to be a pretty darn good mom." I decided it was finally my turn.

Now, I've been reading books on how to improve myself and change your mindset and all those good things, but what really gave me the kick I needed was at the 4 Percent conference, where I met Forbes Riley.

Forbes pulled me out of an audience of 600 to 700 people. I was nervous when she asked who wanted the little thing that she was holding out because I was behind the VIP people, and when you go to these events, VIP people get the first shot, but she pulled ME out. She pulled me up on stage, and I talked for 10 minutes. I will admit that it stressed me out, and I had to leave the room because it was just too much for me. You have to understand that after being told for years that you're worthless, that no one wants to hear what you have to say, that your words mean nothing, and you're unimportant, to comprehend that people now people want to talk to you and listen to you and hear your story and that you are an inspiration is a mind-blowing experience.

Lesson #1: Find your voice and own it

I've learned that even a crooked-legged little girl with no voice who was rejected all of her life can find her voice. If I can find my voice, anyone can find their voice and own it. Use your voice only for good.

Lesson #2: Ask for help and accept it

Learn to ask for help. Even if everybody says no, keep asking. Someone will say "yes" eventually. We all need help, and accepting help from others is actually a gift to them. We all need to give and receive, that's how life keeps working for us all.

Lesson #3: Keep trusting others

Trust people even if your trust is totally obliterated from past experiences. Keep trusting people, because eventually you will find people you can trust, and they will make your life so rich and beautiful just by being in

it. You don't have to have a big circle of trust, but everyone needs a small circle of trust.

What have I Forbes'd lately:

I found my voice, and it changed my life. You will see me on the banners of Forbes Factor Live. I am the lady in pink. I do not look like that anymore, and it's been less than six months. People did not recognize my picture. I went to another event, and they asked me for my Facebook page, and they said "That's not you anymore."

I've met people from 71 countries in the last week, and three people have approached me to work on projects, international projects, in real estate. These projects and the lessons I learn are going to change my life. It all was because of Forbes pulling me up on the stage and welcoming me into her world of pure empowerment and transformation.

Forbes gave me the courage and the steadfastness to keep me going on the route I have set for myself. For example, I attended in LA, where I met a lot of people and one of them was a CEO of a company out of Norway. This CEO had come out for a breather and he always saw me in the middle of the group of people always talking. Now he sees me on the side by myself. I was just on the side because I was talking to my boyfriend, and I just wanted some privacy. After the call, I sat there thinking for a second, and I didn't even hear him come up. He asks, "Lari are you okay because you're sitting here and everybody else is over there."

You can imagine how touched I was that this gentleman from Norway, who runs his own company and only knew me for this past few days, was concerned enough to come to check on me, because he already knew what kind of person I was and that I had to be in the middle of everything. I was never in the middle of anything growing up, and that this person who I just met already knew me a little bit better than I actually I knew myself. You are supposed to be over there not over here. When I was saying goodbye to him I told him how touched I was. He just said when you come to visit me, I will show you Norway!

I started a real estate business, and here is my real estate business plan: I buy tax deed sales, and I flip those homes. Then, I buy some more to fix up for people on Section 8. Once I reach a certain amount of units, then 50 percent of the income will be going into building homes for homeless vets and other homeless people.

Lari Thomas

transitioned from being a court reporter to a successful health insurance saleswoman. Over the last 5 years, she grew her company and became an independent contractor, working on various housing projects.

As a contractor, she especially enjoys fixing and flipping houses and working on housing developments. In her free time, she fulfills her passion for riding motorcycles, as well as enjoying her family and friends.

Sadly in 2019, Lari lost her battle with cancer and we miss her and send prayers and love to her family.

What Have You **Forbes'd** Lately?

My name is Leah Holmes, and I Forbes'd my fitness business. Don't run from your gifts, even if they scare or intimidate you. I asked the people around me what they thought my gifts were, and so many of them told me that sharing my knowledge on health and fitness was one of my greatest ones. Sharing and communicating that passion and understanding with others inspired them. I inspired them! My fitness coaching and lifestyle business came from that. I had only been focusing on my own training and athletic development before, and now I'm helping others!

On Track for

$UCCESS

By Leah Holmes

I was always a tomboy, raised around a lot of really athletic guys. When the guys were playing sports I would have to join them, playing with dolls was not for me. I was the girl who wanted to play in the mud and watch the guys race up and down the driveway. And because my competitive spirit was strong, I won many of those races. From 6 to 8 years old, I was just one of the boys, but then I started "developing" into a girl. For me, that was when my competitiveness really began to shine, and it became fun for me! I'd hang out with the guys all the time, so we put a running team together. I remembered my mom and uncle watching track and field, and I didn't know what that was. They just had me sit down and watch it.

I got excited, and I realized—that's what I wanna do! So, I asked them who was on the television screen, and they said: "That's the Olympic team." From then on I set my goal on becoming an Olympic track runner. I thought I'd practice a lot, so any opportunity I'd have to go outside and race with any friend, neighbor… anybody, I took that opportunity.

Eventually, I got to middle school where track and field were offered as a sport, and I thought I needed to have clear goals to get to the Olympics. I said, "First, I'm going to do whatever I can do to get on that track and

field team, whether it's boys only, girls only or both boys and girls team, I don't care! I just want to run and be on that team." I felt like I practiced already, because in my after-school center there was this kid, Bobby, who played football, and one day he said "Let's race to the park."

So, every day after school, we would race to the park, and I would win. I thought I was already a track runner. Now, I wanted to try out and join a team, and I figured I'd win every race! I felt like I was on top of the world.

Lesson #1: Don't give up—power through

In my second year, I lost my first race. It was 200 meters, and my friend Monique passed me, giving me my first loss. I didn't know how to take it. I didn't want to give up, so it made me push harder. But, it was a serious lesson for me to learn. It was definitely hard, but I realized that I needed to continue to work at this if I wanted to keep winning. I already loved to run, addictively at this point, so now it became a serious activity to push myself.

That mentality carried me over to high school, where I competed in track and field meets, but there was an emotional strain that wasn't there before. My mom was a single parent, and she was unable to make it to many of my track meets. I really needed her support, and her not being there actually hurt. I saw my teammates have family there, and I was one of very few that didn't any family to support me. I would look up and see families cheering and singing and dancing, and it made me miss my mom even more. My mom did the best she could, and she would make it to as many meets as possible, but it wasn't the same for me. It felt a little lonely to be a part of the team, while being one of the only ones who didn't have anyone there to cheer them on. So, frankly, the reason I quit the team was that my mom told me she couldn't get off of work in time to pick me up from the track.

While I still had this strong desire to continue to run, and I begged and begged, I even asked my grandfather to pick me up from school late, but he refused. I wasn't able to continue the sport at school, and it really hurt. I decided to find another way to solve this problem. I never looked at it with the perspective of "just because someone said no, I couldn't do

it any longer. So I thought "I'm going to take the bus and/or find a ride home or get a ride from my friend".

My mom would not allow me to ride the bus, but she would allow me to get a ride from my friend. Once I had my friend agree to give me rides, I joined the team again. I was really excited to be back! I was a junior in high school at this point, and my coach welcomed me back, and I started practicing while that competitive nature just came right back. I started working out with the female track team, and I won all of the races. I wanted to be challenged a little bit more, so I started working out with the guys. It's interesting that some of the guys played multiple of sports like football, baseball, and they would make these childish bets like "you owe me a cookie" or something like that to keep it fun, and a little bit to keep score.

Then, something happened. It was about midway through the track season, and it was incredibly cold outside. My friend Johnny and I were running together. And I'm not kidding—it was painfully cold, as we're running. But, as I'm running along the track, I felt the tear on my bone, and I lost control of my legs, and I just collapsed. Johnny, did the same exact thing, and we stood beside the track and we stretched for the next hour. We just sat there, and we cried a little bit because we didn't know when or how we were going to be able to run again. I became more upset as I sat there thinking about it, because he played football, but for me, that was the end of much my career in high school. So, I had to hang up my shoes and my shorts, and I left running alone. From there, I just focused on studying and getting to college.

At the time, my family was looking forward to me going to college, so that was what my focus became. I did go to college, but I also started to eat really poorly. I slipped into this really sad mental state—something I had never experienced before—and I was depressed. I did know that I caused this to happen in my life, and despite my injury, it healed, and it was time for me to get back to what I love doing—running.

So, I went out and did track and balance to work out, I'd jog here and there, too, but it wasn't the same for me. I got myself back into the gym to doing something active, because that's what I needed in order to get back to who Leah was. Then, the oddest thing happened, I honestly

could not move. I felt frozen when I walked into the gym. I decided to just go and sit on the machine and not budge. I was really in a low place. I decided to talk to a mentor that I worked with, and her name was Mrs. Jane. She was my supervisor at my work-study job, and I decided to talk to her about how things were affecting me. Things like my fitness level, being away from home, and not really knowing what to do.

Mrs. Jane just gave me that listening ear I needed and the mental strength to go back to the gym. I decided to use self-talk to guide myself through this obstacle- let me figure out how to train myself again, back to the place where I know myself and let's see what can happen. So I returned to the gym, regularly, but my eating habits were very poor. I was not a water drinker, instead, I was a sweet tea drinker—at least 3 to 4 times a day. I didn't know what healthy eating was. I was just a typical college student who went to the cafeteria.

Lesson #2: If you don't fit in, create a group where you do

I was sad and felt like I didn't fit in, and that I was in a strange place I didn't know. I just got angry, and I didn't know where to go. There isn't a place for an 18-year-old girl to go to figure all of this out. I did jump back in the gym, and I met some friends there. We decided to go to a group fitness class. We were all freshmen at Western Carolina University, and we decided to join the recreation center there. That was the most fun that I had since the day I injured my leg in high school!

We were all over the place, but we had a fun time, and that mattered most for the moment. I knew that there was a part of me that was given a gift of loving to feel fit and challenged, and sharing all of that with other people. I made that a part of my daily routine, and whether I was joined by my friends or not, I learned to just enjoy the time to myself. So, through my first 2 years in college, this helped me to sustain or bring me back to the "me" I knew.

Later, I decided to transfer and move to the middle of Carolina, and so I enrolled in the University of North Carolina at Greensboro. There were no check-ins there, so I didn't have to worry about going back to the state of mind where I couldn't work out on the track, because I wasn't able to sprint the way that I wanted. I also decided to devote

myself to other types of work, such as service work, volunteer work with homeless, or other activities in order to discover other things that were important to me.

Then, in the summer of 2008, something alarming happened. My sister and I were home for holiday break, and I remember just jumping up and down and feeling really hot. I didn't understand what was going on, but I felt something in my chest. I said to my sister, "This is awkward," while feeling my chest.

She said, "what's wrong ?"

"Just place your hand on my chest, it feels like a lump," I replied.

She said, "I'm not going to touch you, don't bother with it."

"Okay well, I need you to help me out."

Finally, she felt my chest and said "Oh my, yes go and call mommy and see what's going on!"

I went to my mom, and she brought me to a doctor. I was terrified as a 20-year-old with this sizable lump in my chest seemingly appearing out of nowhere. After the examination, we learned that I had a benign tumor. I had it removed, and I felt like everything was okay. Soon after, I was accepted to my first exchange program, and I went to Lima, Peru. I was there for six months, and it was the most beautiful experience because it was my first time living overseas by myself. I went there to learn Spanish, and I lived in an amazing international house with 35 other beautiful people from across the world who really exposed me to different cultures, and I just loved the whole experience.

Eventually, though, I became really homesick. I started to drink coffee there, and I went to Dunkin Donuts almost every day. I found one not far from our house in Lima, and I would go all the time not realizing that was my comfort, or my way of soothing my feelings of being homesick. I didn't usually drink coffee until then, but my mom did, probably around six times a day. I guess that Dunkin Donuts coffee made me feel close to my mom—the smell and familiarity.

When I came back to the states, I jumped back into my studies, but I felt another sharp pain in my chest where I had a surgery scar now. I learned after my surgery that it's common to have healing pains here and there for some years after the procedure, but I went back to visit my doctor to get it checked out. They did another ultrasound, and this time I had nine cysts. I was devastated. I didn't understand what I had been doing incorrectly with my diet or just in life to make this happen. I learned later that it was something hereditary, as one of my family had to deal with this too.

This really distracted me, and it was affecting my studies, so I decided to go and have a conversation with my doctor. He sat down with me and said that although these cysts are benign, he did not want them to potentially develop into anything that could be much more harmful in the long run.

I said "Okay, but what does that mean going forward? How do I take care of myself?"

He said, "What I need you to do is exercise and eat healthily." That was it, and I said okay, then I walked out the door.

I didn't really know what that meant. I thought I had been eating healthy my entire life. I was raised with starch on your plate, something green and meat, and always with a side of bread. I usually drank sweet tea, and I'd add a dessert. That's how I structured every meal, and most of my meals were full course meals. I know for a fact that I ate at least four times a day, so that's basically what went into my body. Well, breakfast was a little different. It was also a full course meal that would include eggs or ham or sausage, a biscuit, cereal, yogurt, and sweet tea.

Honestly, I thought that was how we were supposed to eat. Then, I would go to the gym, but when I looked in the mirror, I didn't like the girl I saw. I was someone who was used to being the best sprinter, but now I just couldn't move. I kind of freaked out, and I felt sluggish all the time—no energy and a little sick. I started to do a lot of research about what it meant to eat properly. I was surprised by what I learned so fast with just a little digging. For instance, sugar was always a big part of my diet. I thought I was doing the right things eating protein bars and

granola bars. I would always have a cookie or grab something sweet after a meal. I looked at myself, and I didn't like that girl physically. I learned that my food choices had nearly everything to do with what I saw that I didn't like.

I'm basing this on the physique that I had always had, eating exactly the same way, but going into my twenties my metabolism changed, and poor food choices were starting to add up with added weight gain and low energy. I didn't understand what I needed to do going forward, so I continued researching and I looked to my fitness community. I started to learn through other people's good nutrition habits.

Also, when I came back from Peru, my mom invited me to Zumba classes, and I didn't like it. I thought that "I was a timid, shy girl- a wallflower who just ran track, whose hips just went forward, never swaying side to side," and that Zumba was way too uncomfortable for me. But my mom continued to encourage me to come back to these classes, so I did. Then, I started to go to other classes, and the instructors would speak with me afterward. They would tell me that I was really good at Zumba, and that I should look into becoming certified teacher, and be a fill-in teacher for some of their classes.

At that time, I didn't have that level of confidence where I would attack that or jump right into the opportunity. Instead, I ran from even the thought of it, but it was constantly asked of me, and I constantly said "no".

Well, persistence won—theirs not mine. When I turned 25, I made a promise to myself, that every year of my life from here on out, I would step out of my comfort zone. So I got certified to teach Zumba, and I was invited to a charity event to teach, which was my first time officially teaching a class. I just jumped into this charity event, and I taught it alongside other Zumba instructor friends that I had made along the way, and I absolutely loved it! I loved it because it became not about me, but about those smiling faces that came to support the cause or support me while I was teaching. I learned that I have a gift of making people feel encouraged while they're in the gym space or when they're not as comfortable with doing those types of activities. And that positive energy flowed both ways—it energized me too. I decided to continue

with teaching Zumba, and members of the classes would constantly reach out to me when they started to see my body change or get results.

I made it my mission to learn how to teach as many formats of Zumba as I possibly could, so that I could train anybody. I even decided to teach children, and I started to teach teens, young adults, middle-aged groups and up to seniors. Then I started teaching people with special needs. Everybody deserves to live the most of their life that they can, and if I can have a part in helping them change their life in some way or contribute to their life in some manner, then that's very important to me.

Lesson #3: Do not run from your gifts even if they scare you

Do not run from your gifts. I went to a conference once, and at the conference one of the instructors there said, "When you get home, ask five people who know you very well what are your five gifts. They can base it on their interactions with you, things that you talked about or what they've observed." All of them said of me that my gift was my level of fitness and sharing that with other people no matter what fitness level they're in. The next gift they said had to do with how I can help people transform themselves. They also mentioned how well I work with children to help them learn about fitness and getting them excited about movement and about sports.

That was a huge lesson that I had to learn because it was something that I did try to run from, but when I surrendered myself to understand that those were my gifts, everything started to come into fruition. I understood that was my purpose.

Now, 7 years later as a professional fitness trainer, I've had the pleasure of training hundreds of people of all ages and walks of life. As the founder of Body By Leah, my programs can now reach countless people around the world to share excitement about health and fitness.

Leah Holmes

has an energy and passion for fitness and was known as the "energizer" growing up in Asheville, NC, where her love of fitness was forged in track and field. She excelled as an athlete and had Olympic dreams, but they were put on hold when she was injured in her first year of college. Attending her first aerobics class inspired her and set her on a new trajectory in life studying the personal training industry, and developing a curiosity for helping people get fit. Her professional fitness career began in 2012, and she has helped hundreds of people reach their health and fitness goals.

Leah's drive for success has resulted in her obtaining her Personal Training and Health Coaching certification, as well as a Bachelor's of Arts degree, a Master's Degree in Liberal Studies, and a Global Studies Certificate from the University of North Carolina-Greensboro. She is a digital marketing specialist focusing on fitness marketing and delivers routine "Health Talks" at gyms, churches and health centers to spread her message of "great living through health and fitness".

To learn more about how Leah can help you reach your fitness goals, download her free gift at:
www.FreeGiftFromLeah.com

To learn more about Leah, go to:
www.BodyByLeah.com

What Have You **Forbes'd** Lately?

My name is Lisa Paul Heydet, and I Forbes'd ZizzyBee Bags! ZizzyBee Bags is my company and product line that helps families get organized in a fun, very useful and creative way. My first important lesson in business was about the power of choosing perseverance and determination. Friends would ask me why I'm still doing my business after all the setbacks I have experienced, and how do I keep going? It's too easy to give up when challenges stare you down, but the truth is that it's a choice, and that it's about not giving in when your heart tells you that you're on the right path.

Success!

"IT'S IN THE BAG!"

By Lisa Paul Heydet

Toy cars, Legos and doll pieces...my house had become a sea adrift with miniature kids' toys strewn all about. I was constantly battling to keep my head above the rising tide of these miniature toys and my only life preserver was single-use, plastic zip-bags, the ones normally used to store food.

These bags served me in my initial desperation to gain control over the relentless waves of scattered toys throughout my house. But I loathed using these plastic bags, which were dangerous to kids, and end up clogging our landfills and polluting our oceans. Did you know that there will be more plastic in the ocean than fish by the year 2050? There are 3.5 trillion fish in our world ocean just to put this in perspective. I don't know about you, but I don't want my kids to have to scuba dive for plastic instead of beautiful fish! And this is a real problem close to home. There are currently five floating garbage patches in various locations in our oceans - the biggest being between Hawaii and California with plastic waste weighing as much as 500 jumbo jets and spanning the size of two Texas states. Fish, whales, seabirds, turtles and more have bellies FULL of plastic and 1 million marine animals are killed every year because of plastic waste entering our oceans. So, yeah, I loathe using plastic. In fact, since this is such a problem that is only going to get worse without action from all of us, we launched a movement called Take The Plastic

Pledge to motivate people to swap plastic items for other alternatives while raising money for ocean clean-up.

I had always been a problem solver and my entrepreneurial mindset led me to develop a solution for a convenient, environmentally-conscious organizing tool- the "ZizzyBee Bag". I started my company when I was going through a bad divorce. I wanted an alternative to single-use plastic bags to help keep these endless little parts from my kids' toys organized. I had many reasons to find a better solution -- first, the plastic zip-bags were not safe for my daughter when she was a toddler because she could put it over her head and suffocate, and second, single-use plastic zip-bags weren't durable, either. The bags would rip easily, and you'd have to throw it away and get another bag. I was surprised that there weren't any other organizing products for kids' toys besides bulky bins. As a mom, it was frustrating to have clutter everywhere with no good storage solutions. Plus, I really wasn't happy that we kept throwing plastic bags away, which I knew was bad for the environment and wastes a ton of money. I even learned after launching my company that we use single-use plastic sandwich bags on average for 12 seconds and then end up polluting the environment.

So, I set out to find a solution. I knew that as a mom we are always trying to find a way to have a little less chaos in our lives, and to make things easier for day-to-day living. Let's be honest, when moms are happy, everyone else in the family is happy, too! I was motivated to design my own washable, reusable, eco-friendly storage bags. First, I came up with a list of the features I wanted the bags to have. I wanted them to be made from durable white mesh; being see-through would allow you to see what's in the bag. I also wanted an easy zipper pull, which was suited for kid's small hands. The bags also needed a handle for hanging and for easy storage on a wall, closet, in a kid's room, at the gym, or in a playroom. I also wanted bright colors for the accent material to make the bags modern and trendy. Finally, I needed a fabric that was strong enough for matchbox cars and heavier toys, and I found all the materials in the USA. On one of my first expeditions for a suitable material, led me to mosquito netting in Florida. It was exactly what I was seeking - strong and durable. With the mesh bag material identified, I then interviewed eight mom and pop factories in Portland, Oregon to sew

and manufacture my bags. At that time, I named my company Bambino Toy Bags. I decided to have an initial test run of 1,600 bags produced. I knew the labor costs were higher in the U.S., but I needed to test the bags. On my first test, the bags sold out and were a hit! I then decided that I was going to go overseas to look for a factory to produce my bags. I looked at China, Taiwan, and Vietnam.

By this time I had to change my business name because my mom customers were using the bags for so many different uses in addition to toy bags. Plus, I knew that I was going to be selling in retail distribution so having legal rights to a name is really important. Wanting to do it correctly, I hired a lawyer and decided to trademark my name. I followed my gut and decided to move forward with retail distribution. You need to have a trademark so that you don't get sued for your name. This process was tedious—it was countless hours of writing company names down, and then my lawyer would say, "this sounds like a certain name that was already out there". So, I had to go back and be creative, to think differently about names. Then, I came up with "ZizzyBee Bags." Soon the bags were selling all over the country, then across the world! We had sales in England, Canada, and Australia. However, business took a turn downward as 30 percent of my inventory had a color defect from the factory in China. That was a big issue for me because our sales were great, we had been on the Today Show, and we were getting great press and interest—and sales. My choice was I could either quit or could keep going. I decided to keep going as this was my passion, and I believed in my product.

Perseverance and determination = success

My first lesson was about the power of choosing perseverance and determination. Friends would ask me why are you still doing your business after these problems, and how do you keep going?

The answer is that the alternative would be an insult to all of the work I've put in to this business, and to all of the people who believe in me. Upsets and defeats, in fact, make us stronger, and you learn a lot more from them- more than you do when everything is going so smoothly! I recently went to a conference and heard many business owners share

their stories of ups and downs and the struggles of running a business. Take Airbnb for example. They shared at the conference that it took them four years trying to convince investors, and it finally took off right at the end when they ALMOST gave up. Now they are a multi-billion dollar company. So yes, there were many ups and downs, and you have to react, but you get to decide how you react. Do you make these trials a positive or negative? It's all based on the way you frame them in your mind. I knew that my bags were helping so many people and making an impact. I needed to forge ahead, but also decided to take the summer off to gather my thoughts and spend quality time with my kids. People kept asking me when was I going to bring my bags back. "We want your bags," they would say. "We are excited for them." After doing critical research on potential manufacturers, I found a new one, and I picked everything back up again.

Starting over is a success strategy

I was basically starting over at this point. I had to build a new website, because my old website wasn't mobile-friendly, which just shows you how much changes in three years. I realized, looking back, how much I had learned not knowing exactly how to start a business. I'm so glad that I was able to figure it out on my own. I was a business administration major and a communications minor, but I went back to school to relearn how to write a business plan and learn some technical lessons about being an entrepreneur. Then, I was selected for a 10-month business entrepreneur scholarship with the Small Business Administration. Finally, the momentum was building again.

Know your business

Looking back, I'm glad I had completed and fought to overcome all of those steps. My best advice is doing your market research and learn as much as you can about your business field. Also, when starting your own business there are going to be unknowns, and you need to be prepared to just learn as you go. You can't control many things, and it really helps to have the personality of being laid back and going with the flow, controlling what you can, managing the stuff you can't, and enjoying all the many good surprises along the way. At this point, I felt like I was really ready to move forward, and I had already learned

the process of dealing with China where my product was made. The good thing about finding my new manufacturer is that they handled the communication with China. So, I negotiated with them, and they would communicate with China for me. Originally, I was dealing with China directly on my own, and my last representative in China, named Arnold, spoke little English. We would have to communicate back and forth constantly calling and emailing each other. My kids would ask: "Is that Arnold calling?" because he would call either when they were going to bed or getting up in the morning, and that became our joke.

We re-launched ZIZZY BEE Bags in January 2017, and it was very exciting after not selling for a year. However, I had stopped all of my marketing, so I had to restart and do everything as if it was all brand new, and I needed to really believe in myself and ZizzyBee to make this happen. The next thing I knew, both former and new customers started buying bags. I tested some new marketing ideas, and then we launched on Amazon.

I had an unwavering belief in my product; I didn't listen to all of the criticism and negative opinions out there—I stuck firmly to my business plan and did the work. I really think perseverance and determination kept me moving forward. I didn't want to quit what I had started, and wasn't done making a product that people loved. Customers would tell me how organized they felt and how much better that made them feel. My customers make me happy, and I feel really good about what I am selling. That is why I get up every day and do what I do, because who knew organizing bags would make a difference in people lives? I learned that when customers feel more organized, they feel better about themselves, and it's amazing to know that I did something to help make that difference for them.

The real backstory here is that ZizzyBee started as a toy storage solution company. Since then, we've grown into organizing travel supplies, toiletries, makeup and purse clutter, art supplies, sports, snacks, pool and beach gear... the uses are endless. Anything that might have been resolved by a single use plastic-zip bag, ZizzyBee is the better answer. A 3-pack of ZizzyBee Bags save 1000+ single-use, plastic zip-style bags a year per household. Now is the time to take action and win the war

on plastic. As we shared before, we started a movement called Take the Plastic Pledge. By taking the pledge people promise to make at least one plastic swap. We even launched the Swap Shop where we partnered with amazing brands that have eco products to replace plastic items or have products made from recycled plastic. A portion of profits are donated to The Ocean Clean Up. Our goal is to get one million pledgers and raise one million dollars to donate to ocean clean up.

Customers love our reusable, see-through mesh and washable bags, which not only helps the environment, but it saves them money by using a permanent solution that works better in their lives.

The bags go through TSA easily, and our bags are far more durable— they don't rip or tear apart like conventional plastic zip-bags. What's been amazing is that I started a company to solve one problem, and then as we've grown, and my kids have gotten older, the uses of the bags have changed and so have the product offerings. Customers who buy our bags tell us all the different uses they have for ZizzyBee. Sometimes I'm surprised to hear a ZizzyBee used in a way that we hadn't thought of. (One woman used the bag for her nurse gear – her hospital badge, stethoscope, and more. Everything she needs in one spot easy to find and carry or hang.)

The challenge of having your own company is that you need to adapt and come up with new product ideas to keep your brand fresh and to tap into new target markets. For instance, I thought it would be fun to sell a "dirty laundry bag." I came up with this idea after traveling, and I never had a place in my suitcase to store my dirty clothes. I would just grab the plastic bag in the hotel room, and stuff my clothes in there. So, the dirty laundry bag was born from a need I had. The amazing thing is that we put it on Amazon, and it sold like crazy all over the country. Who knew! We sold nine hundred in almost six months on Amazon, and it's just a basic dirty laundry bag. It lets you come home from traveling, feeling super organized, so that you can just take the breathable dirty laundry bag straight to your washer, and not have to worry about what's left in your suitcase.

Now we're turning into this travel organizing company because we found a niche in the market. From listening to our customers, thinking

out of the box, and doing market research, we need to be on top of our brand and responsive to market needs. We are going to be launching our travel line, as well as locker bags for gym/school, and toiletry bags as we identified that there's a need out there.

Lesson #1: Juggling is practice and planning

I've always been a multi-tasker, and I believe that you can make anything happen. Whether it's day to day with my kids' schedules, work, or juggling after-school activities along with owning my own business and being a single mom, I always figure out how to make everything work, because that's just how I am.

Sometimes I say "no" so that I don't spread myself too thin. I also believe you should ask for what you want, be direct and make it happen.

Lesson #2: Find what motivates you

Don't listen to everybody else, because many things happen that are out of your control, and your instincts will guide you better than the negativity and fear of others. Surround yourself with a team of qualified business consultants, lawyers, mentors and people that you can trust, who aren't family and friends, as they have an objective opinion. They will even serve as a great sounding board to bounce ideas off of because when you have your own business it can be isolating and lonely. When you don't go to an office every day and have a team of people right there dedicated to their work for you to keep the energy flowing, it can be tough. I sometimes spend time in coffee shops because the energy of other people help keep me motivated. Mostly, though, the motivation comes from my customers—I know that customers love ZizzyBee Bags, and that's what keeps me going.

Lesson #3: Surround yourself with the best people

I really believe in networking and reaching out to people, because I know that I don't know everything. I like to be a sponge and surround myself with people that know more than me and reach out to people that know more than I do. I would say that education and networking are really important before you jump in to start your business—take the time to do both. Often people don't want to do that part,

because they might see it is a waste of time, think of it as socializing or empty knowledge that's obvious, and nothing could be farther from the truth. Doing as much as you can to learn from books, classes and most importantly, from mentors and coaches who have achieved success will help you sprint ahead and weather some tough storms. Weathering storms also has to do with perseverance and determination

and knowing you can't quit. Some people have it in them innately, and some people don't. Those other people need to figure it out fast, or it's going to be a tough, tough, long road ahead.

Personal perspective

I learn quickly, and enjoy being a problem solver. Reflecting on my childhood and early adulthood, it's clear that I was really meant to have my own business, as I have the patience, curiosity and drive to keep my business going no matter what. It also requires flexibility to sustain the day-to-day operation of the business that people don't see. They see the end product, but the daily grind has made me more appreciative of small and large businesses. I also have a deeper knowledge of how people create products and services based on industries, and all that goes into executing it. It's tough, but so, so rewarding.

Then there's the exit plan. You need to have goals for the future, because people start businesses all the time, and then they jump on to another one, and on and on, without really powering through the barriers to achieve success on their first business endeavor. Then, once everything is moving somewhat smoothly, and you're selling your product, you need to just keep going, as more opportunities will present themselves. I have created a business that makes people feel really good, and that keeps my energy flowing to be able to tackle the next challenge. Be organized and believe in your dreams!

Lisa Paul Heydet

graduated from the University of San Diego and has acquired extensive marketing and advertising experience with the Colorado Rockies Baseball Team, Ogilvy & Mather, Adidas America, and as a residential realtor.

Her creative thinking lead her to develop ZizzyBee Bags, the ecological alternative to conventional single-use, plastic bags. ZizzyBee bags are reusable, washable, see-through, last forever, have a convenient zipper, and also have a convenient loop making them easy to hang or hold. A 3-Pack of ZizzyBee Bags saves 1000+ single use plastic bags a year per household.

Lisa is committed to protecting the environment and realizes the world is losing the war with plastic. But she has taken a stand against the polluting effects of plastic by launching the "Take the Plastic Pledge" movement, which has partnered with numerous eco-friendly brands to offer a one-stop shop of plastic alternative or recycled plastic products. 10% of all Swap Shop sales are donated to "The Ocean Clean Up Project", with a goal of raising one million dollars and to obtain one million pledgers.

To learn more about Lisa and ZizzyBee Bags, go to:

www.ZizzyBeeBags.com
www.TakeThePlasticPledge.com

What Have You **Forbes'd** Lately?

My name is Makenna Riley and I Forbes'd allowing myself to be confident.

I never let fear stop me. My mom taught me at a young age that overthinking is the only thing that would ever stop me from reaching my goals.

How it

HAPPENED

By Makenna Riley

There are many things that can make a kid in high school unique, such as sports accomplishments and academic awards, but not many can say they started a business at 13 years old. I grew up in a very business oriented household with my mom being the "Queen of Infomercials" and the $2.5 billion dollar sales women. This required her to travel often, which meant if I wanted a relationship with her, I would have to go with her. This prompted me to grow up on the back of TV sets such as QVC and HSN. The interesting thing about those companies is that they would only air live television, so this led to me being on those sets almost every night just watching the magic happen. From this experience I learned the art of the perfect pitch by just constantly hearing different ways to do. One night I was sitting on the set doodling on a yellow notepad when I noticed the camera was switching to the models who weren't ready, so I took notes and gave them to my mom when she was done. Turns out she was very impressed with my feedback at age 6. At 8 years old, she began to value my opinion.

One afternoon my mom called me into one of her meetings where her team was trying to figure out how to lower the cost of a product for a discount sale. All the adults in the room couldn't figure out what to do as they were focused on pricing and stuck saying things like,

"I just don't know what we can do." I chimed in and suggested that they take out the Neoprene bag that carried the product. It ended up saving them $48,000 because taking out the $.65 cent bag on an order of 75,000 units makes a big cost difference. Soon after this, my mom started taking me to trade shows... where I would usually outsell the hired adults.

It became apparent that her products needed to start hitting the online market, but since she is sort of old school, I took it upon myself to do it. At 11 years old, I learned to create landing pages, websites, and code security software. I even built her first online store which began generating money and changed the way my parents do business.

I realized that I had a knack for building platforms online and started my own business in 2015 that focused on internet marketing. So far I have built pages for superstars like NFL Legend, Joe Theisman, built an ecommerce around a woman who had an amazing book and clothing line and of course, my own stores and funnels for a variety of products and services.

All I know is, the best is yet to come.

Life Lesson #1 *Don't let fear stop you.*

The only thing holding you back is the lack of confidence towards the goal you want. For example, I was given the opportunity to meet Russell Brunson the multi-million dollar creator of Click Funnels. With a crowd of people around him, I went up and struck a conversation, which lead to him asking me what I like and don't like about his platform. I began to talk about all the success it gave me, but also how it could be improved. He was so intrigued with our conversation that it lead to me being on their national podcast as guest talking about being a junior entrepreneur. That's not the best part though... when he was on stage in front of 10,000 people he gave me a shoutout! This ONLY happened because I had the courage to go up to him, but even though I was nervous meeting someone I admired, I didn't let that stop me. The only thing standing in your way is yourself. One thing I live by is not doing something because I am afraid of what others will think or to not being afraid to be embarrassed. Embarrassment is a state of mind and your mindset is how the rest of your life will play out. If you see someone you would love to meet or talk, go up to them with a goal in mind. When I was just starting out in internet marketing I met a man named Adrian Morrison who had recently built a funnel that grossed $9 million. Being the curious kid I am, I wanted to know exactly how he did it and how I could potentially do it. It resulted in me simply walking up to him and asking him all my burning questions. This lead to us on his computer showing me exactly how he did it. The point of this is that I was able to replicate his funnel and sell his training from which I made $5,000... in just one day.

Think of all the missed opportunities you have because you were simply too scared or didn't want to embarrass yourself. These things turn into regrets that will haunt you down the line. In reality, life is based off connections and if you can't simply ask another person a question or start a conversation... you won't go very far. I am glad I learned this from a young age and I hope now you can understand that no matter what, you should always do the things that push you outside your comfort zone.

Life Lesson #2 Use the Lens of a Child

Never grow up. Stay curious. Keep the mentality of learning. A huge issue I find among many adults is that they are not open to learning new things and taking risks. Many feel that they know better and "What else could I possibly need to learn." Let me tell you a story about how my mom wishes she had listened to me as a kid. I remember coming to my mom in January 2013, (I was 10 years old) and I was so excited about the new craze Bitcoin (it was $100 a coin then). If you don't know what bitcoin is, it is an online currency that is like stocks, but without any type of insurance. You can make a lot of money with it though if you do it right. A couple months after I urged my mom to let me buy just 1 coin, which by then it was worth $500, but it was still a dismissed no. Then it grew to $1000- $5000 and by the time she was ready to take me seriously it was worth $10,000 per coin -- if I had bought just 10 coins when I first heard about it, it would be worth $100,000. Later on it reached $20,000 in value and I was still stuck with $0 worth. This goes to show that kids see things different than parents because they haven't been jaded by the limiting beliefs so many adults live by. Trends move fast and start young, like Pokemon GO or SillyBands. Understand that they might be younger, with less life experience, but that ignorance towards the world and "how" things HAVE to happen certain ways is simply not true in a kids mind. If your child is into technology or comes to you with a great new idea, don't put them down just because they are a kid. You never know if your kid will bring you the next bitcoin...

Life Lesson #3 - Give Back

When you give what you have been so blessed to receive, no matter how or what it is you will be rewarded. There are many reasons to volunteer. One being that you are able to learn what you community wants and needs by giving away your time. An example of this is me and my friends like to go out to our beaches and clean them up. I learned that because we are doing this, it is busting tourism which boast our economy making our city better. Even though this is not a direct effect on myself, I will eventually begin to see how well our impact is on the grand scale of things.

Having a stake in your community is powerful and good for your health. When you have relationships with more than just the people you work around, you begin to feel a different type of "being at home." An example of this is I raised $10,000 to donate to 'Boat Kids' which takes lower income kids or disabled kids out on boat rides. On these boat rides it gives me the opportunity to meet people I would have otherwise probably never meet.

www.MakennaRileysBoat.com

When giving back the community it is important to think about the ones you are helping but also about yourself. You should enjoy whatever you are doing to help the community because the most genuine part of a person comes out when they are happy with what they are doing. An important factor in life is the relationships we surround ourselves with and the kindness in our heart. At the end of the day it really comes down to how you feel your life went and how others will remember you.

Makenna Riley

is a 16 years old business woman… who's a junior in high school. She knows what she wants out of life, but only time will tell as she moves out into the world. She certainly is a teen to watch, as not many kids her age have a thriving business and interviewed celebrities like Shark Tank's Kevin Harrington, Motivation Guru Les Brown, Fitness Legend Jack Lalanne and many others. She is a genius when it comes to all things technology which gives her a leg up in the internet marketing world. She is skilled at funnel building, email marketing, advertising, and even coding.

The list goes on with all the skills she has picked up in the last 5 years in the Internet Marketing world. She learned from the best in the business and with this, she is working towards generating different recurring incomes, as well as spreading her knowledge to others.

Born in Los Angeles, she and her twin brother, Ryker were raised in St. Petersburg Florida.

To contact Makenna please visit:

www.FreeGiftfromMakennaRiley.com

*Do or do not,
there is no try*

- YODA

What Have You **Forbes'd** Lately?

My name is Maria Loya, and I Forbes'd finding the best environment for my child, against many barriers and obstacles. One of the most critical lessons is that we're all different, and we're each struggling with something difficult. We're all fighting some battle most people know little about—this fact actually makes us all the same. When you treat others the way you want to be treated, you prioritize kindness, compassion, and collaboration. When we have each other's best interests at heart, the world is just better.

A New
NORMAL

By Maria Loya

As we go through life, our inspiration for growth comes from many different directions. It may come from a book, a conversation with a friend or from listening to someone we look up to. Often times we overlook the inspirational sources that are right in front of us. But, not me. My daughter, Kassandra, has taught me incredible lessons, and has allowed me to discover many of my strengths, including the passion I have for fighting for what I believe in.

Kassandra crawled, walked and was potty-trained at a normal age. When she was just one year old, she could successfully feed without a bottle. By the time she was in kindergarten, there was no evidence to suggest that she may have any cognitive difficulties. Even her pediatricians found her to be growing normally during routine check-ups. As the years went by, there were occasions where my daughter exhibited certain characteristics that did seem, well, different.

Battle Number 1: There's a problem

When my daughter began a Kindergarten program, I noticed that her voice inflection was different compared with other children near her age and grade level. She wasn't fully speaking. I challenged the school system and told them that my daughter's language skills were being

delayed because she was learning two languages at the same time. Certainly, her speech was lagging because learning two languages was difficult for her, and therefore she was struggling at school.

We agreed to retain her in kindergarten for another year so she could catch up. I was confident that she would catch up with the rest of her class in that year's time. Then, months went by, and the school year had ended, and Kassandra's speech was not where it should have been, even having that extra time.

The school explained to me that an IEP, or Individual Education Plan, would be the best way to proceed with adapting to Kassandra's needs and abilities. To start her IEP, Kassandra took many different tests to measure her learning ability. She scored very low. In response, the school recommended that Kassandra be reviewed by medical professionals. However, I was very apprehensive because she had been previously examined by her pediatrician who had no concerns and said her development was normal.

I reveled in a tumultuous mix of emotions, from frustration, anger, to denial. I could not believe this was happening to me and my daughter, and I began to convince myself that this school was on a crusade against my child. Frustrated, and fully convinced that this conspiracy was a reality, I made another appointment with her pediatrician. At the conclusion of her appointment, her pediatrician again said everything was "fine and normal."

That fueled my fire, and I vented with those close to me, who was familiar with the situation surrounding my daughter-that the school found her learning to be below average and wanted her seen at the children's hospital for further testing.

Yet, her pediatrician advised me to proceed with the testing, saying that it wouldn't hurt, but that he would also send all of her previous medical records indicating everything was fine with her development. As a decidedly pissed off parent, I took the pediatricians findings to the school, but I also agreed to proceed with the process. After all, my daughter was fine.

My daughter and I had an appointment with the Children's Hospital in Colorado. She had lots of tests- so many different tests. I cannot even begin to describe them, as there were so many tests that were administered to see what was wrong with her. All of the tests results returned with "normal" results, except for one. The last test, they explained to us, was the one that keeps track of her brain function while she is sleeping. I had learned that when forming thoughts, both the right side and the left side of the brain connect and form a complete thought. However, with Kassandra they would connect and "jump," and the thought process would either not complete or lag. Ultimately, she was diagnosed with "Mild Retardation Cognitive Disorder."

My husband and I were devastated. We had no idea how to explain what happened. So, we began by blaming each other: "Maybe it is your fault" or "Maybe it is YOUR fault!" and "What about your family?" or "Maybe it is because of YOUR family?" Still fixated on denial I exclaimed, "It can't be! It can't be!!"

Before Kassandra was born, I had two sons whom I felt were doing well in school and could function normally. I felt that it was rational to think that it couldn't be me or my fault because they are "normal." In my ignorance, I continued thinking that it was impossible for my daughter to have a cognitive disability. After all, she was potty-trained, she did everything as any other average child could. And if she had a cognitive disorder, I thought that she would not be able to do all of these things.

By this time, I had been reading all I could about my daughter's diagnosis—everything I could find. In the end, I had more questions than the answers.

BATTLE NUMBER 2: *Show you care*

After submitting Kassandra's test results, we again struggled with the school system. The school system informed us that because she was deemed a "Special Needs Student," she could no longer attend their school. My paranoid thoughts resurfaced, and I felt that I was accurate in my assessment that the school did not want to assist or retain my daughter in their school—they didn't care about her, and they didn't want to help.

The school added that they could not meet her needs because they didn't have a special education program at their site. Because my daughter had special seeds, she needed to work with a qualified professional who could work with children with special seeds. I vehemently disagreed with their decision, and I felt that it was ludicrous. I foresaw the consequences of the school's decision, and was faced with my daughter having to go to another school on the bus all by herself for her first grade. I was afraid for her.

I was angry at the school's decision to not accept my daughter. The school was right across the street from our home, and her brother was also attending that school. For our family, it was a safety issue, and if anything happened, she was accessible for any of us to pick her up or address a problem. Going to another school meant all of us were facing something unknown, added to all of the fears and stress of the unknowns we have already had to accept her diagnosis.

As I recall the conversations we had with the school district, I distinctly remembered that word "special," "special needs," and "special ed." I kept hearing it over and over "special." My distorted thoughts associated with the word "special" with "rejects." I recall laughing later, in disbelief, as I thought to myself, "Special? There is nobody special here, everyone here is the same." We decided as a family that we were going to continue to treat her the same as the others. After all, before we became aware that she had a cognitive disorder, she was treated like her siblings, because she was seemingly advanced in other things.

As my husband and I visited different schools, my fears and anxieties became more apparent. I was seeing that these schools were so far from home, and not only was she too young at the time to understand all of this, but now she was also "special needs." Finally, after a much-heated debate and probably being considered in secret a difficult parent, we negotiated to move her brother to the same school so that he would be allowed to ride the "special needs" bus with his sister.

Battle Number 3: Your problem is not your identity

After some time, my denial started to fade into resolution, then my husband and I decided that we needed to focus on our daughter. We

were faced with a new question: "What do we do with this?" We could either help her have a normal life, or we could be bitter and make things worse.

Before being diagnosed with an illness or disease, we live our lives normally, but after a diagnosis, when we become aware that something is wrong, we label ourselves with whatever it is we are diagnosed with. Instead of thinking of ourselves as people first, we now tend to think of our illnesses first, we let that define us, and others treat us as such. Soon, we noticed people feeling sorry for us, and then we ended up feeling sorry for ourselves. I use myself as an example often, because I also have an illness, but that's for another story.

Kassandra, just like any other kid, had chores, she was grounded when she needed to be, just like the other kids, and she was talked to as a normal kid. She learned to do her laundry and make herself small meals like the other kids. When going to others' homes, even though they knew something was different, they weren't aware of what was wrong with my daughter. She was already being judged by others' ignorance, and as her mother, I felt that she did not need any more of that in her life.

Battle Number 4: Things are not as they seem

When we bought a home in another county, Kassandra was in elementary school, and we again encountered issues. For us, this was a brand-new school, a charter school that provided preschool all the way through 9th grade. Kassandra and her brother were again able to attend the same school, which was helpful to us. At first, this school welcomed special needs students, until it was too much for them. Then, they wanted these kids transferred to public schools. Once again, my child was being rejected from a place where she was already comfortable. And here we go again, to another IEP meeting determining why she would be better off at a public school.

IEP meetings can be intimidating, because it's just you, your spouse, and your child against 6 or more professionals that specialize in whatever it may be that is the topic of discussion. Some of these so-called

specialists mainly focus the negatives versus the positives for your child. "Oh, hell no!" was my position. Again, I'm the difficult parent—AKA "pain in the ass parent." Why do I need to be difficult to get experts in the field to listen compassionately? These systems and experts really need to change, and they need to be more sensitive about how they are addressing the needs of our children, especially when being done in front of our children. As a "pain in the ass parent" fighting for my child against all of these jerks, I asked, "So now that you've spoken to all my daughter's negatives, please give me the positives."

The room became silent until her brave teacher spoke, and she shared the positive experiences she has had with my daughter. She was her main teacher who spent more time with her and knew her better than all these others who thought they knew what was best for my daughter. Ms. Smith was a really great, understanding teacher who also had a special needs child of her own. She understood our situation, and I could tell that she did not agree with the others, but could not risk losing her job and going against these experts in authority. Sadly, when I felt so overwhelmed, I sometimes wished and thought Ms. Smith would have been a better mother for my daughter.

In the end, I lost, and my daughter had to go to a regular public middle school that offered dedicated attention and services that the charter school was no longer going to offer. I later found out that the county I lived in was not going to fund the school anymore for programs that catered to children with special needs. If these specialists would have been more honest instead of placing the blame everywhere else, things might have been much easier for us, because we would have had a deeper understanding of the situation we were facing. Luckily, her transition to the public middle school was made easier because of her teacher, Ms. Smith.

Kassandra began to do well in middle school once she became acclimated. Unfortunately, children with special needs sometimes have a hard time with change. Kassandra was not only afraid of the new environment, but she was also worried that she wasn't going to have any friends. She eventually began to trust her new teacher and school, and things got easier. At her next IEP meeting, it began with the positives and her progress. This time everyone involved was sensitive

and cautious about what they would say in front of my daughter. This IEP meeting was different from the others. Perhaps they didn't want any conflict, but whatever the motivation may have been, it was a very productive change, and that's how all of them should be. Kassandra was asked what she wanted to include in her learning plan. She wanted to learn how to write in cursive, which was no longer taught in schools, but she learned it successfully. She also changed her to name to Kassie, because Kassandra was too long. Kassie completed middle school and went on to high school, was a straight A-student with a 4.0-grade point average, despite having her disabilities.

Kassie graduated from high school, and she went on to a 4-year learning skills program, before going to college for a year. Kassie is still involved with the life skills program and is eager to continue to learn new things. She also is a volunteer at the neighborhood food bank and now has a part-time job for the city cleaning a government office, which hopefully will turn into a full-time job. Because of the great teacher she has at the life skills program, she has learned to do many more things on her own, such as ride the bus. If I had to ride the bus, I would probably get lost.

Kassie is a very happy young lady and is really excited to go to her job every day. She takes care of herself and her personal needs, and is fully aware that she is different. Many years ago, when my sister and I were having a very difficult day, Kassie was at my office and made a comment to my sister and me. She said, "Sometimes, I think my brain does not work very well."

My sister and I started laughing and my sister said, "Mine does not work very well, either."

I told her the same thing. I said, "Mine does not work very well, either, especially today."

Kassie then went on to say, "Oh, so I am not the only one who has this problem?"

We continued to all laugh and I said, "No, daughter, you are not the only one who has this problem. Now you know our brains do not work very well sometimes either".

What Kassie has taught me is that some things that seem impossible for me are easy for her. She does things without a big fear quotient, something foreign to those of us who are normal, or in this case "supposedly normal" like me. She has no fear in doing things that would frighten me, like when we talked about college, I asked, "Kassie do you want to go to college?"

"Yes, I will," she responded without hesitation. When we talked about her wanting to get a job, she was enthusiastic. She puts no limitations on herself and is unafraid. She will just do it. I really admire her because there is a lot I could learn from her—it's not just her learning from me all of the time. And, when I am feeling down, and when I am feeling like everything is difficult or impossible, I think about my daughter because she has done so much.

One recent example is her incredible self-discipline. Kassie wanted an expensive iPhone—it's about a thousand dollars. I told her that I couldn't buy her such an expensive phone. Kassie said, "That's okay, I will save all my checks that I get from my job so I can get the iPhone." Kassie also worked a few hours at my office before she went to her part-time job to save more money so she can get her iPhone sooner.

Once again, I was amazed that she demonstrated her ability to manage her money, worked to earn more to get closer to her goal faster and saved. I mean in my case, sometimes I am having hard time-saving money because it seems I spend it on something I really do not need versus saving it. She was so motivated that she saved her money, and guess what? She got her expensive iPhone on her own.

After that, Kassie said, "You know, if I can do this, I can do other things. I can save and buy other things." My daughter will never be able to drive a car but who knows what she is able to do that you and I might find really difficult? She may have a cognitive disability, but there are so many things the experts said that she would never be able to do, and yet she's doing them successfully. She does not let her diagnosis limit her. She knows what her limitations are, and she prefers to ride the bus because she feels in control that way, but other challenges she'll take on and accomplish because she knows that she can approach it fearlessly, and work to overcome it. I would love to have her courage!

Kassie stated that she will be 22 soon and is thinking, "Maybe I should start thinking of getting my own place?" This is hilarious, because the way she talks about getting her own place, she thinks she is an adult already. "Yes, I was thinking about that, but I do not want to be too far from you, just in case you need me," Kassie continued.

Isn't that interesting? "Just in case, I need her". Yes, daughter, I am going to need you. Plus, if you move too far I am going to miss you. So, my daughter is living a normal life and she is really happy and content with what she has. I think sometimes being normal is not so great after all because you want to have everything—like it's a contest to have it all, and you think too much, which gets you to start second-guessing yourself and that leads to you limiting yourself. In her case, she does not think too much. She does not have fears, and she just gets her goals done. Kassie also dreams about having her own business. She doesn't know what kind of business yet, but she wants to have a business. She does not want to have a hard business like her mother, but she wants a business.

Kassie has taught me so much. I really admire her and so do her teachers and the people who work with her at her job and food bank. It is so wonderful to have Kassie at the food bank because you know, not only does Kassie do her job well, but she still finds time to volunteer and help us. Kassie also volunteers for activities at her old high school—activities that are held for other students who also have special needs. She is the first one there. She says that she wants to help motivate other kids like her.

When I am feeling down, and I don't think I can keep going on because things are so heavy, I look at my daughter and I say to myself, "Wow, look at me? Feeling sorry for myself and my daughter just keeps me going and going and going." I have also learned through her example that fear is just what it is. It is just fear, and it is merely a limitation we allow to be put on ourselves. When you take away the fear, you have no limitation-your abilities are limitless.

In the process of attending conferences and meetings so that my husband and I could educate ourselves more on how to better meet our daughter's needs, we met many similarly situated parents. And I noticed

something very disturbing. Many of these parents not only treated their children differently, but also behaved as if their children were a burden, and felt they had little support from the school system. Unfortunately, the systems that are currently in place tend to disempower the parents, as well as the children they are actually intended to help. In fact, they often leave both the parents and children with low self-esteem, and without any feeling of power over their situation.

I have always been an advocate for my child. I cannot imagine what other parents go through when you are already intimidated by the system. Instead of giving you options on, "What you could do with your child." They pretty much demand, "What you should do with your child." Many parents face this, and they think that they have no options. Always remember, we have many options, and your child needs your advocacy and support, so stay strong for them. And, in turn, they'll become much stronger knowing you're in their corner!

Lesson #1: Treat others the way I want to be treated

We're all different, we're each struggling with something difficult, we're all fighting some battle most people know little about. In fact, this actually makes us all the same! When you treat others the way you want to be treated, you prioritize kindness, compassion, and collaboration. When we have each other's best interests at heart, the world is just better.

Kassie may have been treated badly at times, but she never used that as an excuse to treat others badly. Her courage is a constant reminder that I can do better. How we treat one another is one of the most important things in life—be kind!

Lesson #2: My family is first

There is no question that my family is my first priority, but sometimes the pressures and responsibilities of work and even the distractions of life can interfere with our mood, our time and our commitments. I dedicate myself to keeping my priorities in check, even when it's difficult or seemingly impossible!

Lesson #3: Feel the fear but do it anyway

Kassie is my hero, and she taught me this lesson more profoundly than anyone else ever could have, as she powers through challenges every day no matter her level of fear. It is inspiring to see her set aside her fear, and focus on what she wants to achieve and the steps she needs to take to get there. Imagine how far we would go if we all dedicated ourselves to that? Sure, you're afraid, but so what? If it's how you get to your goal, just go through the fear and get to where you want to be!

Maria Loya

is the Director and Owner of La Trenza Counseling Center in Commerce City, CO since 2006. She is a bilingual (Spanish) family therapist and an addictions counselor with over 26 years of experience working with individuals, groups, and families.

Maria has worked at schools, women's shelters, as well as outpatient and inpatient facilities. She strongly believes in focusing on authentic relationships, in addition to promoting freedom and growth. Maria has had her own experience with anxiety, depression, trauma, self-esteem, stress, relationship issues/relational conflict, substance abuse, multicultural/diversity issues, growth and development. She is also trained in motivational interviewing, therapeutic groups, and crisis intervention.

Maria belies that everyone is meant to grow and succeed in life. She is passionate about helping others identify the things, people and habits that keep them from becoming successful.

To learn more about Maria and the La Trenza Counseling Center, contact her at:

latrenza@comcast.net

You never want an autograph on anything except a check

- Forbes Riley

What Have You **Forbes'd** Lately?

My name is Maria Lucassen, and I Forbes'd carving out my own path for success. I learned lessons from being laid off three times by the same company. I recognized the need to look at how to make money and enjoy what you do. It's important to have multiple streams of income, especially if you're single and don't have another person helping you financially.

Using the Past to

SHAPE THE FUTURE

By Maria Lucassen

My life had been going great. I had a job I loved, plenty of adventure in my life and my dream of moving to the United States had finally been granted. Then everything turned upside down. I got laid off three different times by the same company before I finally told myself, "Enough! Do not accept another position with this company."

I had tolerated this back and forth with my job because of my love for travel. While growing up in a rural community in Holland, my family never really went on vacation. We took day trips to the zoo or the playground. Traveling wasn't as common as it is nowadays, especially by plane. For us, we didn't even own a vehicle, so traveling by car was special. Imagine my excitement when we were invited to spend a few days with a relative, allowing us to go to a different house and eat different food.

Then when I was seventeen, my family went on a "real" vacation to Germany for five days. We had a great time, particularly my dad, since this was the first vacation he had had in twenty-five years as a farmer. This trip inspired us to travel more and we looked for new places to visit.

In the summer, my younger sister and I were allowed to ride our bikes to France, Denmark, and nearby countries and stay in their hostels. This gave us the opportunity to meet people from all over the world, while enjoying cycling. This experience increased my desire to travel, something which had started to take root after completing middle school.

Embracing the Wanderlust

My eyes had been opened to the possibility of having a career that could feed my wanderlust while attending a food preparation training program at a vocational training school. I was required to do an internship and write a report about the hospital and its organization, so I interviewed the hospital's hotel catering manager. I asked him where he had gained his experience. When his response was "a large hotel in Hong Kong," a light went off in my head. *Hong Kong!* Back in the seventies when I was young and dreamed of discovering the world, Hong Kong was exotic. Unfortunately, it doesn't have the same attraction nowadays.

I couldn't get Hong Kong out of my mind, so I began to think about switching my career to the hotel industry. It would allow me to travel to Hong Kong and other places. The thoughts and possibilities inspired me to study, and I became a lifelong learner. I attended evening classes and earned my high-school diploma before applying to a hotel management school. Although my first application was declined, I applied again the next year and was accepted.

Now I had to make a decision that would affect my career. The hotel management school offered two programs, one for hotels and one for hospitals and nursing homes. The Taurus in me can be stubborn in different areas, and I have a hard time letting things go. So, I chose to stick to my original plan and stayed in the hospital and nursing home industry. As it turned out, I never worked in any of those institutions after graduating.

My first job was as a floor supervisor in the housekeeping department at one of the bigger hotels in Amsterdam, but Amsterdam wasn't "abroad". I wanted to work in other countries. Although I spoke fluent German, I wanted to improve my knowledge of French, so I was offered a good

position at a hotel in the French-speaking area of Switzerland. This led to my working abroad in many European countries where I was able to acquire a wealth of experience and knowledge.

Setting Sail

Then I made one of the best decisions in my life and worked on a cruise ship for a while. The ship sailed during the night, and the next day, you found yourself in another port in another country where you could go onshore and explore. However, as part of the staff, I didn't have as much freedom because I had to work without any days off. Still, I was given a few hours to explore a new place, a new city, and shop or go to lunch with some coworkers. It was exciting just to be in different countries.

The last ship I worked on was Queen Elizabeth II. In addition to transatlantic crossings between New York and the United Kingdom, that ship cruised the world, including Hong Kong. We would have two days at a port to discover the city and shop. The best experience was when working on a world cruise, I was able to disembark in Hong Kong and go on a vacation for 5 weeks. I took the train to Beijing, and then the Trans-Siberian train to Moskou, Berlin and then to Hamburg where I lived. I finally rejoined the ship in Southampton (UK).

Then I decided it was time to settle down and find a job ashore so that I could meet a significant other and have a family. I landed a job in Cunard Line's travel reservation office in Germany. This position allowed me to still travel on one of their ships and stay connected to the industry.

Coming to America

Another one of my dreams has always been to live in America, the land of opportunity. I had submitted my application for the U.S.'s green card visa lottery before going to Britain for a supervisory assignment with a new German-speaking team in the reservation office. The lottery randomly gives a green card to 50,000 people who qualify. Even though I had applied in the past, I never won. In fact, I had forgotten about applying until I got a letter six months later asking for documentation. Believing things happen for a reason, I complied with their request and got accepted for a green card.

Telling my new friends on my team goodbye was difficult. I took the chance in 2000 and moved to Miami, Florida, where I continued working for the same company, Cunard Line. I serviced companies wanting to charter one of our cruise ships. Fortunately, I knew a lot of my coworkers from working with them on the cruise ships. They had been my friends and helped make my new life in the U.S. very enjoyable.

The First Time

Everything was going well. Then one Friday in 2001, my manager approached me and said, "Maria, I have bad news. I need to talk to you." I followed her into her office. She told me the company sold three ships in their fleet. They had to lay off people. Because I had a green card, I was one of the 300 people who was let go. I thought that at least I was better than my coworkers who had work permits. I knew they wouldn't be able to find work, whereas I had a visa. I believed I should be able to find another job, after all, I've worked all my life, and I've never been unemployed.

I had already booked flights to go home to see my parents in the Netherlands, which would be my first trip home since coming to America. I didn't want to go home and tell my parents, "Hey, I'm enjoying my life in the United States, but I don't have a job."

Cunard Line had given me a severance package. Fortunately, it had a group program that included resume writing assistance and job search training. I was optimistic and took advantage of both.

Then on September 11, 2001, the World Trade Center towers were attacked. I happened to be at an unemployment office when the news of this tragedy was broadcasted. As a result of that 9/11 event, the cruise and hospitality industries were not hiring. I was still without a job. Although my severance package helped, I had to rent one of the rooms in my home to assist me in paying my lease because unemployment benefits in the U.S. are the worst.

I couldn't find a suitable job, so the unemployment office offered me a skill assessment test. As a result, I learned that I was good at bookkeeping, which didn't surprise me because I always liked accounting. So they

sent me to school to earn an associates degree in accounting. This was a huge step backward for me after having earned a bachelor's degree in hotel management twenty years ago. I was starting all over again from scratch because none of my credits were accepted.

Rehired and Laid Off...Again

Then things started looking up. Within ten months of being laid off, I was able to return to Cunard Line and start working there again. I spent the next couple of years working and studying and working and studying because I still wanted to become an accountant. Accountants can work anywhere.

The economy was still not good, and the cruise line was again forced to look for partners. Cunard Line merged with another cruise line, so in the last quarter 2004, they announced they were relocating to Los Angeles. The merger didn't offer any job openings in middle management in its new location. I was laid off from them again for the second time!

I wasn't as worried as before because I was studying for a new profession. I felt I would find a job in Miami, and I was right. I was offered temporary accounting contracts so that I could gain experience.

After earning and receiving my bachelor's degree in accounting in 2007, I was offered a steady, nice job with a company close to my home. It gave me the opportunity to really learn the ropes in accounting. The company took good care of its employees, and I had wonderful colleagues and acquired a solid foundation in my new profession. The downside was that I had less vacation time than I had with the cruise line, and I missed traveling and the long trips.

A few years later, a former coworker from the cruise line called me out of the blue. She had been working for Cunard's smaller sister company. She asked if I had completed my accounting degree. I said, "Yes."

She said, "Guess what. We're looking for somebody with your degree to come work for us in our office because the person who had the job is leaving. We need someone soon. Would you want to come here for an interview?"

For the Third Time

I agreed and connected immediately with the people at the interview, as I had previously worked with them at Cunard Line. Within three weeks, I was back in the cruise industry, working for the same company, but this time in the accounting department. I was using my new skills and accounting experience, helping and supporting a great department. I couldn't have been happier.

My happiness was short-lived, though. If I had known what laid ahead, I wouldn't have left my previous job. Just three weeks into my new job, management announced at a Christmas luncheon that the cruise line was moving to Seattle, Washington, due to another merger. I couldn't move with the company because only managers and directors could apply for positions in Seattle.

After four months, the cruise line laid me off for the third time. I knew I could never go back. Being laid off so many times is very difficult, especially if you're single, and it's the only income you have. Of course, the company offered severance pay, but I didn't get much because I hadn't worked there long. Furthermore, unemployment benefits in Florida were still as bad as they were ten years ago. I couldn't pay my mortgage, so I had to use my savings to survive.

Alternative Income Sources

Then a friend introduced me to network marketing. Although I had never considered this as an option, I could see how I could make money outside of traditional employment. So I pursued it in my spare time. As it turned out I immediately became very successful, but I was not good at sales, and I was fortunate to find people who helped me make money. While I started seeing more and more how successful someone could be if they were good at network marketing, I never was able to reach the level that supported me. I had to find a job, and I ended up with a great one that pays all of my bills!

From World Traveler to Retirement Coach

My experience in network marketing opened my eyes to alternative income sources should I find myself unemployed again. Fortunately,

that has not happened because I've been working ever since. I hope I don't lose this job, but I want to be prepared in case.

With the Internet, I continue to research opportunities and successful people who can help me consider options for the next chapter in my life. I'm nearing retirement age, and I want to be able to retire at 62 years old and then travel the world. To make that possible, I need to have income because I can't live just from social security. I'm learning to become a certified retirement coach, which will help people just like me.

What I've discovered is that a lot of people retire every day, and not all retirements are voluntary. Even if you choose to retire, you can still face challenges. Retirement is scary for many people because they don't know what they're going to do. They want to make sure they can maintain their lifestyle, and they don't want to lose the friends they've worked with at a job.

Applying Lessons Learned

I learned lessons from being laid off three times by the same company. I recognized the need to look at how to make money and enjoy what you do. It's important to have multiple streams of income, especially if you're single and don't have another person helping you financially. Income from sources like investment dividends and/or books royalties will help, but they may not be able to provide enough to survive hardships that can come from losing a job. The only way to become financially independent is to find something that can make money while you sleep, otherwise known as passive income. There are many avenues to accomplish this.

Lesson #1: Find your purpose

However, you may find yourself "stuck" in a job you started a long time ago because it was what you studied in college. The older you get, though, the faster the years pass by, and your life continues to change. Consider what you really want to do with the rest of your life; think of your real purpose and what you want to leave as a legacy. Pursuing your original dream or following your gut feeling for what is important, as it

can give you new energy. A life-changing experience of job loss can give you the chance to start fresh.

Lesson #2: Learn to see possibilities

My past has made me passionate to help those who are in the same situation as I was. I want them to see the possibilities and find a happy retirement. I can share my experiences as an entrepreneur and in starting a business as a certified retirement coach to facilitate change for them. I want to help them make their journey to become whatever they envisioned to be in that next stage of their life. My ultimate desire is to assist those career women, who are tired of their nine-to-five job, transition to something meaningful.

Lesson #3: Embrace opportunities

I learned so much when I was searching how to become a better person and finding ways to earn money while creating my legacy. If not for the help of my coaches, Toastmasters friends, and professional groups and masterminds, I wouldn't be the person I am today. Embracing the opportunities to meet other people and support one another is what makes this journey enjoyable and successful!

Maria Lucassen

obtained her Bachelor's degree in hotel management in her native country of The Netherlands. She worked in the hospitality industry for 20 years, traveling to Switzerland and Germany, as well as aboard the famous ocean liner "The Queen Elizabeth 2". Luck eventually came to Maria when she won a drawing in an annual Visa lottery and received her Green card. Maria pursued a career change and at the age 54 earned a Master's of Accounting degree from Florida Atlantic University. She now works as a Corporate Accounting Manager for a large private company that provides turn-key operations in hotels and casinos.

During hurricane season, Maria volunteers as a shelter manager for the American Red Cross. For many years, she has applied her vast tax knowledge as a volunteer in the Volunteer Income Tax Assistance (VITA) program for the IRS, which helps elderly and low-income families file their tax returns for free. One of Maria's core values is giving back to her community.

Her new passion, as CEO of Maria Lucassen Coaching, is to help career women shift their perspective to living a blissful retirement after they leave their 9-to-5 job and is seen as the go-to expert for anyone who wants to transition out of corporate employment.

She organizes workshops for those ready to plan their retirement. One that fun, purposeful and affordable.

To learn more about Maria, go to:

www.MariaLucassenHQ.com
lucassenm427@gmail.com

What Have You **Forbes'd** Lately?

My name is Mariano Padilla, and I Forbes'd having a dream and getting to fulfill it while still in my twenties. I was inspired by Forbes after hearing her speak at the LEAP Foundation, and again at 10X. I've Forbes'd shedding limiting beliefs. The dreams that I've had of my future are now becoming my reality.

Dream Big, Hustle Hard,
MAKE IT REAL!

By Mariano Padilla

My name is Mariano Padilla. I'm in my mid 20's. I currently live in Southern California, and grew up in the West Covina / Baldwin park area.

Often times, a lot of people ask me where I get all my energy, inspiration and drive from. Truthfully, it's been ingrained in me since I was a little kid.

I remember being a youngin, going to a private Christian school and I remember the song, "I'll Do My Best." To this day I remember ALL the lyrics because it's been deeply ingrained within me. When I was young, I learned to give all I've got.

That's what I do now.

When I was younger, my dad painted a vision inside of my head: my dad drew this pyramid, kind of like a triangle of success pyramid. What he said was, "There are people at the top, there are people in the middle, there are people at the bottom. As a family, we are currently between the middle and the bottom."

That really stuck with me.

I was like, "okay cool?" Then he said this to my sister and me, "But you guys are young, you guys could go anywhere you want. You two can go to the middle. You two could go all the way to the top."

He inspired us with stories of how people that are on the top have their own movie theatres inside of their own homes, they have their own pools, they have everything! They have control of their life.

That's really what intrigued me. Hearing that from my father really turned me on to the idea of success. He often reminds and encourages me saying, "You are still you and you CAN do whatever you want." He also told me the best path is by going to college. I can do that... I'm going to make him proud.

I remember being seven years old and becoming overly obsessed with just growing as a person. I didn't know about "personal development" at the time, but I knew that action was the key.

My father also told me to "know your numbers because numbers equal dollars. People will pay you good money to do the math for them." This inspired me to get really good at math when others weren't good at it. Outside of playing baseball, I was always playing around with numbers and calculations. I've been doing it since I was little. I've always had that drive, but unfortunately...

I was taught a big fat lie.

Growing up, I was always taught that I had to go to a certain college, get good grades, and only those two metrics would dictate how much money we would make in the long run.

Because as an athlete we're trained to eat a lot and put on weight, I was always that skinny guy that couldn't put on any weight and so I stopped working out and dropped out of baseball because I went through some frustrating injuries and couldn't play at the time I was coming out of college. (FYI, I did play my senior year injured). I let my body rest and I created a habit of not wanting to workout anymore because habits are key and I'm gonna talk more about habits that drastically changed

my life at the end of the story but long story short I was at twenty-two percent body fat. I got fatigued very easily and I found myself aging.

It's a lie!

Since the second grade, I've been working my tail off. I always had the vision of going to college. I saw myself playing college baseball because baseball was a passion of mine. Literally I remember sacrificing so much, even backing down from fights to increase my chances of getting into a good college because I didn't want to get in trouble.

Long story short. I graduated with incredible success coming out of high school. Top twenty-five of my graduating class with a high GPA, and as tri-athlete in football, basketball, baseball. That combined, landed me an academic scholarship to go to a private school.

Going into my freshman year, however, I choked. I was working two jobs at the time. One as a full-time manager for a theme park, the other time as an umpire, just to make extra money to make ends meet. Exhausting and frustrating I ended up changing my major three times and finally just got to the point that I didn't know what I wanted to do. Now mind you, I was not one of those people that decided to go crazy when they got into college and party hardcore. I wasn't that person, I never took a sip of alcohol or puffs of marijuana or cigarettes... nothing like that.

It all kept piling up though, professors were telling me as a freshman that I wasn't cut out to graduate and most of the time I was beyond stressed out. At the end of my rope, I was thinking, what the heck am I gonna do with my life? I felt like I was living like a slave with no free time, people telling me I wasn't good enough and just overworking myself. I hit a wall. Hard. Like a dog chasing its tail.

Life does that though... pushes you until you hit rock bottom and then as if by magic a solution appears. Going into my sophomore year I discovered motivational speakers. I watched an Eric Thomas video and bam! that gave me the inspiration I needed to shift.

My cousin texted me and shared an opportunity that opened a new gate towards my future. He introduced me to the world of network

marketing. I quickly met a lot of the mentors from the network marketing industry and that totally changed my mindset, big time. I learned about personal development, business development and how to connect with customers. Honestly, it did change my life for the better and allowed me to see a bright future.

I didn't create rags to riches story just yet, the company folded but the lessons rang loud. Senior year I played college baseball and it definitely helped me grow as a player too.

I've always had the drive but not always the luck.

I actually got cut from the baseball team during my senior year in high school. That's okay, I remember thinking. My DESIRE to play college ball was SO high that I started researching other high schools that I could transfer to, so I could play my senior year. Back then, even though I didn't know the saying, burn the ships, I was willing to do it for my opportunity to play and live out my dream.

I was about to transfer to a school three cities away, the coach from my original high school gave me another tryout and bingo, this time I made the team.

College baseball was definitely more intense than high school. My desire, work ethic, and grit got me games and we won Conference Championships in my junior year. Unfortunately, as a collegiate athlete, we're trained to eat a lot and told to put on weight. I was always THAT skinny guy who couldn't put on any muscle and THEN I got injured in my senior year. To let my body rest I slumped into a habit of not wanting to workout anymore. Good or **bad habits** will make or break you and I'm gonna talk more about habits that drastically changed my life at the end of the story.

Then the question loomed -- what to do with my life?

I found myself living out of my car and using the gym as my place to shower up daily, not to workout.

I knew that something had to change. I remember doing a work task delivering a product to a low-income apartment complex. A "middle of

nowhere" type of hood area. As I entered the building I saw a guy with a ski mask breaking into an apartment. He hears me, and he makes eye contact. At that moment it looked like he was about to pull a gun or something. I RAN! to my car and took off. I didn't look back.

At this point in my life, I was at an all-time low. I remember I had the highest body fat percentage than I've ever had. I looked a lot older than I was. If I were to show you a before picture you would guess I was 10 years older than my age.

On top of that, I was $20,000+ in debt living out of my car wanting to file for bankruptcy. But at that time I was just wondering who I was, what's happening with my life? Where did I go wrong? I was living in regret. I was blaming everything on me but I just didn't know how to go about fixing everything, I was just overwhelmed.

I kept thinking I am better than this. I knew I was made for more. It was at this point I discovered journaling. Suddenly everything began to get clear my mind. I just thought about what I was doing with my life. I shut off for a few hours.

I focused on the business training I had received, began to cultivate mentors and started doing public speaking engagements to share my story.

I listened to inspiring podcasts and one that cuts through the noise was 75 Hard from Andy Frisella. I listened and heard of this mental toughness challenge. I felt like it was calling to me. I thought it could be the perfect training. It talked to the basics. The basics began with drinking a gallon of water a day. No sweets and no alcohol. For myself, I decided to add, no fried foods like Mcdonald's, In and Out or anything like that.

Another basic was working out two times a day for 45 minutes a day. One of those workouts had to be done outside. Last Basic, was the toughest one for me... this challenge was to read ten pages a day. This one may have been tough but it changed my life forever.

I went all-in with this challenge. I treated it as if my life depended on it. The challenge was to do these things every single day for seventy-five

days straight. I started on March 14, which was a random Thursday, I didn't wait until Monday to start.

I saw a vision within myself. I saw myself not only completing the challenge but creating a big mastermind group out of this... and that's literally what I did. I dropped down from twenty percent body fat to between eight percent and ten percent body fat now and I was able to put on a good ten pounds.

Funny how this journey had become my destiny. As I posted the challenge daily and my progress a lot of people on my social media began reaching out to me. *What are you doing? What's your diet plan? What are you consuming?*

I cultivated amazing habits from my commitment and success with the challenge. Now here I am doing speaking engagements for big groups of people. Telling people how to change their habits to manifest success.

I now focus on the business training I had received, cultivating mentors and I have an online business. I see myself doing a lot of big things.

My message to you guys is just by changing your habits and taking action even when you are uncertain you are gonna gain clarity out of it. You may be uncertain now but by you taking action today. It's like jumping out of a plane and just FIGURING OUT how to land. This is something my baseball coach always preached to us throughout my four years of college baseball is FIO - "FIGURE IT OUT".

You may not know it but "figure it out" this current moment. How do you figure it out? How did I figure it out to get the physique I have. I reached out to people who were buffer than me. I reached out to friends who used to be skinny like me and they're buffed out now. So I did their workout to ask them what's your diet like I ask them questions. My willingness to learn was high and me taking this challenge to heart, it definitely changed my life for the better and they say everything happens for a reason. I'm very grateful.

What I have Forbes'd into my life lately. I've created a new physique that I've never created throughout my years of playing college baseball,

playing 3 sports in high school sports. I've never had this energy before. My strength has improved both mentally and physically.

Lesson #1: The Pyramid of Success

The lessons from my dad to paint the vision that you can rise to the top. Maybe you weren't born with a silver spoon in your mouth but don't use that as an excuse for playing small.

Lesson #2: Networking is the key to success in life and in business.

It's not what you do some of the time that matters, it's what you do ALL of the time that adds up. I have a nickname, Super Connector because a lot of people know me as THE networking expert. People remember me just because I'm good at making them, showing them that they matter and just remember little things like remembering their names but one thing I'm definitely an expert at that I want to share with you guys.

Lesson #3 : Habits -- They make you or break you.

One thing I definitely wanted to share was that habits are something that I've definitely mastered and this is just the beginning.

I Forbes'd attending Forbes Factor on a scholarship. I originally met Forbes Riley when she was a keynote speaker at the LEAP foundation Teen Leadership building camp I attended. I ended up getting her attention in the audience and she inspired my to find my truth. I then watched her speak to a crowd of 10,000 in Las Vegas... but here's the cool part. When I approached her, she remembered me. Attending the 5 day training in St Petersburg was the icing on the cake. It allowed me to truly see my potential and discover that I am unstoppable.

The experience gave me clarity and now I'm living purposeful. Looking back, it's like what Forbes Riley says, "You get what you tolerate."

I'm only tolerating the best and I'm on a mission to inspire the masses and to change lives for the better.

Thank you to Forbes Riley for playing a huge role in my life! She is by far one of the best mentors I've had in my life. Even though I've only known her for 2 years, she has played a huge role in my life.

Mariano Padilla

is a millennial leader who believes in teaching others how to cultivate habits that allow them to become the person they desire to be, or at least better than they were yesterday.

His Teachings are based on The five BIG key pillars of living a quality life; Faith, Family, Health, Wealth, and Happiness!

Currently, he has a full time business in the Alkaline Water Industry and his company's mission is to spread true global health.

He also has a Global Mastermind Group dedicated to helping the people with limiting beliefs achieve THEIR highest potential. Dream Big, Hustle Hard, Make it Real!

To contact and learn about his programs, follow him on Instagram:

@MarianoVPadilla

If you don't build your own dreams, someone will hire you to build theirs

- Tony Gaskins

What Have You **Forbes'd** Lately?

My name is Pat White, and I Forbes'd a world traveling lifestyle and business. Since I was a child, I loved to travel, and that love of adventure carried through all of my years. Now, my family and I have learned how to make world travel and dream vacations our career, and it's extraordinary!

Journey The

GLOBE

By Pat White

As far back as I can remember, traveling was a huge part of my life. I loved it! My curiosity and passion for learning about new places, cultures, and languages was something I recognized early in my childhood. And through my adult life, I have had the opportunity to experience some of the most amazing places on earth.

One of my earliest memories of traveling was going with my dad every Memorial Day weekend to his hometown in upstate Pennsylvania called Warrior Run to visit his family. We would go to different lakes, visit with other people and watch a wonderful parade. My dad had three siblings who were scattered throughout the country. He would see his sister that lived in Harrisburg, PA often, in fact, we'd visit her every Easter.

My dad's brother lived in New York. And when I was about five, we went to visit him over the Fourth of July. We went to Coney Island, rode the Cyclone, and we went to the beach. One of my fondest memories was getting lost on the beach of Coney Island for an hour—I'll never forget that!

My dad's other sister lived in Miami, FL. When I was six years old, my cousin, Merle, was getting married, so we flew down for the wedding. Leading up to the trip, we would sit at the dinner table and pretend we were airplanes!

The youngest of nine, my mom, and the majority of her family lived in Philadelphia or in the surrounding area. My mom's sister had a house in Wildwood, NJ. Starting at the age of eight, we would spend our summers there. My other aunt and her daughter also spent the summer there, and then on weekends, the place would get packed!

A lot of people would go down for the summer and work. They came from all over, including places like Canada and Ireland. I thought that was interesting, and I liked to talk to them about the different places they were from. I always looked forward to traveling with my family and being with everyone, while learning about them and being connected to them.

Many Sundays, my dad would take us on a drive. During one drive, he took us to Asbury Park, NJ. Yes, the hometown of Bruce Springsteen! We went in the winter, and it was very cold. When we came home, my dad asked us which place we liked better, Wildwood or Asbury Park. I said that I liked Wildwood better because it was warmer!

When I was ten, we went to Niagara Falls, Canada. That was great, but sometimes just looking forward to these trips was a thrill. One time we drove on spring break, and we left at night time. I'm not sure what time at night, but my sister and I had pillows, and we slept in the back seat of the car, and when we arrived it was daytime. It was in March, so the falls of Niagara were still a little frozen. You couldn't get down and take the boat ride on the "Maid of the Mist." It was there that we ate french fries with mustard instead of ketchup!

In my twenties, I would go down to the Jersey Shore all the time. I remember I booked a three-day cruise, and I went down to Nassau, Bahamas. I always loved traveling—it was part of who I was.

When I was 28, I enlisted in the United States Marine Corps. There I worked full-time and put myself through school. I spent 16 years in the Marines, and I finished my last four years in the Air Force. During my 20 years in the military, I traveled extensively. In total, I have been to about 29 states and five different countries. I would find out what was there before I arrived, and I would plan it out to make sure that I could see as much as I could.

New Mexico was the last place I went while in the military. It was incredible! I was working in a place called Gallup, NM, where we were building homes for an Indian reservation. While I was there, I went up to Santa Fe and Four Corners. I also got to meet a Navajo code talker, which was an incredible honor that I will never forget!

Also, while in the military, I met my husband. Fortunately for me, he also loves to travel. We were lucky enough to come across a travel club that has incredible prices and experiences. We get to stay at four and five-star hotels at two-star prices! We have been to Italy and Switzerland, and flying over the Swiss Alps was a sight to see! I just can't wait to get back there. Italy was breathtaking. We have been to Rome, Naples, Pompeii, Gaeta, and Casanova. You read about these things in a book, and here we were just walking around, experiencing it all—the food, the culture, the people, and the history.

Our first Dream Trip was to Orlando, FL. We stayed at the Gaylord Palms Hotel, and the hotel was beautiful! Our room had a balcony that overlooked everything. You didn't even have to leave the hotel, because they had everything. Included in our trip was breakfast every day. It wasn't just coffee and donuts—it was in one of the many restaurants in the hotel, and it was a buffet. We spent one whole day at one of their two pools. It was the adult only pool with a bar, and someone brought drinks to us. One day we spent at Universal Studios, and another night we had dinner at the Hard Rock Cafe.

We also went to Cancun, Mexico. This trip is so great that we go every year! We stay at the Hard Rock Hotel, and every little thing is included. So every year we get so excited about this trip. We are treated like royalty, and it is amazing. As soon as we get off of the plane, they pick us up at the airport, and then someone is in the lobby waiting for us to make sure we get in our room. We even get to attend a welcome party where we meet members of the travel club—it's like being a member of something so exclusive and cool, and you can experience things together, or go off and explore on your own if you want.

The Cancun trip was spectacular because every single thing is included. Every single drink, every single bite we put into our mouth, and they had a gorgeous pool with two bars at the end. Plus, it was right on

the beach. For a snack or any of your meals, you could have anything you like. They have seven restaurants to choose from and some snack stands. For lunch, we would usually get a steak or chicken kabob. My son stuck with a hamburger, french fries, and a coke.

Our son's birthday happens to be during the time we go, and he likes Hibachi grill, so we go there for his birthday dinner. On one trip, the cooks brought him up behind the grill and had him put on a chef's hat. They even spelled his name with the rice. When we went back to our room, someone from our travel company had decorated our door. When we went to our room, they had it decorated with balloons, a cake with his name and a bottle of champagne with two glasses!

You don't even have to leave the hotel if you don't want to, but you should. The excursions are a blast! When booking this trip, we received $750 back to spend! I usually get several messages while I'm at these resorts. My first year, I got to cross off something else from my bucket list—swam with the dolphins. These memories will last us a lifetime. My son is always talking about these trips and planning our next adventure.

We couldn't believe that we had never heard of this place before, and we were just so sorry we hadn't joined 10 years earlier, because these trips are phenomenal.

"We live in a wonderful world that is full of beauty, charm, and adventure. There is no end to the adventures we can have if only we seek them with our eyes open"—Jawaharlal Nehru

Life is short. So often we think, oh one day I'd like to travel. People on their deathbed have said they wished they would have traveled more. With this amazing company, you don't have to lose your life savings to visit a few places. If it comes down to $300 shoes/outfit or a vacation, I'll take the vacation any day!

Pat White

is a veteran having served a combined 20 years in the U.S. Marines and the U.S. Air Force. In addition to her extensive service to her country, Pat has helped change the lives of children as a special education teacher with the Philadelphia School District for 20 years. Her passion for teaching and the military has led her to write and publish a children's book, "Molly the Marine", which is now available.

Always looking forward, Pat applied the drive she had in the military to pursue a multitude of creative ventures, including a soon to be released movie and TV series. Pat has also found success as an entrepreneur, where she has leveraged her passion for travel and cultures to create a successful business with World Ventures. When she is not traveling, creating or changing the world, Pat relaxes by practicing yoga as a certified instructor.

To learn more about how Pat, and the incredible trips you can take with World Ventures, go to:

www.patwhite.worldventures.biz
opbart@aol.com

What Have You **Forbes'd** Lately?

My name is Renee Barnes, and I Forbes'd my voice. Two years ago, if you had asked me to speak, there was no way I could've overcome that paralyzing fear that used to wash over me. I wasn't ready, and I didn't have the tools to eliminate the overwhelming limiting beliefs that kept me in a dark space. But today, I'm ready. It was an amazing journey to get to this point—it was challenging, but more importantly, the messages I need to share are popping up now, and I'm sharing them, empowering others around me with all that I've learned. What got me to this place? Forbes Factor Live.

Lost & Found:

THE MIGHTY VOICE

By Renee Barnes

Ten years ago, my brother's death was the biggest loss that ever happened to me. You see, he was also my best friend and soul mate. And yet, it wound up being one of the best things that could have happened, as it transformed me!

I realized that before his death, I wasn't listening to where God was trying to tell me to go. But the loss of my brother made me realize that I needed to heal from past childhood traumas, to stop being a victim and to move forward in life. In other words - to let go of lower energy. I began healing through meditation and other tools. And out of that I opened up my mind and heart, and I started discovering my true voice!

Occasionally, things happen, memories brought up through little events, certain words, etc, which brought back some of the memories that kept me "stuck" for so long. But now the fear is no longer there. That extreme pain is no longer there. You see, I have discovered tools to move forward, which have lifted up my energy, and allowed me to speak out and help others open the door to their more empowered voice and life.

Ten years ago, if you asked me to speak, there is no way I could have overcome the paralyzing fears I had. I was not ready, and I didn't have

the tools to overcome my overwhelming limiting beliefs that kept me small and in hiding. But today, I'm ready. It has been an amazing journey to get to this point —it was challenging, but more importantly, the messages I need to share are at the forefront, and I'm sharing them, empowering others with all I've learned.

What was the catalyst for my "breakthrough"—from what source did my newly discovered voice finally emerge? Forbes Factor! It's like Survivor if I think about the intensity of the challenges, and the camaraderie developed, but it's not punishing—no one is sabotaging you or voting you off of an island. Instead, everyone there supports you and including you, yet challenging you to become your best self, believing in you even when it's proving difficult to believe in yourself.

That summer I experienced the most profound, life-altering, game-changing experience of my life attending Forbes Factor by Forbes Riley. Through Forbes' teaching, I was able to fully reconcile with my energy that had been trapped inside, and dormant for so long. I found this amazing part of me that had been hiding, and I was able to lift her up, allowed her to become empowered and gave her a voice! I realized that my experiences and my ability to thrive through the dark times made me an expert, someone of great value to others who may be dealing with similar pain.

Through this process of working with Forbes, I discovered the following lessons:

Lesson #1: life happens for you, not to you

That lesson was definitely a big one for me because if you think that life happens to you, you tend to be more of a victim in the world, always wondering - why me. But if it happens for you, you can use that. A perspective that life happens for you, for something greater than the moment you're in, to give you strength, tools, and purpose for you and others, that's a whole mindset shift into living a life with purpose and gratitude.

Lesson #2: Stay young at heart

I had a lot of trauma in my life, and my inner child never fully grew up, because I was hiding to protect myself. And now that child is growing up and being able to grow and learn, and speaking up, learning to not be so tiny, I'm finding that there are a lot of qualities in that inner child that I really like, including

playfulness, curiosity, and even trust. Staying young at heart keeps you connected to those very important qualities that you might have hidden deep inside yourself.

We have a choice to live in the light and not be hidden, and we have a choice to be in charge, to make decisions. And until I gave myself permission to let my voice rise up and take a leading role, I don't think I realized that these were all choices that I got to make for myself. It feels so much better to feel empowered!

Lesson #3: Your past does not have to dictate your future

My past doesn't have to dictate what kind of energy I put out, and your past does not have to stop my voice from being free and bold. For me, expanding on my voice is a huge life lesson because the voice is attached to the brain. At heart, no one can control your brain but you—no one can require that you live small and in silence but you, and you can make a decision to live boldly with greater purpose, letting your voice be heard if you choose. That's what I choose for myself going forward - to live a purpose-driven life and to empower others to do the same with my voice!

I'm not a psychologist, psychiatrist, therapist or counselor, and if you need someone like that definitely engage in those services to get the help you need. But, if you're like me, and you have a voice inside you that wants to come out, and maybe that voice has been silenced for too long due to fear, trauma, and pain, I need you to know that I understand you. I was given permission and specific tools to empower my own voice, to unlock it from the fear and pain that kept it silenced. That's a gift that I can give to you, too—the permission and tools to find your voice and to let you speak with a purpose to empower you in your life.

What energy is blocking you from achieving your goals and living your most powerful life? That's the work that you can do. With the tools that I have garnered through my journey, including the lessons and grace that have been given to me by experts in this field, I would be honored to have the opportunity to work with you to peel back your own layers and to give your voice the power it deserves. I know what it feels like to think you're small, that your voice isn't important, to let your fear and pain keep you silent when you have so much to say and give to the world.

Renee Barnes Orozco

has always been fascinated with overcoming life's obstacles and challenges. Her passion for personal growth fueled her to become a certified high-performance coach trained by a world-renown speaker and coach Brendon Burchard. Her coaching technique is an amalgamation of foundational scientific principles and her own life experiences. Renee's coaching is tailored to the unique needs and goals of her clientele, including those that may have only just started on their journey to become their true self.

Renee's focus is unrelenting, as she assists her clients gain clarity on who they are, their core values and the vision of what is most important to them. Even more importantly, she develops a clear plan forward for her clients, by guiding them through key areas of their life, which include energy, courage, productivity, necessity and influence. Once the plan is developed, then it is explored on a deeper level to reinforce her client's path to empowerment and their mastery of it. Renee's passion for life is reflected in her mantra, "Each new day is a new opportunity for possibilities!"

To learn more about Renee, go to:

www.PeacefulMindJoyousHeart.com
facebook.com/renee.rbosuccess

What Have You **Forbes'd** Lately?

My name is Robbin Fortier, and I Forbes'd a positive mindset that overcomes all challenges and allows me to manifest solutions and success. I used to think I was the unluckiest person on the planet until I learned how blessed I truly am. Meeting Forbes Riley in 2017 turned out to be the blessing I needed and I'm pleased to have her as one of my mentors. I've downloaded the Forbes app and often listen to her inspirational quotes, and I listen to her "comments" for the day whenever I get time.

Success in a

DRESS

By Robbin Fortier

"Life isn't about waiting for the storm to pass. It's about learning how to dance in the rain."

~ Vivian Green

This inspirational quote by Vivian Greene has changed my perspective on life and has taught me many valuable lessons. I learned that without the hardships in my life, I could not have moved forward. These lessons happened "for" me, not "to" me. The challenges I've faced in life have served as stepping-stones to advance my career path and my success.

I've titled this chapter "Success in a Dress", as I hope it will be a tool for every saleswoman out there. Those just beginning, and those seasoned with tests of their own. I use the term saleswoman because we all have a product to sell. The absolute most important product that we sell is ourselves!

Everyone carries his or her own baggage. Instead of leaving it behind, you should pack it up and make the most of these experiences to empower you. Use these lessons to define goals and then plan a roadmap to turn those dreams into a reality. The difference between a goal and an accomplishment is discipline. Without a clear roadmap, you have

no direction. Without discipline, there is no road and there is no goal. Here's a secret, learn it early because "it won't be easy."

Whether your goal is a new job, a promotion, or perhaps you are an entrepreneur, you need to market yourself. Success is possible and worth the effort. Break down your major goals into smaller tasks. Whenever you achieve a milestone, it'll motivate you to move forward towards your next benchmark.

My Life Story

My childhood was fairly average. I had a group of sincere friends, and I excelled in education as well as in sports. What I didn't realize was that my father was an alcoholic and a gambler. He never really cared about us as a family. My early memory was us living in what I later learned was Glenview, IL, a suburb of Chicago. I guess I was about four when we had to sell our home to pay off his gambling debts. We had to move into The City of Chicago in an attempt to start afresh. My mother not only had to work long hours, but had to endure our father cheating on her. In his drunken state of mind, he'd even given those women our home phone number. You can imagine my mother's frustration, which was usually directed at us.

He'd gamble and drink away his paychecks, leaving nothing for our family. If not for the kindness of our landlord and friends, we would have surely been homeless. These circumstances paved the way for insecurities and mistrust. It was something that would harden me, so I kept most people a safe distance away.

In order to start our lives over yet again, my parents decided to move to Miami, Florida. My father's aunt, Helen, lived there. She always helped us out of financial hardships, and assisted my mother by keeping my two brothers and I safe. Since I had no family living in Chicago, I had no choice, but to move. I was just 13.

I attended school at St. Hilary's with the same classmates. My class would have all graduated together at the end of my eighth-grade year. I had planned on attending high school at St. Scholastica, but my parents shattered those dreams. In fact, within three years of this move, I had

dropped out of high school, was permanently injured in a motorcycle accident and was abusing drugs.

It was extremely difficult to adjust to the public school system of Miami, after studying for so long at a private school in Chicago. I was way ahead of my classmates as far as my education. This added to my boredom and frustration with school. I had no long-term relationships or friends, so I felt completely lost & alone.

This was the summer of 1969. The era of hippies, drugs, burning bras rock & roll and the Vietnam War. To me it brought along a world of stress and anxiety. I was 5'8", had curly/frizzy hair, and a slight case of acne. I also didn't have much self-esteem, like most teenagers. I just began hanging out with other misfits, sharing the same boredom and frustration with school and our lack of strong family ties.

I began to skip school and started smoking pot. My parents weren't there to support or guide my two brothers or me. The reason for this lack of support was that they were too busy enjoying the nightlife of Miami. At that time, Miami was a haven for drug dealers and life in the fast lane. I found it fascinating. I wanted in that lane too.

Crazy as it sounds, back in those days, the government forced black teens from surrounding areas to attend our high school. It was referred to as "Busing". Busing was implemented in 1971. It was to achieve racial desegregation in the schools. These students had to travel sometimes for hours to reach our school. Because of it, we formed a diverse student body. I appreciated the early immersion into multiculturalism and the people of many countries.

If I were in Chicago, I wouldn't have had free access to drugs. But in Miami, life was very different. My classmates and I were all getting high. Being young entrepreneurs, we started selling the drugs that we had easy access to at very low prices. None of us understood where this path would lead.

Eventually, I reached high school, but it didn't change my lifestyle. It did, however, change the boys at school – they became increasingly more aggressive. Aside from the typical, "kissing" or "necking", I knew

nothing about having sex. My mother had never sat down and explained sexual intercourse with me. I hadn't really experimented with sex just yet. Some of my friends, who got pregnant, traveled to New York for abortions. I stayed away from sex due to the fear of getting pregnant.

One night, when I was 16, I went to a party. The young man that I was dating couldn't join me at the party. It was there that another male student, who was a football player, started to flirt with me. Well, who doesn't like that? The next thing I knew, I had been drugged and I found myself alone with him in a hotel room. Suddenly he was on top of me. I knew better than to fight, I was no match. Plus I was too high to resist. This was what every mother feared would happen to their daughter. This was a painful and humiliating experience to lose my virginity this way. It seemed like everyone in my high school was aware of what had happened.

For a very long period of time I felt so alone and ashamed that I couldn't share the incident with anyone. My "boyfriend" heard what had happened to me. He went to fight the other guy, and he ended up getting hurt himself. That's when I decided it was time to quit school. I just couldn't take all of the drama. I was about to learn that my road was going to get even bumpier.

Do you remember when you were seventeen? Just out of school, got a drivers license and you wanted to explore a bit. Maybe your first venture was out of town and away from your parents. For me, at seventeen, I was headed to Naples, FL. with a friend on his motorcycle when a car hit us. I went flying off the bike much like a rag doll. Seeing that we were injured, a man came over to help us. I asked him to hide some of the needles that I had stuffed into my tube top. He silently agreed and accepted a small stash of needles that I had crushed with my bare hands. He quickly left the scene of the accident. By this time my drug abuse was completely out of control. I was in terrible pain, but I had to stay focused. I also had a small stash of Seconal sleeping pills on me. Boy, that was some tub top! I hid that stash of pills in the ambulance, and the driver questioned me about the pills. I denied that they were mine, but they knew they belonged to me. They didn't pursue it due to the severity of my accident. I guess that they felt I had enough on my plate.

This was life and death, and my head was clouded. I wasn't sure what was going to happen. Remember, I'm seventeen and all of a sudden, my world is changing every second. I've had issues no seventeen-year-old should ever face. At first, the doctors wanted to amputate my left leg at the knee, but my father wouldn't allow it. Next, I was transported to a hospital in North Miami. We later discovered that I had shattered my hip into three pieces and broke my femur bone. I had pulverized my left kneecap and tore my peroneal nerve. I endured surgeries, three months in traction and months of physical therapy and rehab. I had to wear an orthopedic shoe with a brace that would flip my foot up so that I could walk. It was difficult at first. Making matters worse, I was embarrassed by the gear I was forced to wear just to walk. At first, I was angry that this had happened to me. Without parental guidance, I had raced into adulthood without the maturity to handle it. Now, stuck in traction, in pain and full of pity, it looked like a very dark future for me.

The distance and cold behavior of my parents was a huge impact on my life. My father's infidelity and gambling habits angered me and created a wall between us. "How could he use my mom as he does?" "Why doesn't he care about my brothers and me?" Questions I knew I'd never find answers to. I had built very high walls to try and protect myself, but they weren't working. I traveled in a small circle, but in the drug business that's pretty much the profile. I had moved away from my parents' house a few years earlier. But now, I was forced to return home so that I could recover. I thought of returning to school, but I had fallen so far behind that I couldn't convince myself to go back. Life at home was no better and I was looking at a very long recovery.

The day I recovered from the accident I was back out on my own. Starting over again was something I was getting good at. Now, I just needed some time, some space and something new. Little did I know, that the perseverance to get up and out would serve me later? Looking back, many teenagers would have just stayed home and watched TV and stayed in a dead-end existence. This, of course, wasn't my decision. My decision was to pick myself up, brush myself off and move forward with my life.

Little did I know that I had contracted hepatitis C from using needles. It's a chronic disease that I live with today. I knew that I was out of control and most of my friends knew it too. The problem was that we were all in the same boat, and it was sinking quickly. My druggy lifestyle wasn't over. Not just yet!

A few years down the road, I met a man who I fell in love with. I know what you're thinking, what happened here? He was a kind and caring man. We had a lot in common. But he too was in the drug business. For me, this was a step up to bigger opportunities and bigger dollars. At the height of the operation, we brought freighters in from overseas, filled with drugs. Originally we were involved with bringing in freighters loaded with marijuana. By the age of twenty-three, I owned a 1955 MGB TF series, a Mercedes Benz and was living on the Intracoastal Waterway, in Boca Raton, Florida. We had our own sailboat in the backyard. Our lives were consumed with parties and drugs. Eventually, we started bringing in cocaine, and that's when our world changed for the worst. We had no idea what was about to come down, but it wasn't good.

The danger was closing in. We watched our druggy circle one by one, disappear. They were dying from gun violence, overdoses, crazy accidents, robberies, and just plan greed killed many of our friends. We were living in the shadows trying to stay alive and out of jail. However, our lifestyle was extravagant. Some of my friends had children with their drug-dealing boyfriends, but I knew better. I understood that this lifestyle would come to an end, but I was caught in the net too. I couldn't stay away from drugs.

Within a year, my father and boyfriend would be dead. My younger brother went to jail. My world was quickly falling apart at the seams. Something had to change. But when? How?

If you don't know who Geraldo Rivera is, take the time to look him up. He has had a long career of making false accusations against others based on hearsay. He'd been removed from several stations for poor reporting and flat-out falsehoods. In 1986, Geraldo Rivera busted my younger brother and friends on national TV. Previously, Geraldo had experienced the worst nightmare of his TV career. Of all people, he was

the one who going to open "Al Capone's Hidden Vault" to discover all these supposed long lost treasures. This event was live on television and created incredible hype. When Geraldo opened said vault, it was empty. This was a humiliating moment for Geraldo, and it was captured on live television. In order to protect his reputation, Geraldo decided to do another show to make up for lost revenue. But what would bring in the viewers? Nancy Reagan was leading the "just say no to drugs" campaign and created a lot of heat for drug dealers and users everywhere. Geraldo began to work with the police to bust drug dealers and addicts on live TV once again for the ratings, the hype continued.

Geraldo Rivera came to Fort Lauderdale and immediately posed as a drug dealer. He wanted to purchase two kilos of cocaine, and wouldn't you know it, he found us. After an initial meeting, it was agreed we would move forward with the deal, and my brother, along with some friends, went to a predetermined location to sell the cocaine. Within moments, local and federal authorities jumped them. They were all arrested right there live, on National TV. This was no intervention. The police couldn't arrest me though. Back then there were no cell phones. The drug deals went down using pay phones. There was no way the police could connect me with this deal. But they knew that I was involved. They knew I was on the other end of the phone making the deal.

The problems started right away. We only had one kilo of cocaine to sell, not the two kilos that they had requested. Because the local police were also on the take, they thought that we had hidden a second kilo someplace. And they wanted it now! My brother was the star of this show. The cops took him and beat him senseless to get the location of the other kilo of cocaine. They wanted to sell it themselves, which was very typical of the times. When my mother went to visit my brother in jail, she feared he'd lose his eye. He was beaten that badly by the cops. Now, I was really alone and once again my mother refused to help me. I had never seen her so angry. I was supposed to help my brother, but so was she. I had nowhere to turn. My friends couldn't afford to be seen with me any longer. I was too hot. Eventually, my mom's friend, Gloria, came to rescue me.

In my despair, I couldn't help but wonder, "How did I end up here!" Maybe I hit the snooze button on the other wake up calls, but this one was real. I had to reinvent my life. My drug-dealing career was over. Quickly, I looked over my options, not many for a girl with only a high school diploma, let alone college. I went into survival mode and hit the books. I trained myself, by studying to get a real estate license. Education was the key to spring me from the life of a drug dealer. At the time, housing was booming. I had figured out that I was good in sales, so why not join a real estate agency. I was 30 years old. I had a lot of catching up to do.

I learned to support myself legally. I was able to get a few clients, but then the real estate market crashed. Had I completed my education, I would have known that recessions strike the real estate market every 7 to 9 years. So, I was yet again seeking a change, a new job/career. I had the trust in myself that I had plenty to contribute. I knew that my discipline, education and trust, or DET principle, would be my strongest attribute. I maximized my DET principle to carry me forward.

While working on that change, I went to work at a Five Star restaurant on Hutchinson Island. There I met a couple, they were both named Michael. We turned out to be great friends, and soon one of them had been offered a new job in San Francisco. The two of them were setting their sights on moving to the West Coast. Here was my break. I needed an opportunity to get the hell out of Florida. With confidence I didn't know I had, I sent the same firm my resume, and I got an interview and the job. Florida was in the rearview mirror and I headed to San Francisco. I had the self- discipline to "leave the known for the unknown."

My new job involved providing cost estimates for relocating our client's household goods to their new residence- both domestically and internationally. I met fascinating and successful women during this portion of my career. They saw something in me, and every one of these women encouraged me to get my degree and continue on to a master's degree program. Oh, how right they would be. And oh, how thankful I am to those ladies today! There was no time to regret the past mistakes I'd made. I viewed the accident and my bad choices in friends as learning experiences. I was focused on the future now. I was

inspired, so I enrolled in a college program. It was difficult, demanding and intimidating. I was 37 now. I didn't give up and I worked hard. I knew that I had the discipline, education, and trust in myself to know that I would succeed. *I would be a success in a dress.* (DET)

I had a good career going and a roof over my head. I was meeting goals and setting plans for my future. Through my friendship with the Michaels, I was fortunate to meet a wonderful group of other professionals in The Bay Area. They were all extremely supportive of my educational goals. Unfortunately, the Michaels couldn't change their lifestyle. They have both been dead for a very long time. They were too young to die. Their path was tragic. I was one of the lucky ones to escape the drug scene, finally. My path was education, and it took me to both personal and professional success.

Are you stuck in a rut, due to poor life choices? Where do you see yourself heading? What steps have you taken?

I eventually received my BSBIS and MBA degree a month before turning 44 years old. It took six long years, but I did it. I worked full-time as well. Education helped me build up my self-esteem. I knew it was time to move on from San Francisco and looked for new career opportunities. After all, I had achieved my dream of completing my education. What was next? Complete one goal at a time. Remember those stepping-stones.

In April 2002, my firm sent out an internal email, stating that they had purchased an existing business in Los Angeles. They needed a marketing/salesperson down there. I asked for the opportunity. Don't forget that people are not mind readers, so speak up when you want something. The Los Angeles area offered plenty of opportunities. I was willing to take the risk and wanted the change. "No pain No gain", right? It was around that time that I started making a path for myself. I was writing down realistic goals. Stepping-stones would present themselves, but as I stated in the beginning, you can't see a stepping-stones if they lead to nowhere. I decided to open myself to newer possibilities and bigger responsibilities.

Ironically in 2002, I had knee surgery to repair my shattered kneecap. I also now qualified for a titanium hip replacement. This was going to be big! Fortunately, my company's group insurance policy covered previous injuries. In November of 2002, I got my new hip. Finally, after thirty long years, I was able to walk, pain-free. The recovery process still required a lot of physical therapy and hard work. Following this event, I was ready to move down to sunny Orange County, CA. It was now January 2003 and I was to start over yet again. There was a big difference this time though. Now I had the faith in myself. I knew to trust in myself to look beyond the circumstances and move forward. No matter what.

I always loved the beach, and one of my goals was to move back to the beach. I found an apartment in Huntington Beach, better known as "Surf City" USA, and I settled into my new place, making new friends. You see, I didn't really know anyone when I had moved from Florida to San Francisco; so starting over again wasn't new to me. I enjoyed the changes. Huntington Beach wasn't as diverse as San Francisco, or as cramped. I was able to settle into my groove, enjoyed my recovery and my new start. I even met a really sweet man, named John. We are still together to this day!

My new job was going great. I had made new friends through both work and external relationships. There was much to learn about the area, Los Angeles and Orange County are large territories to cover. Now that I learned the job, and was finally settled, it appeared my strong goal setting and academic achievements were paying off- the DET Principle.

Unbeknownst to John and I, "The Storm" was just around the corner. The trust and confidence that I had in myself was now going to be put to the test. We had been together for about three years when out of the blue, I was diagnosed with breast cancer. Despite having insurance and going for my mammograms every year, cancer had been growing inside of me for about 7 years. It had gone undetected. Once we did the MRI, it was discovered that I had 13.5 cm of cancer. The average is 3.2 to 3.5 cm. I was diagnosed with stage-three breast cancer. Suddenly, my life took on new and dramatic challenges.

Doctors, clinics, blood test, and shots- it was all so new, so scary. John and I had been together for some time, but even so, I was nervous as

to what would happen to our relationship. What was going to happen to me, my looks, what about my hair? What would John's response be? All too often, men are known to leave their wives or girlfriends at this time. It's all so much to handle. I had so many questions and concerns. I bottled a lot of this up and kept it to myself. But with the help of my new doctors, and John going crazy with research on the topic, I decided, at some point, to take on this cancer and fight it with everything I had. My decision was made and my new battle would begin. If things weren't bad enough, right on cue, the kicker. I needed a full hysterectomy. Surprise!

I learned the news about my breast cancer and the action plans for the recovery over the phone. I felt like collapsing when I heard the "C" word. And by the way, it's difficult driving when you're crying! I had never been sick before, at least nothing like this- cancer. I didn't really know anyone dealing with cancer. I had been down before, and it was time to get up and out just like I did when leaving the druggy lifestyle, as well as Florida and San Francisco. Each of those decisions had a puzzle and no answers. With my treatment in hand, I was able to make my way forward. Cancer was just another unknown. The big "C" was hard to process but was better than not knowing. It was time to weather this storm with new goals, not academic, but physical goals to achieve and conquer. No one else really notices what you are putting into your success. It is a lonely journey at times. It is your journey.

Though I was frightened, I knew there were treatments available, so I remained calm. This event helped improve my relationship with my mother. Although she didn't treat us well during our childhood, I knew it was useless holding grudges, and therefore, forgave her and myself. There was a blessing in there. She did have a funny line about the turn of events. When I told her that I was diagnosed with stage-three breast cancer, she replied suspiciously, "who told you that?" Like I was consulting with my gardener for my medical advise. She was a funny lady.

John was with me the entire time. We constantly talked about what was happening and what was ahead. The first surgery was awful. I had drainage tubes coming out of my breast, so moving was very difficult. I had staples where they had performed the hysterectomy. It

was extremely painful. John was there to support me, along with some friends and even a few colleagues.

From the get-go, I started off with an infection. I spent every day at the hospital having antibiotics pumped into me. You want to go through your cancer treatment procedure quickly and leave it behind. But the doctors couldn't start the treatment due to the infection. It took some doing, but we got rid of that infection. I was now ready for the chemo. I chose to keep my bald-headed look instead of wearing a wig. I thought that I looked like a drag queen in the wig. As my sister-in-law, Janet pointed out, that was a much easier look to pull off in "LA". Once the chemo was completed we moved on to the radiation treatment.

I knew that I was in trouble as soon as everyone went running out of the room during the radiation treatment. Once again, it's a challenge, but it was easier than the chemo was on my body. Radiation treatments take a toll on your body. Your skin gets burned and it actually hurts.

You must stay healthy and exercise during your cancer treatments. You must be a partner in your recovery, not a victim of the disease. It is both physically and mentally hard on you. It takes a lot of strength. Once the treatments were completed, we took off to Maui. It's the perfect healing paradise. My plastic surgeon advised me to wait for a year before having the reconstruction surgery. My hair started to grow back. I got color and eyebrows back on my face. I learned how to dress and conceal my scars. Finally, after a very long time, a smile returned too.

A year passed, and I had breast implant surgery over Memorial Day weekend. A follow-up surgery was to be performed in September. In the meantime, I had planned to celebrate my mother's 80th birthday in June. We would all be there. My brothers and my uncle with their families all participated. It would be the last time that we'd all be together. It was during this visit I realized how precious life was. How fleeting life was & how quickly time passes. Don't forget what's really important in your life. Part of setting goals is to remember to include time for your family and friends. Realize the responsibilities one has to his or her partner, family, and friends. Make the time.

Now, I was thinking about a peaceful life. We expected this next surgery to be the last surgery, and I imagined what it would be like to not have to see any more doctors. Right on cue, following the follow-up surgery in September, my recovery wasn't going as planned. My skin wasn't healing due to the radiation treatments. My right chest area was so badly damaged the skin was actually burned. We were trying desperately to get my skin to heal. I even endured several visits in a hyperbaric oxygen chamber to assist with healing the skin. I'm unbelievably claustrophobic. I had to trust.

To my own amazement, I worked through all 9 of my reconstructive surgeries. I had too. I could not sit still and watch. I had to stay focused on what I could control. I immersed myself into work. In fact, I was scheduled to speak at a convention in Las Vegas. The day prior to my speaking event, John and I had dinner and went to bed early, as we had an early morning the next day. The next morning, I pop up out of bed and jump into the shower. While bathing, I realized I had fluid pouring out of my breast. It was hard to tell at first because of the water from the shower. John took a look and he could clearly see directly into my chest. We called my surgeon immediately. She told us to drive back and that she'd meet us at the hospital. We rushed back to Newport Beach. She took out the implants, placed in smaller implants and stitched me back up. I was horrified and wondered if I was cursed.

This quick fix didn't work. By the end of October of 2008, I was left with nothing in my right chest cavity, just a sunken hole, and a very large scare. My depression actually hurt. My focus on DET had to pull me through one more time. I had the discipline to follow the doctor's orders, educating myself about the disease and trusting that my positive attitude would see me through. I had to save my sanity and life!

The surgeon referred us to another plastic surgeon. She told us I had a chance at a full recovery and told us to wait for 9 more months for the next surgery. My skin needed to heal and so did my soul. I got used to wearing turtlenecks to hide the condition of my chest. Turtlenecks in July, oh my!

During this time, I focused on my mother and step-dad. Their health was deteriorating quickly and they were severely ill. This also diverted

my attention away from my problems and onto them. There wasn't anything that I could do until the next surgery. Unfortunately, my stepfather Bernie passed away in March 2009, and in July of the same year I lost my mother. I'm so grateful that we had our time together.

Once again, my surgery in August 2009 had failed. Thankfully, my mother had passed. I don't think she could have handled it. After all, it was her daughter's body that was being brutalized. None of us had ever heard of breast reconstruction surgery being this complicated. It was a difficult time for all of us. It was hard to face everyone with yet more bad news. Everything was becoming more and more difficult to deal with, so was especially my depression.

Another surgery was scheduled for November 2010. Suddenly, walking on a shattered hip for 30 years seemed like a piece of cake. I felt defeated, but with the support of John and friends, I was able to overcome these challenges.

Finally, November 2010 arrived. I underwent a huge surgery. They replaced the damaged radiated skin with skin taken from my stomach area. They had also taken a vein and some fat to place in my right chest cavity. A tummy tuck at 54, sweet! The surgery was successful. We knew right away. We could hear the blood running through the replaced vein. I've always enjoyed music, but this is the best music I had ever heard. Finally, we could close this chapter. I could move forward and again chase my dreams.

We all are tested in our lives. I have hit the lowest of lows. I have been the loneliest woman on the planet, but I never gave up. As you can see, each small success has lead to large successes. I have much more to accomplish in my life and have been prepared for the future by the past. So if you're determined, nothing will stop you from moving forward. Take that baggage that you've been dragging around and jump high on top of it. Use it to reach for the stars and soar with the eagles.

Life Lessons I've Learned

Life has taught me that I'm much stronger than I ever thought. I successfully overcame drug addiction, defeated cancer, and completed my education in my mid-40's. This boosted my self-confidence and gave me the motivation to focus on my goals. My experiences, whether good or bad, have contributed to where I am today. So just take the first step, it's the hardest. Implement your DET principles.

Today I'm healthy, happy and eager to learn, much like a child. I appreciate my life and am always improving and moving forward. My next step is to complete my book and use my experiences in life and sales to help guide others to their success. After all, we are always prospecting for new opportunities, presenting/selling ourselves, closing the deals, constantly learning and taking care of ourselves.

What Have You Forbes's Lately?

The Forbes Factor Live event has positively influenced my mindfulness. I used to think I was the unluckiest person on the planet. But when I listened to the stories of others, I realized everyone has their own set of problems and miseries. Meeting Forbes Riley turned out to be the blessing I needed, and I'm pleased to have her as one of my mentors.

I've downloaded the Forbes 360 app, and often listen to her inspirational quotes while I sit in the "Corona Crawl", our local term for the traffic on the 91. Since I'm in sales, I try to listen to her "comments" for the day whenever I get time. Her three-day event in Long Beach inspired me to become the woman that I saw in my dreams and the desire to help others.

Robbin Fortier

has realized that everything she thought happened "to" her happened "for" her. She has beaten drug addictions, cancer, crippling accidents and more using the DET Principle of "Discipline", "Education" and "Trust".

Robbin has overcome many obstacles in life, and now holds a Bachelor's Degree in Business Information Systems (BSBIS) and an MBA. She also has a successful career in information governance, outside of sales. This has allowed her to have an abundance of opportunities to speak in front of professional organizations.

Dedicated to giving back to her community, Robbin was the president of the Orange County ARMA, and is currently on the board of The Greater Los Angeles ARMA. She has also been awarded the Michael Hanahan Award for her many years of volunteer work with the Orange County Special Olympics. Not only does she assist with the Orange County games, but she also oversees venues for the State Games. Robbin has also been the stage manager for the past 9 years for the "Long Beach Searches for The Greatest Storytellers", which has allowed her to sharpen her stage presence.

Robbin is now on a mission to assist those willing to improve their lives by using the basic sales principles of prospecting, presenting, closing deals, continuing education and health & beauty.

To learn more about Robin, go to:

www.SucessInADress.net
robbin@SuccessInADress.net

The key is not to prioritize your schedule, but to schedule your priorities

- Stephen Covey

What Have You **Forbes'd** Lately?

My name is Shelly Stucchi, and I Forbes'd being a badass mom and being a major player in a Fortune 500 corporation, all while building a lucrative real estate portfolio on the side. People think that you can't be both a good businesswoman and a good mother, watch me continue to prove them wrong! Because of who I am, because of all I've been through, I know that my daughters will have the best life, while I still manage to be the best wife! I Forbes'd the ever elusive term for most, I Forbes'd balance.

Imperfectly
PERFECT

By Shelly Stucchi

I still remember the night we landed in this country. We were in New York City, spending the night at a hotel near LaGuardia before our connection to Boston Logan Airport. My dad rounded my brother and me up, and took us to the bathroom. It was there he proclaimed, "In this country, hot water automatically comes through the faucet and you can drink the water right out of the tap!" I thought he was fucking crazy. Hot water on call? Drinking water without boiling first? Imagine that! When he saw the doubt in my eyes, he took the cup next to the sink and filled it with water. Slowly, and never breaking eye contact, he lifted the cup towards his mouth, and right before it touched his lips I shrieked, "NO DAD!"

I was eight years old and far too young to not have a dad. In fact, I had just met him two years ago and it was sort of nice to have a dad like the other kids at school. Prior to my 6th birthday, he lived in the United States with my mother working to establish a foundation in "the land of opportunity" so that they could bring my brother and I back on firm footing once the US State Department approved our permanent residence applications. Still, everybody knew that drinking water straight from the tap was a death sentence and I wasn't going to allow it under my watch. He laughed with that gentle smile of his, and calmly

explained that it was indeed safe and that's precisely why we're moving here- For the great water! He took a sip while I held my breath, and when he didn't drop dead I became an immediate believer that this was indeed the most amazing country ever.

Once we settled, life fell into a series of routines. My parents were partners in a local Chinese restaurant where they devoted almost all their waking hours to the establishment. Back during those days, we barely saw mom and dad during the week, as my brother was 12 and was assumed to be capable of watching me after school while our parents slaved away. On Saturdays we would ride to the restaurant with them, and by nine-years old I was packing take-out and answering phones while my brother bused tables. For a little while my parents had Sundays off and those were the days we'd spend as a family running errands. I remember the rare occasions when my dad would take us fishing... those were fond memories. However, by the time I entered middle school, my relationship with my parents had morphed into an employee/employer affiliation. The time we spent together outside of work was minimal and mom and dad never engaged in emotionally connecting experiences with me. We co-existed professionally, and although I recall yearning for a more heart-filled bond with my parents, the doors were just never open, and I never asked for the keys.

During that time, my parents also decided to go out on their own and open a restaurant without partners. There was no doubt that the work ethic they had alone would deliver success, but to ensure it my parents tapped into the strength of a family operation. While my parents worked every single day for almost a decade, it was expected that my brother and I would be there to help every weekend and holiday as well. This expectation, of course, made getting the occasional Friday night off to attend that Valentine's Day dance arduous, and always lead to fights and guilt-trips. We'd be reminded that we didn't come to this country just to forget our roots. We are Taiwanese, and a life lived in pursuit of happiness was selfish and frankly absurd. "Having fun won't pay the bills" they'd say, and we would begrudge every word.

By high school, my relationship with my parents had become even more distant. I met my obligatory duties, worked when I should and endured the backlash when I had the rare alternative commitment that impeded my availability to the restaurant. It felt like they didn't know me and didn't care to. I dealt with it the best I could by constantly picking fights with them, breaking curfew and sneaking out with friends who "actually cared about me."

And then one random night in the summer when I was going into senior year of high school, things came to a head. After coming home from hanging out with some friends on a Saturday night, I walked past my father who was watching TV in the dining room and before I could turn the corner to go upstairs, he called out my name. When I turned around he plainly asked what my plans were for after high school. Perplexed by this question I muttered with obvious "um... college?"

That's when out of nowhere he laughed out loud with a snarling undertone and said "COLLEGE! How are YOU going to get through college? HAH! I would actually bet money that you can't get through college. Only successful astute individuals get through college." (Mind you, despite the partying, I was a National Honor Society, honor roll student, being recruited by universities (and some Ivy's) for my track and field + academic successes during this time) .

I can still see myself, frozen by the attack. I remember all I could think was "WHAT. THE. FUCK?!" When I finally collected myself, I asked him "what the hell are you talking about" and "what do you want to bet on?". And after some hurtful words were exchanged, we settled on a car. A brand-new car upon college graduation. We shook hands on the bet and I ran off to cry myself to sleep. They brought me to this country for "a better life". But my assimilation with "weak Americans" whose misplaced priorities on "happiness" and "passion" had clearly softened me. Is that true? All the societal praise was nothing more than a mirage of real success because the standards of this culture is so low? Or was my dad just an asshole? I remember refusing to believe these thoughts that had begun to surface from my subconscious. So, I suppressed them by choosing the latter reasoning and became angry with my father. We didn't speak for months and it broke my heart because it appeared no

skin off his back. When I graduated from both high school and college, he was not there. Nor was my brand-new car.

The danger with not confronting the legitimacy of his words was that those very words were able to take permanent residence in my subconscious, and were capable and accountable for leading me to the self-sabotage I had experienced for subsequent decades. It nurtured my unsustainable drive for perfection and constant self-doubt in the face of accomplishments. And no matter the success, it was never enough.

It wasn't until I attended a life-changing business training in St. Petersburg, FL that I truly began to heal something that was never broken. Me.

For days at Forbes Factor, classmate after classmate told stories of their horrid childhood in small trembling voices, and as I cried for that lost and broken child in the tale, I wondered if the story was my own. Maybe. But as each one of them stood in front of me, strong, beautiful, alive and thriving, I couldn't help but recognize that our pasts weren't the only parallels we shared. Each one of them, so successful in their own rights, were unable to see their mark in this world because they chose to focus on an unchangeable past. But the 5-day training was intended to arm us with the powerful tools to shift that oppressive focus and free us from the self-imposed shackles to pursue our true potential. And those brave enough to allow it, did break free, but not without first paying the price of confronting these villains from the past and extending the necessary empathy in order to move forward.

I guess you can say I was one of the brave ones. I left Florida that stormy day in September without the shackles I'd been carrying for so long.

For the first time, I truly opened my heart to my parents and contemplated that loveless childhood I clung on to. Was that what really happened? I allowed for the empathy they so deserved to flood my being and considered the facts. I recalled the story my dad once told me about his five-year-old self. It was back in the 1950's and while walking home from school a few classmates asked if he wanted to go play some baseball. Oh, how my dad loved baseball when he was a boy. But the problem was that my dad was the eldest son of 6 growing

up in Taiwan, a few years after the Chinese civil war had ended. Life was harsh and survival had to be earned. He lived in a dirt shack and was expected to run the household and take care of his siblings, while working to weave nets for local fishermen for a few pence after school each day. So that day, at five years old, the invite to play baseball presented an especially tough predicament for my father. As anyone could imagine, the allure of recreation for a little boy was hard to pass up. But the beatings my grandmother would serve to him if he didn't show up on time was frightful. As my father explained, at this time he had already developed an amazing fear for my grandmother's beatings, but reluctantly agreed to play baseball by rationalizing that he would only stay for a few minutes. That afternoon, he ended up playing longer than the intended 5 minutes, and returned home 15 to 20 minutes later than expected. What awaited him was the beating of his life. When he told me this story, I remembered seeing him close his very sad eyes as his face twitched with agony recalling the gruesome details of his lashings. It was endless, he recounted. He actually thought it was going to end his life. If it wasn't for my grandfather who ultimately interrupted the discipline, my grandmother might have never stopped. The beatings persisted, and decades later when she was confronted by the guilt of the abuse she inflicted on my father, my grandmother actually tried to take her own life. Not only was there physical abuse throughout his early childhood, but whenever she felt a surge of frustration build up due to my father's inability to perform to her expectations, she would tell my father that he was worthless, useless, and might as well go kill himself.

I thought about how that boy turned into a young man and married a beautiful girl from work in his early 20s. How he initiated the courtship by baking her a birthday cake, and unbeknownst to him, was the most special thing anyone had ever done for her. Because until that day, nobody had ever valued her life. In fact, she believed that she was worthless. To be clear, her existence was so inconsequential that she didn't actually know when her real birthday was, as her gambling addict of a father never registered her birth with the country until months later. Instead, because of that loser father, she spent her childhood on the run with her family from bookies looking for repayment of his debt or their lives. She was just another daughter in a male dominated culture, identified at best as property and at worse a burden. And although she never

endured the physical abuse that my father did, the emotional neglect was enough to cultivate a misguided rulebook for human connection for decades to come.

So when these two humans connected and embarked on the journey of parenthood, what could anyone expect? It's true that I have no memories of my parents ever hugging me, kissing me or telling me that they love me. As Maslow dictated, it's quite possible I will always yearn for those basic needs. But taking the time to reflect on my parents' own journeys and their relationships with their parents, I can't honestly say I should have anticipated more from them. To expect my mother and father to speak a language they were never taught or be angry with them when they communicated love in another language... the only language they've ever known, is pretty selfish and frankly has caused me a lot of unnecessary pain.

When I think about what I've Forbes'd lately, there's a lot. But the most life changing is the simple recognition that my parents are owed an overdue appreciation because the truth is what they did give me, is a whole lot more valuable than hugs and kisses. The countless years of work at our restaurants allowed me to accumulate over 10,000 hours of execution and public speaking practice. Before I even turned 21 years old, I was more comfortable with operations, project execution and communicating in front of an intimidating audience than any of my peers. I can up-sell anything to anyone. My emotional intelligence soared to new heights. And as a result, I've enjoyed tremendous professional success as I continued to build on this foundation years later. But up until Forbes Factor, I couldn't clearly see all these gifts. I was so stuck on what I didn't have, when what I have received from my parents was actually what I had wanted all along, just in a format I didn't recognize.

Today, I'm free from the shackles of perfection because I finally realize my parents never expected it. I'm able to accept my successes and that acceptance is what has allowed me to pay it forward, and coach others on how they can overcome limiting beliefs and design a life worth living. Until I saw it as a gift, I couldn't give it to others. I see now that while working for a Fortune 500 company, my abilities to effectively negotiate contracts with foreign governments around the world, worth over a

billion dollars, while managing a high performing team and executing to incredible profitability was no accident. I had been running businesses since Junior High and such real-life experiences had armed me with more business acumen than my MBA ever did. Moreover, and most importantly, my parents taught me that life was about eating a lot of shit, but if you are strong enough to endure it, not physically, but mentally, success will follow naturally like the law of gravity. Today, I really don't fear falling because I've always gotten back up and soared. After Forbes Factor, I'm able to thank my parents for the countless opportunities to feel the bottom. After all, it has taught me ways to fly and has given me the assurance that I won't just survive but thrive through any storm. I'm not sure how many people can actually say that, and this very mindset is what's enabled me to build a real estate business with my husband that will give us the financial freedom to be with our children without the 9am-5pm corporate restrictions.

When I look at my kids, I often wonder if I would have had the strength to leave them for several years to build a new foundation in another country - if it meant ensuring their happiness in the future. Their energy, laughter, and love are so addictive, would I really be selfless enough to do that like my parents did? I'd like to say yes, but I don't know if I'm strong enough. Truthfully, at the end of the day, this consideration is all but moot because I won't ever have to consider that. My parents sacrificed and endured heartaches to raise me this way so I'm equipped to build a business that doesn't earn just money, but more importantly time with my amazing family. Isn't it ironic that my parents always told me to not focus on happiness but that was all they were trying to give me all along? They gave up everything so I can actually have it all today. All parents are misunderstood. My parents are the worst victims of them all, but thankfully for Forbes Factor, I'm able to course correct and build the relationship with my parents they had always intended. With love.

Shelly Stucchi

is a mother, wife, investor, consultant, health enthusiast and lover of tacos.

Shelly is an industry recognized, award-winning, corporate professional who is responsible for profitably developing and directing international programs worth billions of dollars for Fortune 100 companies... her job takes her all over the world, flying over 150,000 miles each year.

However, it wasn't very long ago when Shelly and her husband, Craig, were stuck in the "rat race" of trying to juggle life with two children under the age of 5, demanding full-time jobs, self-managing multiple rental properties, and pursuing additional avenues of income to enable their release from their corporate handcuffs. It was overwhelming, and the sickening feeling of constant drowning had become apparent.

Together she and her husband developed the 25th Hour System, a revolutionary productivity framework that ensures the alignment of goals with daily tasks through reclaimed focus and massive action. Based on Agile, a software development methodology, the effectiveness of the 25th Hour System is maximized with concepts from today's thought leaders in psychology, leadership, productivity and success. Since the development of the 25th Hour System, Shelly and Craig have enjoyed helping individuals and organizations eradicate that lost and overwhelming feeling by realigning their priorities and focus to develop an actionable path forward.

In addition, Shelly is a successful real estate investor who is passionate about sharing `her knowledge and experiences to empower others.`

To learn more about Shelly, reach her at:
shellystucchi@gmail.com

*Go as far as you can see;
when you get there, you'll
be able to see further*

- Thomas Carlyle

What Have You **Forbes'd** Lately?

My name is Stacey Saintz, and I Forbes'd my Incredibly Connected business. Forbes built an activity that demonstrates to people that often when they're dreaming bigger and bolder, they fail to take action on those dreams because they're seeking permission—from their boss, parents, partner, friends, peers, colleagues, etc. Forbes figured this out and began a movement that grants people permission to start believing in themselves, allowing them to go after what they really want in life. That exercise, along with so many other lessons learned and experienced through Forbes Factor Live, changed my life, radically.

Incredibly
CONNECTED

By Stacey Saintz

The Formative Years

How much do you remember from your childhood? I don't remember much, and I have often times wondered why. The question certainly doesn't come up much in everyday conversation. Although, when I have asked other people, I've been amazed at how much they remember, and it's in very vivid detail!

I have come to believe that the reason I don't remember much is that I have merely "existed"—just gotten along to the best of my ability, given my circumstances. I don't particularly recall any traumatic experiences. There was no abuse or outright neglect, but I feel like I have had just very few peaks and valleys in my life because I have lived my entire 58 plus years in "the comfort zone."

I grew up in a little community within Seattle called Ballard. It was mostly made up of descendants from Scandinavia back then, including my family. My grandparents were Norwegian and Swedish. Both of my parents grew up in Ballard, and they actually lived across the street from each other. Interestingly, our family home where I grew up was ½ block up the street from their childhood homes. My father was 18 months older than my mother, and they knew each other from the time my mom was about three years old. When they got married in 1956, Mom

was 20 and Dad was 21. Mom was the eighth of nine kids and Dad was the sixth child of seven.

I am the oldest daughter in our family, the second child of four siblings, alternating boy-girl between 1957 and 1962: Mark, Stacey, Stuart, and Marcey. During a Forbes Factor event with Forbes Riley, she asked me about my first memory from childhood. Since I actually have a preoccupation regarding my <u>lack</u> of childhood memories, this was a really odd question to have to answer. I could recall a time when I was about three years old, laying on the living room floor, drawing tiny little connecting circles. My mom later told me that I spent considerable time doing that. I have recently concluded, based on that information, that I just got accustomed to being alone and working through things in my own head. Also, I was "painfully shy," which my mother often told people when we met them. I guess that made it okay to just stay stuck there, hiding within myself.

This is mostly what I've been told about myself, though. I honestly don't recall much from my childhood. There were some pivotal moments in school that set the stage for who I was to become, which I do remember. In the first grade, Miss Cadwell's message was that nothing less than perfect was acceptable or good enough. She screamed at several of us 6-year-olds for coloring outside of the lines! Along with that, the fact that I was always tall for my age made me "different" and therefore not welcomed into the little girl groups at school, and because I was "painfully shy," of course I did not assert myself.

To further differentiate myself from the crowd, in the second grade, I had to wear an eye patch (over my good eye) and "cat eye" glasses in an effort to strengthen and correct the "lazy eye" that had not been caught earlier in my life. This combination of "oddities" made me somewhat of a social outcast, so I just focused on getting good grades. Overall, though, elementary and junior high school are somewhat of a blur. I got decent grades—mostly A's and a few B's. Then, later in Sixth Grade, I felt extremely blessed to connect with another tall girl, Anna, who became my very best friend throughout junior high and high school. A year after graduation, at my wedding, she was my maid of honor! We are still very close to this day, although she lives across the country from me, and has, since 1979. We did lose touch for several years, given

each of our moves in our respective segments of the country. And of course, communication over that period was via "snail mail" and/ or very expensive long-distance phone calling. Thank you, Facebook, for helping us find each other again! My sister and I visited Anna a couple of years ago, we spent four glorious days together, and it was like we never missed a beat! We picked up right where we left off, and of course, we reminisced about some of our antics from "back in the day."

Anyway, back to my childhood, things started to get more positive for me in high school. Mr. Logan, my sophomore year history teacher, was something special—a bright spot in the midst of the school years storm. I am 5 foot 11, he was like 5 foot even. He had a Texas accent, and he spoke to his students as if we were real living, breathing, thinking individuals (imagine that!). He called us "folks," and he taught in such a way that history actually made sense, and it was interesting for the first time in my school years. He connected current events to historical events in a way that made total sense, which was actually of real value to me! Before and after meeting Mr. Logan, I always thought history was pointless, because the other teachers merely taught from a textbook, and they had us focus on memorizing people, events, and dates just to pass tests. After that one semester in high school, I moved on to other teachers, and it was back to just facts, data and memorization; and, of course, it was about getting good grades for just the sake of it during my junior and senior years.

One thing about high school that sticks out is that I was very excited to learn to type and run office machines because that was going to be my post-high school employment ticket! Really, my entire school experience was such a mundane drag, I don't recall any real conversation with my parents about going to college. If I had been interested, I would most certainly have had to pay for it, and I really was just "done" with school and ready to pursue life as an income-earning adult.

Throughout my childhood, I received mixed messages from my parents. I quietly did my best, and as I said earlier, I was painfully shy. I didn't want to bring attention upon myself, so I got mostly A's and a few B's, and I didn't get involved in many activities. I was a tap dancer from the age of five to twelve or so, and I was very good at it. However, I quit when

the other girls quit, because for me, it was all about the community and connection we had.

The message that I heard off and on throughout childhood was "children are to be seen and not heard." My Dad's perspective seemed to always be that my best can always be better, and so I never felt good enough to measure up to his high standards throughout childhood or even well into adulthood. My Mom was at home in our early years, and she would pump me up and tell me, "Oh, you can do anything and be anything you set your mind to!" But at the same time, she'd characterize me as "painfully shy," which seemed to contradict her belief in me. It was confusing to say the least!

My mom went back to work when I was 13. From then through high school, I was the evening meal preparer, which came with an extra allowance. Our meals consisted of "fancy" processed foods like Hamburger Helper, macaroni, Rice-a-Roni, and similarly delightful and cheap chemically laced food crap. I say that now, though at the time it tasted decent, it was quick and easy to prepare, and I was used to it.

The values I grew up with were: work hard, do your best, and always be better than your best—though, I'm not quite sure how that last part works. Along with that, I was taught to be loyal; honesty is the best policy; get good grades in school, then go to work for a big company; mind your Ps and Qs, and you'll have good benefits and the amazing reward of a decent paycheck. Maybe I'd even get recognition for perfect attendance and years of service, and then someday I'd get a grandfather clock or some other cool thing like that for retirement. My parents never talked about dreams or goals or any of that "fluffy" stuff, so the message was one of duty, and cause and effect: "Do this, and you'll get that" …kind of thing.

"Independence" and Early Marriage

I was "done" with school, and I was emotionally ready to get out of my parents' house at age 18 (it was a different reality financially). I got my first job with the telephone company in October, 1977, making a whopping $149 per week, plus paid vacation, healthcare and dental coverage! Now I've really arrived, right? I'm on my way toward independence and prosperity, I remember feeling. I saved up for

a down payment, and I bought my first car four months later. A car that I couldn't even drive because it had a stick shift! That was fun and exciting—it even felt a little defiant! My boyfriend, Loren (now my husband) was incredibly patient with me, and he taught me to drive my new, manual transmission, 6-cylinder hot rod, Plymouth Duster! WooHoo!!

When we got married in November of 1978, I was 19 and he was 20. I went from living in my parents' house to a honeymoon to being married and living together with my husband. Thus, I have never lived on my own.

Because we were underage, and we were living paycheck to paycheck, we took an Amtrak train from Seattle to San Francisco for five days for our honeymoon. The southbound coach train trip extended to 24 hours (several extra hours), due to an insane amount of snowfall and related delays for clearing of the tracks. Once we got to San Francisco, we walked to our hotel (no rental car because we were too young and broke). Between walking and the cable cars, we got around the city and saw the sights. We were young, naive and probably oblivious as to the potential dangers of walking in that area after dark at that time. In fact, a really uncomfortable situation occurred on our return from dinner one night. Thankfully, nothing bad came out of it!

The Corporate Career Years

In October, 1977, my first full-time position was as a Senior Typist, preparing correspondence to telephone company customers, usually about billing issues. Then in September of 1979, I accepted a lateral transfer to an administrative assistant position, where I was actually replacing my mom, as she and my dad were moving to New Jersey for a rotational assignment he had accepted. In that clerical position, I supported groups of managers, including some district and division levels, which were the highest level supported by a clerk at that time. Then, in June of 1988, after proving my skills and talents to the "powers that be," I was promoted to management as Executive Secretary supporting a single Vice President, which was a huge success for me! I was so excited and proud! By then, my dad had returned from New Jersey. He worked for the phone company a total of about 35 years, and

he worked in the same building as I did. I went to see him and invited him to come to meet my new Vice President boss -- and it was clear that he did not want to come. Given my history with my Dad, I took this to mean that he didn't believe I deserved to have that promotion or position, though he didn't say that to me.

I found out some years later, however, that Dad had actually said the words "you aren't worth that" to my older brother when he excitedly announced he was being hired for $11 an hour at his first full-time warehouse job back in 1976. Those words had a lasting, damaging effect on my brother and his relationship with our Dad.

In August of 1990, I was promoted again to manage an outside crew of pay telephone coin collectors. Over the ensuing nine years, I got the added responsibility of managing the coin counting center, where we counted and banked over $100,000 in coins each day from payphone collections in four states. A few years later I was given responsibility for a small crew of pay telephone installation and repair technicians in the Puget Sound region. At one time, I had 24 direct reports; both inside and field employees. I truly enjoyed that time in my career, the people I worked with and the continuous learning I experienced!

Then, in May of 1996, while I was still working for the phone company, I became a Mary Kay independent beauty consultant; mostly because I had a good friend who was in the final days of a challenge to promote herself to a sales director position.

In June of 1999, the Public Communications (payphone) department was downsizing, and they had a separation package available. Cell phones were beginning to make an impact on payphone usage, and it was only a matter of time until payphones would become like the dinosaur, or at least close to extinction. I was one of three managers in our group, and they were cutting down to two. I had been feeling like I was missing prime years in my kids' lives by working full time away from home. At that time, they were 14, 11 and 8. The teen years can be very trying for some, and I wanted to be home with and guide our kids. After discussing and agreeing with Loren, I volunteered to leave the company, "retiring" from corporate life at age 39. Fortunately, between my separation package and his income, we could still pay the bills.

Loren and I worked, paid bills and saved what we could for a number of years, and by being at the right place at the right time, we were able to purchase our first home on a "lease option" deal in June of 1982. The interest rates on home mortgages at the time were in the 17% range annually, and builders were unable to sell their new construction. The builder offered us a 4-month lease option at $801/month; $1 for rent and $800 towards the down payment!! Who knows how much longer it would have taken us to become homeowners had we not gotten that deal! We closed in October at an APR around 15%!

We welcomed our first child, Joshua, in June of 1984. The very day he was two weeks old, my mother took an intentional overdose of medication and was nearly unconscious. I had to leave my two-week-old son at home with Loren to go help my dad.

In December of 1986 our second son, Nicholas came into our lives!

Between 1984 and 1989, my mother suffered a total of 8 overdoses. I went to my parents' house to help my Dad on most of those occasions. A huge part of the problem was that Mom refused to take her medication, which sent her into a spiral, which resulted in her overdosing. She was in and out of mental hospitals, and I was the primary support for both my dad and, as much as I could be, my mom as well. I knew she suffered from mental illness. Still, I was very angry with her for those overdoses, because of her refusal to take her medication and the havoc it wreaked on our entire family. In February of 1989, my dad separated from my mom after 32 years of marriage and her eighth overdose. My siblings really weren't in contact with Mom much at all, so that whole burden was mine to bear, also. I stuffed most of those emotions, though, in order to help her cope with life as a divorced woman who lived alone for the first time in her life.

In June of 1989, we sold our first home and purchased a bigger, nicer home about six blocks away. I was pregnant with our third child at the time, and we needed more space. Our daughter, Amanda, was born in December of 1989.

Mom was lonely and lost after Dad left. She was convinced he would come back. She never took another overdose after he left. My parents' divorce was final after nearly two years. Mom never ever got over it, and never got over him. Dad moved on, married Vonda, a very nice woman with whom he was very happy, and he made a new life for himself.

In June of 1998, we moved to our dream home, which was about 12 blocks away, with almost 3 acres of land and an in-ground swimming pool! We hosted many fun family and friend gatherings and enjoyed that home immensely.

Our sons graduated from high school in 2002 and 2005, and Josh moved out in 2003. In 2005, we sold our dream home for a 100% plus profit—another "right place-right time" opportunity—to a land developer that built a neighborhood of homes on our nearly 3 acres, combined with the neighbor's land. We upgraded one more time; this time moving 18 blocks, again to a home with acreage, which we were able to customize with an in-ground pool, air conditioning, and other amenities.

Coincident with these other events, from her freshman through senior year in high school, our 6'2" daughter, Amanda, was in club sports—both basketball and volleyball—and she and I did extensive traveling to colleges viewing tournaments. During her high school junior year, she accepted a scholarship to play volleyball in Washington. Between that time and Spring of her senior year, she had a change of heart, and she opted out of going to college and playing the sport she most loved. This was very difficult for us, as her parents, to accept.

Our Growing Family Tree

In December of 2007, Josh married Krysta. They had their first daughter, Kaydence, in August of 2008. Their second daughter, Kaelyn, came 15 months later in November of 2009. Daughter number three, Aubrielle, arrived in May of 2012. Baby Girl number four, Briar, blessed us in October of 2014. Then, in December of 2016, their son, Alister was born. He had a twin brother, Hartley, in-utero, that did not survive due to a congenital defect. Thus, Alister's birthday brings mixed emotions, and of course, we are so blessed and thankful to have him, happy and

healthy! He is quite the character! Josh and his family live about 30 minutes away from us.

In March of 2011, in his senior year of college, getting a bachelor's degree in chemical engineering, our son Nick flew off to Las Vegas, using my companion fare, and eloped with Kelsey. Each of them called the other's parents to announce the news! Today, Nick and Kelsey's family includes first daughter, Penelope, born in July of 2012, son Malcolm, who arrived in July of 2014, and younger daughter, Violet, born in September, 2016. Nick's family lives about five hours away by car.

In 2012, daughter Amanda eloped to Las Vegas also, with husband Brian, and they welcomed their son, Levi, into the family in July! Brian has an older son, Jackson, as well. They all live out of state, and we see them as often as we can.

At this writing, we are so blessed to have 3 wonderful, loving, independent kids, their 3 loving spouses, ten grandchildren: 6 granddaughters and 4 grandsons, including Jackson!

My Extensive Entrepreneurial Search

I have always wanted to create something special—an income stream that was independent of an employer, doing something I love... something that would make a positive difference in the lives of other people.

With the Mary Kay business I began in 1996, I had a couple of short spurts of success in the early 2000's when I thought I was really going to grow that business. Then, I got involved in other distractions — mostly our daughter's sports.

In August of 2011, I enrolled in an eCommerce training course focused on eBay selling. In December, 2014, we attended real estate academy training that focused on fixing and flipping homes. In August of 2016, we enrolled in another real estate training with a focus on wholesaling of property contracts. In October, 2017, we took on an eCommerce training program based on Amazon selling. In each of these endeavors, we received considerable education, yet no real traction! In retrospect, I believe that none of these opportunities took hold because they gave

me no sense of contribution to others; to society. They seemed to be just about making money... which of course is not a bad thing. For me, though, without that sense of contribution, I just couldn't embrace those business ventures.

In November, 2017, I formed "Incredibly Connected, LLC." To my amazement, I was able to get both the company name and the URL! A huge mental light bulb flipped on—It just "clicked" with that name. Connection is something that has always been important to me; a focus of mine – and has been lacking in many areas of my life. From the age of 3, drawing all those tiny connecting circles, to being included in elementary school, to finding a peer to connect with in junior high and high school. Connecting was a huge part of how "history" class finally made sense and was of value to me. Later, I realized that I wanted more connection with myself, my kids, and in my marriage. Then, I connected with Forbes Riley and all the love, community and inspiration she brings! I got the business of "Incredibly Connected" started just prior to meeting Forbes Riley, and now things in my life feel as if they're coming full circle.

I don't yet know the final destination with my Incredibly Connected business, but I feel something BIG is over that horizon -- and I am in pursuit of that destiny!!

"Incredibly" -- defined as Exceedingly, Extremely, Not Easy to Believe...

"Connected" -- defined as Joined in Close Association

I am so excited to pursue my new, incredibly connected life!

So, here's the thing about Forbes Riley. I met her in March of 2018 at an Amazon training event, at which she was one of several guest speakers over three days (the most dynamic and impactful, by the way). . When she walked into the room, it was electric for me! Her smile and presence were huge and authentic; the energy, passion, enthusiasm and absolute heart that she leads with are second to none. Just being in her light touched my soul. I have known for many years that my heart "melts out through my eyeballs" (I'm easily moved emotionally), and I had a serious meltdown going on. The way she moved around the room and

engaged with my fellow students and me touched me to the core—like no one has ever touched me before. I scored another huge "right place-right time" moment in my life connecting with Forbes Riley!

Because I have optic nerve damage (diagnosed in my 20's), which means that glasses are of no help, I try to sit in the front when I go to classes and events so that I can capture the maximum information on those slides and whiteboards. It works to varying degrees of success, depending on the size of the room, size and clarity of handwriting, distances to the visuals, etc., but it's my best shot. I was sitting in the front row, on the aisle when Forbes came in. After her opening comments and video introduction, she began to move around the room and talk to people, asking them questions and handing them the microphone. I was one of a group of four that she asked to come up in the front of the room, and she asked us what we were waiting for permission to do. I said, "shine my light." Permission Granted!

Forbes built this activity to demonstrate to people that often when we're dreaming bigger and bolder, we fail to take action on those dreams because we are seeking permission—from our boss, parent, partner, friends, peers, colleagues, etc. Forbes figured this out and began a movement, granting people permission to start believing in themselves and to go after what they really want in life.

Before we returned to our seats, Forbes told me that she wanted to give me a scholarship to her course, which totally blew me away! She has said this is not something she does often, and I am so very thankful to have touched her heart that day because it has altered the course of my life! I noticed that she did other things throughout her two presentations over three days that were seemingly very spontaneous—she definitely leads with her heart!

I had the opportunity to work with Forbes one-on-one in her hotel room the morning after the event. I sensed that she could use a hand, and I was so very grateful for her gift! Thankfully, she accepted my offer to give back! We were definitely focused on the work at hand and meanwhile had some opportunity to get to know each other. I explained my visual limitations (which definitely slow me down), and

she was very patient and understanding. It is a super fond memory I now have, spending that one-on-one time with her.

The Yo-Yo Weight Loss/Gain Struggle

I stayed a few additional days in Las Vegas to attend the vendor trade show. The day after returning home, though, I felt compelled to record a video of myself, spinning around in my underwear in the kitchen, confessing that I realized the choices I've made in my life so far have not served my body well—then I posted it as "public" to Facebook! This bold move was definitely not me, or who I'd always been. I give complete credit to Forbes for the guts and inspiration! It was actually the very first time I have come out from hiding and accepted responsibility and committed to change. I just wasn't sure how THIS TIME.

After the birth of our daughter, and quitting smoking a few years later, the weight just began to accumulate, and from 1990 to today, I have done the yo-yo dieter thing for nearly 30 years! I suspect some of you can relate. You lose 20 pounds here, 40 there, then you find them again, and they usually bring new "friends" to pad the hips, belly, and butt. Over those many years, I have tried so many diet programs, each with temporary success, going back to the days of Dexatrim and SlimFast, Atkins, LA Weight Loss, Hypnosis, other diet pills, and most recently, Ketogenic eating. Each time, after sliding backward from the latest success I had achieved, I would tell myself "well, maybe I'm just destined to be heavy like my mom," who weighed around 250 her entire adult life. At my heaviest, I weighed 347 pounds.

In 2018, I finally decided that it's time to stop my suffering—for good—and inspire others to take charge of their health and life and make it better. My journey began at Forbes Factor class in June – a business class!! We had an opportunity to participate in a metabolic reboot as a group; a 60 hour liquid fast. In all of my years of yo-yo dieting, fasting had never, ever occurred to me. Between June, 2018 and February, 2019, I have shed… released… 105 pounds of stored fat. I still seek to drop another 40 pounds or so, and my journey continues as of this writing. Because I know the suffering from obesity (morbid obesity), I have a passion to help others to STOP THEIR SUFFERING!!

As you may know, ketogenic eating is very difficult for people to maintain. Loren has done it very successfully for two years with very few stumbles, but he has always been super focused with new endeavors. He has lost over 110 pounds, and has seemed to have plateaued at this point, with maybe 20 more pounds to go. I have recently been introduced to a new breakthrough product that helps you get into Ketosis quickly—within 60 minutes—and it helps you stay there, giving you optimal mood, energy, mental clarity, fat loss, and it can even help you sleep better! After his success and plateau, Loren is excited to get to his goal with this new breakthrough product. Ketones are the body's very best fuel, in stark contrast to the debilitating effects of too much glucose in the system! I am logging my journey to my best, along with inspiration and tons of great health and wellness tips at Incredibly Connected Stacey Saintz on Facebook! You can connect to all of my content; websites, blogs, social media, etc. at https://StaceyZ360.com

Incredibly Connected with Forbes Riley

In June of 2018, I went to Pitch Mastery and Forbes Factor (on my scholarship) at Forbes Riley's Florida TV Studio. These two classes were scheduled to be five days long, and I was a bit nervous going into Forbes Factor because I really have never allowed myself to get pushed outside of my comfort zone. This time, I was committed to play "full out!" I knew at the time I enrolled that there were an additional 3 days of Business Mastery class following Forbes Factor. Because I fully expected a transformative experience, I figured my head would be spinning after 5 days with the amazing Forbes Riley, and I wanted another opportunity to be in her presence in the future, so I decided at the time to attend the 5 days only. As it turned out, my experience in those five days was incredibly transformational, and I felt such momentum that I decided to stay on for the additional 3 days of Business Mastery. Yes, my mind is blown. There was so much amazing content, and I have so much to learn and implement!

Through the exercises and support from Forbes and her team, along with this great classroom full of like-minded people. I have finally recognized that I am enough! I do deserve more. I have a story to tell that will resonate with a segment of the population… and the negative

baggage that has held me back, making me live a small, insignificant life, is behind me! It doesn't serve me and my greater purpose in this life. It's time to step into and claim my life! I turned 59 in August, 2018 (born in 1959)—something about numbers aligning like that is fun and intriguing to me. Now is my time to shine my light!!

Another significant difference with Forbes Riley as a mentor is that she actually gave us several opportunities to go out and immediately produce income with things that she is involved with—so many winners! I have attended many different high-level trainings, and nowhere else has such an opportunity been made available to me.

Lesson #1: Love yourself enough to change

One of my favorite quotes from Forbes is: "Your Family loves you the way you are. I love you too much to leave you that way." I absolutely felt that from her, and I am so thankful for the work that she has done with me so far! I'm looking forward to continued inspiration, growth, and liberation from the small, semi-conscious life I used to lead!

Lesson #2: How you do something is how you do everything

Forbes says, "How you do something is how you do everything," and that has been so true in my life. I'm now changing my game because the definition of insanity is "Doing the same things and expecting different results." Today is day one of the rest of my life! I am making new and better choices to create a happier, healthier and incredibly connected life for myself!

Lesson #3: Leap and the net will appear

One of my favorite quotes is, "Leap and the net will appear!" Because I have grown up in such an analytically-based mental state (major overthinker), I am now finally wrapping my head around the fact that I don't need all of the answers before I can take bold action! After all, life is most exciting, with the most growth, fulfillment, and joy, when it is experienced outside of your comfort zone!

Now, at age 59, my new, bold life is just beginning, and I can't wait to see where it takes me. I am breaking free from all that has limited me and held me back. In my next phase of life, I am incredibly connected in every way—In my marriage and long-term partnership, with my kids and family, with myself and my self-talk, with improving my health and body composition, with Forbes Riley and my current and growing network of like-minded people who want more in their life. All of my positive connections are growing and flourishing. I encourage you to step into your life and begin to create and/or unleash your own best self and best life, whatever that looks like for you.

Stacey Saintz

has had a long burning desire to create something meaningful... a business that not only generates income, but that gives back to the world in a significant way. She has a quiet confidence about her, and has always known she was capable of great things. Now, at age 59, by the grace of God, and her recent work with high-level mentors, she has awoken to live a life, unrestrained. Stacey is now stepping into her life, her party, and her purpose in a big way- she is no longer bound by limiting beliefs.

A major breakthrough for Stacey was shedding over 100 pounds in 8 months, overcoming a long standing yo-yo dieting pattern. This achievement has inspired her to help others who suffer from obesity and all of the nastiness that accompanies it.

Stacey is a sister, wife, mother, grandmother ("Nana"), and now the founder and CEO of Incredibly Connected, LLC, an emerging global brand dedicated to connecting people to positive, life changing resources. Incredibly Connected encompasses numerous online communities whose members and visitors share common interests, geography, traits and aspirations. We have only just begun... this is a growing global movement.

To learn more about Stacey and Incredibly Connected, go to:

www.StaceyZ360.com
www.IncrediblyConnected360.com

Life's short,
eat dessert first

- Chuck LaDouceur's Dad

What Have You **Forbes'd** Lately?

My name is Tim Hodgkiss, and I Forbes'd my mentor, Forbes Riley. When I met her, something about that first encounter challenged me to stop living so small and so frightened. The Forbes Factor Live event in St. Petersburg, FL was the most important opportunity I've seized in my life, even more so than graduating from law school! I knew if I let my fear and anxiety take over and rob me from using this experience to the fullest, I'd cheat myself from something that could change my life. That day, I decided to commit myself to living to my fullest potential. Forbes, with her energy, insight, compassion, and wisdom, reached inside all of us in the room, and we were forever transformed.

DREAMREACHER

By Tim Hodgkiss

I was scared for so long… I had suffered for so long… I just wanted to be free… Why me… Why me… Why? I didn't deserve to have to live this way. I just want to live, really live, and be myself…my authentic-self, for everyone to see…free of the cage in which I lived, inside my head. I so desperately wanted to destroy the "shy" facsimile of the person everyone in the world saw because it was not me. My life seemed like a cruel trick…so much personality, passion and energy, but it was all trapped in a mind seized in fear—the fear of judgment from others, the fear of not saying the "right" thing, the fear of not being perfect, the fear of not being "cool" enough. A twisted and elaborate trap has been created in my mind, and no matter how meticulously I had plotted to let my personality escape, my fears would inexplicably appear to drag it back to its cage. My authentic-self was starving to be heard and so desperately wanted to be shared with the world, as the confident, dynamic and exuberant person that I always knew I was. This was the paradox of my life, "How could my mind's vision of my personality be so opposite to the person I was revealing to the world?" But no matter how much I tried to break free, to let my authentic-self be exposed, my social anxiety and fear of judgment would always be there, pulling me back, like gravity, to my insipid existence.

I did have friends and a lot of fun growing up, but I never, ever felt like I was letting my full personality shine. I always felt muted, like my speaker volume to the world was turned way down, while the speaker I heard was blaring loud. The dynamic person I envisioned myself as, was one that showed passion, energy and exuberance; a person that people would remember after they met me, and someone they just had to talk to when I came into a room. But, for some reason, I was too afraid or scared to let others see that part of me. While I struggled with this obstacle for most of my life, I was never going to give up on myself. I never give up on anything - ever. I have always been a dreamer and always believed anything is possible. Any obstacle can be overcome, nothing is insurmountable. If I could just find that key, the one to unlock my mind and release my authentic-self, my true personality, and all of its passion, enthusiasm, dynamism, and energy out to the world, I could start living in a way I never had but so desperately wanted. I could then fulfill my dreams of taking my career and talents to incredible heights while living an incredible life full of vibrant experiences and people.

My quest to unveil my authentic-self and personality to the world was a never-ending roller coaster of emotion. After hearing, "Oh, he is just shy" so many times growing up, I felt like this was just something that I could simply focus on and change. From a young age, I was very introspective, and I would often have an internal dialogue with myself in an attempt to fix those flaws in my thinking that produced my social anxiety. The multitude of those attempts worked for a few fleeting moments, if not hours, giving me a sense of empowerment and confidence, which radiated through me, making me feel complete. But that feeling of confidence quickly unraveled and faded away into the shadow of my own self-defeat. I was endlessly disappointed. My fear of being myself around others, that social anxiety, was the chasm that I needed to traverse to get to my dreams, but it was such a daunting process. My fight to overcome this obstacle led me to see a multitude of doctors over the years, but they all said: "everything seems good!" In my head, I am thinking "Well, great! Thanks for nothing! Back to the drawing board." My frustration, especially with doctors, motivated me to read and study about anxiety, and how vitamin and nutritional deficiencies, as well a plethora of other things could all contribute to it. It was such a complex yarn to try and untangle on my own. But I had

to. I had no choice. At times I felt that I was on an endless journey. No one really understood how I felt or seemed to be able to help me, but I had to continue my fight to find a solution to this bane of my existence.

The inability to conquer my shyness, social anxiety, low self-esteem, or whatever label you want to give it made me a student of human behavior. I would study from afar how people interacted alone, in groups, and in various situations, looking for any clues that could help me discover the key to self-confidence. Strangely, I had always been good at mimicking the expressions and mannerisms of people, and I thought if I could mimic the confidence others had in public situations it would "reboot" my flawed thinking. And while this did help, it was not enough. However, through this process of studying people, I discovered that I am highly tuned to the emotions of others, an attentive listener and an astute reader of facial expressions and body language. This made sense to me, as I had always felt more comfortable talking about deeper topics with people, such as their problems or what is stressing them, rather than superficial banter. While my struggle has been a source of pain, it has taught me that I am very aware of detail, including those details in my environment, as well as the details of people that are in it, sometimes even more than they are.

Even though I appeared "shy" to everyone, I always identified most with celebrities, athletes, TV hosts or anyone who exuded energy, passion, and charisma. They all had big personalities, they stood out from everyone else. It was not what they said that was important to me, but how they said it--their style, their energy, their je ne sais quoi. They knew who they were and were not apologizing for it. I loved that—I wanted that. Infomercials were fascinating to me because they combined charismatic personalities, with my love of new technology and how things worked. Forbes Riley and Tony Little made an everlasting impression on me. I remember raving about Jack LaLane's juicer, and how entertaining Forbes Riley made juicing! In addition to her unique presence and short hair, the name, "Forbes Riley", stuck with me over the years. I remember Tony Little screaming "You Can Do it" as he proclaimed the benefits of the latest piece of fitness equipment. They made it seem so simple to be in front of people and just be themselves. It seemed so easy. Yet, I was struggling so hard.

My passion for electronics and computers led me to pursue a degree in electrical engineering at Ohio University. While I was fascinated by how things worked, I was also very interested in marketing and branding, so I went to business school and earned a master's degree at Youngstown State University. My marketing classes were incredibly satisfying, as it gave me an outlet to write and create. I also took a business law class and fell in love with patent law. It combined my love for the technical aspects of how products functioned with my desire to be creative. My mind was made up, I would become a lawyer, specializing in intellectual property—patent, trademark, and copyright law.

I was excited to go to law school at the University of Akron, but I was still in the midst of my struggle of trying to become comfortable in my own skin and being myself in groups of people I did not know. I was also very nervous because in law school the professors use the Socratic method to teach their classes. This involves the professor asking endless lines of questions to a single student in front of everyone for the duration of the class. A process that I dreaded and never became comfortable with. In every class, I would try my best to make my body disappear into the background, as if I had some invisibility superpower. But it never worked. When I was called upon, I would feel this intense rush of adrenaline and anxiety rush over me. While I was still able to speak, I felt mentally paralyzed and incredibly uncomfortable being in front of everyone. To minimize my anxiety of having to participate in class, I would prepare endlessly for topics the professor may call on me for in the next class. I would prepare and prepare, taking endless notes to the point of taking notes of notes. I figured the more notes I had, the less I actually would have to "think" and react on the spot in front of everybody. Those notes were my crutch, but they were never any help to me. Each time I had finished being questioned by a professor, I felt like I had stared death in its face. Every day I was so uncomfortable, so unsure of myself, so afraid and full of fear of possibly having to be in front of the class. It took all of my strength to fight through that uncomfortability, which I endured for 3 years until I graduated. I did very well in law school, especially in my legal writing classes. In fact, while I completed my degree and was battling my obstacles, I was a law clerk with a law firm specializing in Intellectual Property law, as well as

a judicial extern for the Honorable Peter C. Economus a U.S. Federal District Court Judge.

After law school, I joined Renner Kenner LPA, a highly-respected law firm that has specialized in intellectual property for over 100 years, of which I am now a partner. I thoroughly enjoy the creative process and interacting with inventors. In many cases, inventors don't have prototypes of their device, only a simple sketch of their idea. I then translate that rough idea or concept so that it encompasses different embodiments at different levels of abstraction and detail. As a creative person myself, I also understand the development process inventors go through to conceive of their invention, and the frustrations they have in communicating their structural details and operational benefits. By being a precision listener and having the awareness of fine detail, I am able to adapt to the communication style that best suits each inventor, so that I can elicit a deep understanding of their invention. Those skills have also given me the unique ability and insight needed to readily expand upon an inventor's basic idea to form different abstractions or embodiments of their initial inventive concept. This results in an extremely strong, high-quality patent, which is much more difficult for a competitor to design around to avoid infringement; and is something I am most personally proud of.

While I thoroughly enjoy the practice of law, being an attorney tends put you into a solitary box, where you are isolated from interaction with people. And for the longest time this was great for me, because it allowed me to hide my social anxiety. But, I knew there was more that I could offer the world, I was too full of energy and passion, and was too much of a dreamer to allow my personality to remain hidden. I was only 10% of my potential and I knew it. One day I decided to give another doctor a try. He was different than the others I had seen, he specialized in "integrated medicine", where he treats the whole body as a system, and looks at everything before arriving at any conclusions. In fact, he was so comprehensive, he had ordered lab testing that required me to have 14 vials of blood taken. No doctor ever had done this to me before. In fact, the nurse was exasperated that he had ordered so many tests. But I was encouraged and excited by this. The results showed that my total cholesterol was low, too low, and he encouraged me to increase

my fat intake, eat more meat. He wanted my cholesterol up higher. I had always thought that the lower the better, but I learned that anxiety can be caused by it being too low. In the end, he treated me through a combination of health supplements and diet. And miraculously, over the course of several weeks, most of the social anxiety I felt for so long started to lift away. Mentally I felt lighter, I was not thinking about what I was going to say or how I might "act", I was simply being me, allowing my quirks, personality and attitude to show. The fear of being judged by others was no longer the almighty force it had been all those years staring me down at every turn. I had escaped! I was in awe! I was feeling truly alive for the first time in my life! My personality had finally been liberated, and now I needed to use it to capture my dreams!

I was running through this huge obstacle in my life and was becoming more and more comfortable as my authentic-self. I could now see more clearly how my dreams of success could come true. The problem was that I had spent so much time trapped in the small, confined little world of my mind, that I still needed to retrain my brain to operate on a new set of rules, ones that gave me the freedom to live life on my own terms. I had overcome such a huge obstacle, when many would have given up. I was ready to take steps toward my dreams, but I spent valuable time getting to this point. I knew I was behind, and I needed to make up for lost time.

Inspired with my new-found confidence, and a feeling of urgency to move my life forward, I attended the 10X Growth Conference 2 at the Mandalay Bay Events center in Las Vegas at the beginning of 2018. I knew some of the speakers, but there was that name again, that named, which seemed to follow me through life. It was "Forbes Riley". When she took the stage, the magnificence of her confidence and presence was energizing to me. Her message was not about selling products, but about dreaming and reaching your goals. She said one thing that I never will forget, "The reason I am on this stage and you're not is because I dream bigger". Her words reverberated around in my body, they shook me. Those words made me feel so alive. I had always been a dreamer, but I had not taken steps toward my dreams because of my anxiety. But her message was meant for me to hear on that day because I was ready to take action. Sure, I had become a patent attorney, which

I love, but I always believed I was capable of so much more. I believed this my whole life. But I just could not break free of the limitations my anxiety. However, this time in my life was different. I was ready to take action, and I wanted my dreams. I was there at that conference to move forward on that journey, and it was Forbes' speech that kicked it all off. Her words mirrored exactly what I believed my whole life. I always dreamed big, but I never acted, because I was scared and insecure. In that moment, I knew I had to be a part of what she was doing, because her words aligned so precisely with my beliefs and what my vision for myself was. I knew that I could never go back to the old Tim, and I knew more strongly than ever that my dreams would come true. I just believed and trusted in everything that she said more strongly than anything in life. She was speaking the language of my heart and spirit, one that only a very few seemed to understand. I could have never anticipated the incredible things, the life changing things, that would eventually occur to me after this "moment" in time. But they did, and life for me would never be the same!

Lesson 1: Life Happens in a Moment

I have learned from Forbes that opportunities in life happen in a "moment". Changes, profound changes, in your life happen in brief moments that you must seize to reach your dreams. Having a mindset of action allows you to be ready to step into, and seize, those moments of opportunity without hesitation no matter when they arise. With the clarity of an open mind, one that is ready to act without hesitation, trepidation or fear, you can open up new, incredible horizons, which can profoundly change your course in life.

Lesson 2: Dream Bigger

"The reason I am on this stage and you're not is that I dream bigger."- Forbes Riley. I will never forget her saying those words because it changed my life. I had always been a dreamer, and her message reflected my own beliefs of dreaming, so it was emotionally moving to hear someone else speak about "dreaming" being a key to success. Many of my friends and acquaintances seem to live in a box confined to "reality", resigned to a life whose course is unable to be altered or changed. I understand the need to be "real" at times, but the ability to dream is so

powerful, especially if action is taken toward those dreams. The irony is that if I had never dreamed, my "reality" would have never included getting to have a private conversation with Forbes Riley, asking her to be my mentor, the opportunity to participate in her universe, and to have made friends with an amazing group of like-minded people who understand the power of dreaming. Dreaming is living!

Lesson 3: Make a Decision to Change; Do you differently

Everything is a choice. If you want to change something about yourself, your career, your path in life, or anything, start with a clear assessment of yourself, identify what it is you want to change and make the decision to change it. Simple. Don't give yourself an out to go back to the old way of doing things. Start doing "you" differently. Draw a line in the sand, cross over it, go forward, and never look back. If you are afraid, unhappy, or lacking confidence, you can change your state of feeling in a moment, just by your thoughts, to embody the alternative states of being strong, happy, or confident. You always have a choice!

What have I Forbes'd Lately?

I have always believed I would do incredible things in life, and that my dreams of having everything I ever wanted would come true one day. I had come a long way, the label of "shyness" no longer applied, I was now ready to take huge steps toward my dream. My drive for success was reignited by Forbes' speech at 10X Growth Con 2, and I made the decision right then and there that I was going to get her to be my mentor, I was going to be part of her universe. I had to. There was no choice. I had never sought anyone out as a mentor, but my spirit resonated from her message, her energy and her voice. "Dreaming" was my language and she spoke it. I knew she would push me to give my best so that I could move forward toward my dream of expanding my career and working with incredible people. I was a first generation attorney, I did not have others I could look to for counseling or advice in business or even in life. I knew this was the right time in my life for a mentor, someone that could help me learn and grow. But how was I going to get her attention?

First, I needed to show her how much I believed in her message and how important she was to me. I started following her on social media, and I sent several personal letters to her TV studio recounting my personal story and how I had fought to overcome my lifelong obstacle of social anxiety. While I had no luck hearing back from her regarding my letters, I was not deterred from posting comments and interacting with her on social media. I then learned of the FORBES FACTOR LIVE event at her TV studio in Florida, and I knew that would be my opportunity to meet her. I really wanted to make an impression on her so that she would know who I was before I got there. I had several weeks, so I continued to immerse myself in all things "Forbes" in order to understand her energy and drive, so that when I did meet her I could mesh right into the flow of her communication style. I watched YouTube videos of her past infomercials, interviews she had done, hosting spots, and I watched her "Splatter University" movie endlessly. I was obsessed! At one point, as I was watching some of her Facebook live broadcasts, I heard her mention that she had a new book coming out, called "Virdition". I downloaded it and began reading a little of it each night. A week or so later she asked on social media if people could leave a review on Amazon for the book. This was my opportunity to capture my "moment," like she had said on stage at 10X. I loved the book, but I had never written a book review, and it needed to be exceptional in order to get her attention. I also needed to act fast to grab that "moment" of opportunity. So, while sitting in my office at work, I immediately wrote the review and posted it up on Amazon. I hoped that she would see it, but I knew she was a busy businesswoman, and it would likely go unnoticed, however that did not matter to me. I was genuinely thrilled to just have had the opportunity to help her with her request. A few days later, out of nowhere, while I was watching one of her daily Facebook live broadcasts, she actually mentioned my name and thanked me for the review. I was blown away. It was such an incredible feeling. Nothing like that has ever happened to me. That simple thank you from her told me that whatever I was doing, I needed to start doing more of it, because I was getting recognized. And, oh, by the way I think she really liked what I wrote in the review! I continued to engage with her on social media, and watched as many of her Facebook live broadcasts as I could. She even mentioned me and the review a few more times. I was incredibly excited and looking back,

her kindness had such a positive impact on me. I also knew I needed to make a lasting impact on her if I did get to speak to her privately. So, I put together a customized brochure with her FORBES FACTOR logo on it, which was full of the letters I had sent her, my reasons for wanting her to be my mentor, and the ways I thought I could contribute to her growing business. People thought I was crazy for going to such lengths, but I knew I had to do it, because I could not hold back like I had always done in the past. I was doing Tim differently, and I was not going to hold my personality back this time!

Forbes Factor Live had finally arrived, and it was showtime. Such an amazing event full of emotion and energy did not leave much of an opportunity for me to approach her. I was getting nervous that she may be too busy to talk with me. But I knew I did not come all the way to Florida and not speak with her individually. For so many months it was the only thing on my mind and the only thing that mattered to me. Finally, on the last day of her event I approached her and asked if I could speak with her privately. And you know what? She actually said "yes". Normally, I would be falling apart, but this was Tim 2.0, Tim done differently, and taking control and talking to her was shockingly effortless. I got my chance to tell her privately how much she meant to me, and how much I wanted her mentorship. She even looked through my packet, not so much caring about the contents itself, but more about the effort and passion I put into it. Her mannerisms and facial expression showed her appreciation, and she agreed to talk to me about how she might help me. It was the most amazing thing that had ever happened to me!!! No one believed I could do it. But I made it happen! I was discovering my true power, the power that had been trapped in that cage of my mind for so long. I was radiating energy and things were now happening in my life because of it.

Afterward, I continued to stay in contact with Forbes. And then the most incredible thing happened. I got to speak to her on the phone about my story and what I needed from her with regard to her mentoring me. This was one of the best days of my life, and after that call I screamed "I did it!". I was elated, my work and effort, nearly every day after work, writing letters, putting together my story, the packet of my information

and background, it all worked! Every day since meeting her has been like a dream, but a dream I knew I could make come true. Near the end of summer of 2018, I was at another one of her events in Florida, and she asked if I would like to come to her home to work with her team. I could not believe this, I was jumping up and down in my head! I got to sit beside Forbes in her kitchen and watch her in action working on her business! During the next several hours I was like a sponge, absorbing everything I could. It was amazing in every way. While I was watching Forbes in her full mastery, I realized I had gone from a seat among 9,000 people listening to her in Las Vegas, to sitting at her kitchen table. "I actually did it. I made this happen.", I said to myself. I had "Forbes'd it!" Thank you, Forbes Riley. You have given me more than you will ever know. I am grateful to have you in my life, and nobody, outside of my parents, has made a bigger impact on who I am and what I'm going to do in the future than you have.

Tim Hodgkiss

is a forward thinking, outside-of-the-box, creative visionary with a passion for technology and business. To this end, Tim pursued his Bachelor's of Electrical and Computer Engineering at Ohio University, and his Master's of Business Administration (MBA) at Youngstown State University.

His adept ability to communicate through writing and his love for technology had him pursue a degree in law at the University of Akron in the field of Intellectual Property Law.

Tim has excelled as a partner with the law firm of Renner Kenner LPA, where he has practiced patent, trademark and copyright law for the last 15 years. He has worked with clients domestically and internationally and has had the privilege of counseling some of the most well-known celebrity clients in the world. His commitment to advocating for his client's rights and his attentiveness to their needs is unmatched.

Tim is rapidly building an online platform of courses and educational content, as well as growing his personal brand.

His boundless creativity and diverse abilities have propelled him to embark on various projects outside of his law practice. Recently, he has utilized his writing and creative skills, as well as his precise attention to detail, to assist individuals and businesses advance in their marketing and book publishing ventures to successful completion.

To learn more about how Tim can turn your idea or brand into a monetizable asset Download his FREE guide:

www.FreeGuideFromLawyerTim.com

To learn more about Tim, contact:

tim@LawyerTim360.com
www.LawyerTim360.com

Stay away from negative people, they have a problem for every solution

- Albert Einstein

What Have You **Forbes'd** Lately?

My name is Tucker Wells, and I Forbes'd mentors who helped me always play a bigger and better game. In nearly every area of life where you want to achieve great things, you can find a mentor to help you get there. Role models, teachers, motivators—these are people who have walked the walk and can lead both by example and by imparting knowledge to you that will give you the edge you need to go bigger and truly succeed.

The Payoff of

PERSISTENCE

By Tucker Wells

I am going to give you a glimpse of my personal path to success, and how I got my life on a track. While I have not yet arrived at my destination, I am confident that I am heading in the right direction to fulfill my potential in life. My goal is to teach you what I have learned to this point so you can apply it if you are lacking direction and looking for success in life!

Over the course of the last 4 years, I have gone from being a kid living in Paradise Valley, Arizona with little vision and purpose for my life to having my eyes fixed on a vision that took a long time for me to figure out. This vision is one that I believe will give me long-term happiness and fulfillment; and at the end of the day is what we all long for.

In the new generation, it is often difficult to see beyond your current situation. I found this to be true so many times for me personally- all I wanted was instant gratification! When I was in high school, swimming was what gave me my identity. I was ranked #1 in the state of Arizona in two events for my age group, and the status of achieving that ranking gave me such confidence and satisfaction that I thought nothing could bring me down. All the while, I was engaging in activities with friends that were of no benefit to my life goals, but were actually a huge

detriment to my success. I was so set on gaining social status through becoming something I wasn't. This took me awhile to figure out.

The lifestyle that I was engaging in outside of the pool and in school culminated in being removed from my high school swim team. As someone who was pegged to be a State Champion in two events, this was devastating at the time. Shortly after, I lost my best friend from a drug overdose. This was a moment in my life that tested me to my core. Losing my best friend was especially hard, but it was the consistent negative chain of events that led me to realize that I needed change.

I needed someone who believed in me... and I call those people MENTORS!

As a person, our character is determined less by what happens and more by the manner in which we choose to respond to the hurdles that are thrown in our way. After getting asked to leave my high school and losing my best friend, I was put at a pivotal crossroads, and instead of letting it break me down, I took some time to reflect on what I really wanted in life. I discovered a new opportunity.

Over the past three years, I have been a Division 1 All-American caliber swimmer, the President of the Southern Methodist University Real Estate Club, a full-time student in the Cox Business School, and have 8 internships. All of my aforementioned endeavors have given me varying levels of satisfaction, but none of them have given me the sense of fulfillment, which I have found in my most recent work.

During school, I allowed myself to become lost in the day to day life of toiling with success in a busy college atmosphere, when what I needed was right in front of me the whole time. The biggest asset that I could have had all along was a mentor that cared to invest in me personally and to give me the encouragement I needed to see the broader vision for my own life.

The 3 segments of my story below show how I was positively influenced through mentors, and my hope is that you see the power that comes with surrounding yourself with driven people. As is true for everyone, the term "happiness" should hold personal meaning, because

finding happiness rarely means the same thing for each person. To me, happiness is defined as contrast. Being able to learn lessons from life's most challenging situations is a skill that we should all develop. Along with being driven and focused, I wake up happy each and every day. But I know that one day I may not wake up, so I don't want to take any opportunity I have for granted.

Early Swim Years – Coley Stickels

The first mentor I will be talking about is Coley Stickels. He is the most influential person I have encountered in my life. I encountered Coley while I was a high school swimmer. At that time I did not having my shit together, but he set me up for the massive amounts of successes I started to create.

At this point in my life I was on both the high school varsity lacrosse and swim teams. Because of Coley, I chose to wholeheartedly pursue swimming due to the opportunities that I had in front of me. I could see swimming opening other doors for me in the future. I had the opportunity to train with world record holders and Olympic Gold Medalists in Arizona, and it seemed to me that I would be foolish to shy away from running with that chance! Being able to work with Olympic-caliber athletes on a daily basis allowed me to visualize what I could achieve with dedication and hard work. These were some of the most incredible moments of my life to this point. Olympic Gold Medalist Roland Schoeman was one of the people that were most influential to me during my time training in Arizona, and he played a crucial role in helping me develop into the swimmer that I eventually became.

When I stepped onto the pool deck winning was all I wanted, but Ronald was next to me wanting the same thing, on a World Class Level! I had the opportunity to weight lift next to him, swim next to him, and study how he trained. I took every chance I could to improve my technique from watching him and to feed off of the energy of those around me to push myself to a higher level. Most of all, I had the chance to draw from his intensity and push myself past my pain threshold and into a zone where greatness could truly be achieved.

This was my plan, to show up and repeat this every single day. It's the consistency that I have drawn from this period in my life that I have applied to business because without consistent effort it is easy to get lost along the way. Doing this would set me up for my biggest swimming success ever 3 years later, but getting to that point wasn't to be without its challenges.

Like I mentioned earlier, training with Coley and Roland set me up for my biggest swimming success I ever had. However, three days before my Junior year of college I was hiking, and as I was going down a steep edge of a desert mountain, I felt my ankle crack in half. I could see the bone had snapped. As I slid down the steep cliff, I called my dad and he rescued me and took me to the hospital! At this time, I was the #1 swimmer on the SMU swim team in 2 events and my desire was to lead the team to a conference championship. With a broken ankle, I was looking at months of recovery, and for a swimmer it was impossible to be out of practice for months and come back competitive.

I showed up to the first day of school, post-surgery, in a wheelchair. I was not going to give up on leading my team to a conference championship. Although I couldn't work out with my team, I got up at 5 AM every day and put my leg up for an hour and did abdominal and upper body work to keep up at least part of my strength. I remembered all the hard work that got me to this point, and I wasn't going to let an injury stop me from helping my team win the conference championship that we had been working so hard to achieve.

After 7 months of training like I had with Coley and Roland, I came back to beat all my teammates and finish 3rd at the conference. Although we didn't win, I fulfilled my purpose of transforming into a person who would never give up even in the face of huge adversity. I thank Coley for giving me the gift of pushing me past the point of physical pain. If it wasn't for his coaching, support, and mentoring, I would not have swum that season. Today, I look at that transformation, and think about how lucky I was to go through that pain and come out on top!

In high school, the biggest lesson I learned was that if you want to become the best, you need to work with the best. What Coley did is something I picked up from him that has led me to learn from the top.

Emulate what the top coaches/athletes/owners in the world do and personalize it in a way that you can teach others! Pablo Picasso says it perfectly, "Good artists copy, great artists steal." Meaning, if you shadow and learn about X from Y you have a higher chance of achieving Z. I saw a lot of this philosophy in Coley, and today I currently do the same by personalizing messages from the people that are at the top of their game.

College Years: Tosha Riddle-May

While I was a junior in college, I got into the Cox School of Business at Southern Methodist University and joined the Real Estate Club! At this point in my life, I was looking for a new mentor. I was a member of the SMU Swim Team, however, my swim coach did not believe in me, so I looked for a way out!

My desire was to become a real estate club president! Externally, I wanted to walk around campus and tell people I was President of the Real Estate Club because I thought it would help me to be more employable... Internally, I wanted it to tell my swim coach I was enough!

However, I struggled with a broken ankle in the first part of the year, so I was not as involved as I wanted to be in the real estate club. I was also just partying away and not looking for any opportunities- I just wanted to have a good time!

As my ankle healed from that treacherous hike, I implemented what I learned from Coley: "Go Straight to the Top." The person at the top was named Tosha Riddle-May.

I didn't have a plan at the time, but Tosha was very nice, and I was interested in learning about what she did. It seemed like Tosha did a fantastic job coordinating events, holding happy hours, and paring people up with the most successful people. I wanted to get to know her. I made it my mission! I went to every real estate club event you could think of, and I befriended all the people in the club. Once it came time to run for officer roles in the club, I said "let's go big!" I ran for the President of the real estate club. I remember texting my friends "Hey,

vote for me!" When the results came in, I had a good feeling about it, but I had just gotten into trouble with SMU so I needed to come clean with the people who ran the Real Estate School.

They told me I had won the election, but I had an inkling they didn't believe/trust me. So what does someone do in that situation? I became vulnerable and gained their trust. I broke down and said it would be an honor to become real estate club president, but I need to confess that I do not have the best record at SMU. I have 2 alcohol violations, and I do not want to put you or the club in jeopardy! I ended up getting everything sorted out, gained their trust, and I made it happen! I ended up becoming real estate club President! Wohooo!

That year, I would walk into Tosha's office almost every day and I'd keep my finger on the pulse of what was going on. In fact, she would be setting up meetings with high-powered individuals, and I thought it was my responsibility to do the same! I started calling and emailing all the top dogs in real estate around the country to set up Skype calls, in-person meetings, informational interviews, and the like! I met with 100+ people in all sectors of the industry. Later that year, I won a scholarship for being the real estate student of the year!

All in all, I believe being President, and Tosha's faith in me, turned my attitude around from being selfish to selfless. At the time, I didn't have a job, and I was meeting with these individuals in an effort to get people in the real estate club jobs! I learned you did not have to have a title to meet with these high-powered real estate folks, you just had to show curiosity, ask for help, and be interested in what they do! I made it my mission to help more students, so I developed a how-to book for college students who need help reaching out and becoming more employable!

Post Graduation: Daniel Tovar

I was in quite a tough place having just quit my $60,000/yr. corporate job to make $8/hr at a golf course. I could barely pay the bills, and I was quite embarrassed that I was working somewhere with high schoolers. But, it was then I realized I had the potential to help others. If I could

just find another mentor to help me focus and believe in me, I knew I could become successful again.

By this time, I had just quit 2 high paying salary jobs, and I knew the next career path needed to be closer to what I wanted, which was starting my own business helping to train students to be more successful. However, I was struggling with the fact that I was embarrassed to reach out to my old mentors because I thought they would think I was a failure. I felt pathetic, so I started to network more, hoping to get lucky.

I was at a real estate networking event, and I did what I learned early on- go straight to the top. I made a bee-line straight for the president of the networking event who introduced me to a man named Erik Fulkerson who wanted me to come interview for him. I went in, and unfortunately, I let him know the opportunity did not align with my goals. I emailed him a thank you letter, and referred three of my friends to work with him! He responded back with something that changed my life… "Create a signature on your email."

So I created an email signature that said, "The #1 College Student Speaker," and that got his attention. Erik said his father in law was a professional speaker and he had a book to give me so I went into his office and met my third mentor, Daniel Tovar.

Daniel approached me and said, "So you want to start a business, tell me about it."

I said, "Yes! I want to help students get jobs." We spoke further and he asked me back for another meeting.

My next plan was simple-find a way to work with Daniel Tovar. At this time, I believed my elevator pitch was perfect, as I had been working at the golf course for a couple months practicing it, giving clients a 30 second run through of the business I was trying to start. Then, boom! I started to work at CREST Commercial Real Estate, and better yet, I was solving their hiring/recruiting real estate agent problem.

However, it didn't happen immediately. I was very behind, and I felt like a failure. I got back into that mode again where I felt small, pathetic, and

alone. I was scared every day when I would come into work because I knew I was going to get yelled at or fired! About 45 days into the job, Daniel sat me down one day and said, "I believe in you. You know what needs to get done. Get it done." There was something that embodied me at this exact moment, where I felt at peace, relaxed, confident, and successful.

At that very moment I knew I could accomplish the task at hand. I hired 6 agents in the next 20 days. I had my calendar full every hour for 5 days a week. I interviewed hundreds of people, and the 6 people that CREST brought on, I am fully confident they are at the best place in Dallas, TX to learn real estate. Why? Because the people at the top are willing to train and mentor them. After doing market research for them, it was clear that no one else was giving away that opportunity.

The transformation I experienced led me to give the gift Daniel gave to me, to you. This is the belief that you are enough!

Lesson #1: Find mentors

In nearly every area in life where you want to achieve, you can find a mentor to help you get better—role models, teachers, and motivators. These are people who can lead both by example and through imparting knowledge. They will give you the edge you need to go bigger and succeed.

Lesson #2: Never give up

You will make mistakes, some things won't work out, you'll get discouraged and feel like giving up, but don't. Powering through those critical moments when you think you can't keep going is where you find the greatest success. Get through the hard parts, and at the other end, you'll find what you were seeking.

Lesson #3: You are enough

Believe that—you have what it takes to achieve your goals. Once you really let that sink in, then it's just about learning, planning, and getting the work done.

In addition to the mentors I've mentioned above, I also want to thank my parents, brother and sister, my grandparents, Forbes Riley, Grant Cardone, Phil Puckett, Arne Erikson, and James Ray for pushing me to be better, introducing me to mentors, helping me to think bigger and achieve my dreams.

Tucker Wells

is rapidly becoming an entrepreneurial and motivational force. In addition to the leadership abilities he acquired during college, Tucker has formed strong relationships with high-level mentors to develop his own brand of marketing, sales and networking skills. The skills he has synthesized has allowed him to expand his business IQ by orders of magnitude, enabling him to help grow companies from $300,000/month to $1,000,000/month in sales.

Currently, Tucker has launched an employee recruiting business, focusing on recruiting recent college graduates who feel "stuck" at their jobs or who are finding it difficult to find one. He continues to deliver his sought after message of self-improvement, business growth and networking skills through various speaking engagements. Tucker is passionate about helping others on their journey to success, whether he is speaking to college audiences, or consulting with companies on developing a business culture where millennial employees want to work and stay.

To learn more about Tucker and how he can help your grow your business, go to:

www.TuckerWellsGo.com

One day, in retrospect, the years of struggle will strike you as the most beautiful

- Freud

What Have You **Forbes'd** Lately?

My name is Tyronda Richardson, and I Forbes'd love, forgiveness, and partnership. The lessons I learned from my parents, Leroy and Mae, resonate in my life today - love and commitment. They've been married for 40+ years. I've seen, first-hand, the intricate details of their marriage and learned what it takes to be a loving family; to be a good wife, a good husband, and to raise good children, even when things aren't perfect. I learned to forgive when people make mistakes. The lessons I've learned from Forbes Factor Live showed me that I wasn't living what I learned from my parents. Now, I trust what I know to be true, I've regained my resolve in those lessons to heal and thrive.

Lights, Camera &

TRUST

By Tyronda Richardson

As a wedding photographer, I photograph couples in love. I witness couples getting married, as the highest expression of their love. What a joyous moment! Marriage is a commitment of faithfulness; to love and cherish each other forever. Getting married requires a leap of faith because the unknown future has not yet been unfolded. It is fascinating for me to witness and partake in my clients' blessed and special moment. Unconditional love is what we all strive for in our lives, where someone loves us regardless of our flaws. Is everything picture-perfect in your life? Probably not. But with Tyronda Richardson Unlimited, your picture-perfect photo is guaranteed. Today, I encourage you to seek love in every area of your life. We all want to know what love is. We all want to acquire it and express it. But, we first have to believe love is possible for us!

As a child around the age of 8, one of my first loves was taking photos, along with reading. I remember reading the back of cereal boxes to win prizes and play games as I ate my breakfast. I dreamed of being the winner and getting something new and wonderful, as I was spooning another bite. Then, one day it happened. I was reading the Kellogg's Corn Flakes box early on a Saturday morning. They had a special offer to win your very own personal camera. All I had to do was show a proof of purchase by sending in 2 coupons from the boxes. Bingo, I

had way more than 2 box tops, and it wasn't going to cost any extra! In my mind, I had won BIG! I said to myself, "Oh, I can get my own camera, and I'm only 8! Oh, yeah. I'm on it." And that's how I got my first taste of photography. I took pictures all of the time, everywhere—indoors and outdoors. I took pictures of my family and friends, pets, animals, trees, houses—you name it. I had so much fun. It was the birth of a passion that continues to be fueled deep inside me.

I got to explore beauty, in all its glorious forms, in plain sight. To this day, I love looking back over these early images I had captured, while showing my family and friends, and discovering how much better and more insightful I've become in my photography. I treasure the sense of pride I had doing something as a kid, which has had such a positive impact on the lives of those around me. It makes my family and friends smile, and it warms my heart beyond words with fulfillment, enjoyment and happy memories. The coolest thing is-I still have that camera today, and it serves as my inspiration. It is one of my most treasured memorabilia reminding me of my humble beginnings and for how far I have grown. Since that first camera, it has led me to acquire a large collection of cameras.

What continues to inspire me as a photographer today is my love of seeing and capturing the inner beauty in people, viewing the wonders of nature and securing all the memories that might be lost! Life and its happiest moments should be remembered and cherished.

For the majority of my life I have been taking photos. I fell in love with photography for the enjoyment of taking photos. It was fun and exciting to capture life moments and experiences in time that I could go back and reflect on. It also brought me closer to others, while opening me up to share, collaborate and exchange thoughts- oftentimes with laughter! A photograph helps me see the essence in life!

I look for creative angles and elements that are simple, elegant, and pure, which stand out alone in the light, while showcasing their color, depth, and sharpness. I connect and become one with the photograph the moment I see greatness- the still moment in time where my heart is in awe and my breath is taken away—that's the love I have for my work. I'm crafting stories through images. I have spent years expanding my

knowledge and equipment, and I make it a point to get things right to produce high-quality, beautiful photos. The experience I design will bring your dream to life, and it consists of special locations, props, and accessories, which produce beautiful movie-magic memories that make you feel like a star and that fulfill your fantasy of being in a big production.

During weddings, I photograph you on your most beautiful day, where I focus on capturing an array of genuine emotions from you, your family and friends and the details of your dress, the striking ambience, the alluring location, and pose-worthy shots that make your story unique. This includes everything from getting prepared to the actual wedding ceremony to candid shots of your reception. The details of your magical day will be treasured in albums and in portrait prints, was well as on canvas and film, which can be passed from generation to generation, as a family heirloom.

I was born, raised, and lived in Georgia all of my life. My childhood consists of me being raised in a loving Christian home with both parents and siblings.

Lesson #1: Love

The lessons I learned from my parents, Leroy and Mae, resonate in my life today - love and commitment. They have been married 40+ years. I have seen first-hand the intricate details of their marriage and have learned what it takes to have a loving family, to be a good wife, a good husband, and to raise good children, even when things are not perfect. I have also learned to forgive when people make mistakes.

Forgiving someone is not the easiest thing because you have to forgive often and release the hurt, disappointment, and offense in your heart and decide to forgive, move on and let love flow in your heart. I learned that everything won't go your way, but win/win solutions help make things go much more smoothly. The lessons I've learned from my mom is to love and to put God first. The lesson I learned from my dad is to never settle. My parents showed me love. They taught me to love and introduced me to the Creator, God who is love. When I accepted God's love and accepted Him as my personal savior at 13, I

experienced a great beam of light and love in my heart. I felt lighter like all of my burdens were lifted. From childhood, through today, my personal walk with God taught me that love is the key. God is love. I receive His love for me. All my love comes from God. God is my source.

Lesson #2: Persistence in love

Today, I am married 14 years and have 4 children. I am married to the most loving and patient husband, Larry who loves and adores me. I met my "Mr. Right" 18 years ago in college. When Larry first saw me, he said to himself, "I can go places with her," and the pursuit was on! Larry was determined to make me his wife. As time went by, Larry won me over. We lived together for 2 years, were engaged and then we became one on our wedding day.

We married for love and our love holds us together. When we met, we had a lot in common, but our aligned beliefs keep us grounded in love, and that is what we desire from each other and in life. We are so in-tune with each other. I fell in love with Larry's spirit. We are so connected that when I have a bad day, he will call me and ask, "what's wrong?" before I said anything. He could feel it. These past 14 years we have had our share of unexpected circumstances, however, that has never deterred us from what we believe, our expectations, and our standards. I can't say it's all been "peaches 'n cream," but I can say we are willing to work all things out, even on the days where we don't like each other-we always loved each other!

When we disagree, we give each other space to reflect and come back together to devise a solution we both agree on. We sometimes disagree on friends, child rearing, working too much and spending family time together. For instance, at the beginning of our marriage, my husband was considered a "workaholic". He worked all the time and slept on his time off. I would understand his need for sleep, but I expected his "honey to do list" to still be completed and "family time" to be honored. I believe in balance and encouraged my husband to follow suit. Sometimes he did and sometimes he didn't. These issues have become better over time, but it did not happen overnight.

Our marriage works best when we act as partners. I learned that I had to adjust to my husband's ways and live by the principles I learned from my parents' marriage. But as we come together, we have created our own model that we live by - that's our relationship. Had I not seen a model of love from my parents or experience love from God, would I be able to be the model wife or parent today that I am proud of? I think I would have to work much harder at it. It's easier to replicate love when it is shown to you first, but what happens when it not… you'd have to guess at a lot. Love is a choice. We decide to love. It is great when we feel the love-emotional or passionate. However, love is so much more. Love is loving someone unconditionally flaws and all. True love demands a commitment. Marriage is beautiful when love is magnified, and it's powerful when both parties are on one accord.

When we got married, we promised each other before God that we would love each other for life. We do our best to excel at love and fulfill our promise, and we have both grown together emotionally, spiritually, and physically. We had to keep learning about ourselves and each other because seasons change, we change, and situations change. Therefore, we had to evolve and deal with different circumstances, and we have discovered we view things differently, but we had to come together with our core beliefs. For example, during child-rearing, when our children were growing up from babies, kids, teens, to adults, we realized each child was different, and we had to adjust child-rearing based off of their individual personality. Some were more sensitive than others, and we had to be delicate to instill values without crushing their spirit. We discovered that our success as parents came when we let love be our base to support and heal each other despite our differences. We agree to live peaceably together!

Our lifestyle yields great benefits for everyone, especially our children, to witness and live by these principles, as we value family, marriage, loyalty, reliability, work, community and Jesus Christ. It takes giving all of yourself, energy, time, patience and lots of communication. Love takes work and requires a whole lot of action. You know the phrase, "What have you done for me lately?" Well, love is no fairy tale—it takes work 24/7, when you feel like it and when you don't. Love is the universal language everyone wishes to experience. When couples

come together, they accept each other for who they are. We each come along with our past, our hopes, our fears, our dreams, our insecurities, and our goals. Each couple takes a leap of faith when they get married, hoping and praying for the best. Love is a verb, and it requires action and takes time. Love works best when a couple exhibits the fruit of the spirit-love, patience, understanding, gentleness, kindness, faithfulness, comfort, joy and peace.

Love can be long-lasting when both parties put it into action continually. The joys of love during the best days and the struggle of love during worst days is the test of time, which will reveal your status, and as long as you default back to love you can survive. Expressing love is what we all should do whether we are a couple or not. We should all strive for love in every relationship we have, whether it's parent and child, mother/daughter, father/son, siblings and even our neighbor. Loving is the key that keeps us all together in unison, and it makes our world a better place.

Lesson #3: Trust

Recently, my husband Larry and I attended a class, where I found out he was harboring a trust issue that happened in his past, which prevented him from giving and living to his greatest. One lesson I've learned is that you can't let your past keep you from your greatness. There is a phrase that marriage is 50/50, and that you can't give 50%, you have to give 100%. If each person is giving 100%, then you have a relationship that works.

For years, I felt some resistance, but I didn't know what it was or how to fix it. I thought it was a man thing where he doesn't tell you everything. All I knew is that we loved each other, and that was most important. At times I had some uncertainty, and a little suspicion that something was off, but I knew our desire and love for each other was totally what was keeping us together because we loved each other and believed in one another. The one thing I did know is that love is unconditional. Unconditional love is where I was, and I could live with what he gave because I knew I had his heart, I had his commitment, and I had his respect. I trusted him and I trusted God. I believe love heals

all wounds. I was willing to accept him for who he is- I could live with that. I had taken a leap of faith.

Well, at Forbes Factor, I found out how deep my husband's trust issues ran. It was revealed to me that his mom had left him at seven years old and he had made a promise to himself that he was never going to trust anyone fully. He turned to me and said, "That included you," and my heart dropped. I realized this was the gap that we have been dealing with for a very long time. Forbes Riley uncovered a negative belief that my husband had decided long before we met. Forbes helped my husband reframe his belief to a positive one and then he made a brand new decision. Larry turned to me then, and he looked at me and said, "Forgive me, I promise to give you 100% from this day forth and forever."

As a wedding photographer, I believe in love, families and preserving memories that will last you a lifetime. Love is the universal language, and I believe in celebrating love and the joy it brings to your life. Let me help you express your love!

Tyronda Richardson

lives in Atlanta, GA with her husband and children. She holds a Bachelor's in Computer Information Systems from DeVry University and a Master's in Business Administration (MBA) from Keller Graduate School of Management. In addition, she is an inspirational speaker, author, coach and entrepreneur. Tyronda is also a brand specialist with expertise in photography, videography, and web design. As a brand specialist, Tyronda works with emerging startups and small business owners to develop a cohesive brand vision.

To learn more about Tyronda and how she can help you and your business, go to:

www.TyrondaRichardson.com
tyronda@TyrondaRichardson.com

What Have You **Forbes'd** Lately?

My Name is Daphne Street, and I Forbes'd my best friend. That magical moment when you didn't think it was even possible to find what you were looking for, and you found something better. I found Forbes Riley.

Afterward:

KNOWING FORBES

By Daphne Taylor Street

Forbes Riley has inspired so many of us through the years with her unparalleled ability to form authentic connections with her audiences, whether in front of a camera, on stage or intimately talking one-on-one. She empowers, enlightens and forges a path for others to boldly live their dreams. And, as you've read in the chapters included in this compilation book, the dreams she has helped manifest and the seemingly insurmountable barriers she's helped people overcome, the relationships fostered and the dramatic successes realized, is palpable. The people whose lives she has touched are immeasurably grateful, including me.

That's today, but my story with Forbes began in 2012 when my publisher sent me in to interview her on the topic of her newly built film studio in St. Petersburg, FL. I was surprised to find a jet-set, globally sought-after, award- winning TV host setting up shop here in the small coastal town of St. Petersburg. I soon learned that Forbes' success with Home Shopping, which included a lucrative contract with local HSN, representing several fitness and wellness products, plus her personally branded SpinGym fitness system, landed her here. When I asked Forbes how that happened, exactly, she explained that at the age of 42, she had her children—boy and girl twins—Ryker and Makenna Riley, whom she raised with their dad, Tom Riley, in Los Angeles. And, as the story goes, children change things.

Forbes was born and raised in New York and spent the majority of her adult life in Los Angeles with both locations serving as the backdrop for her career on Broadway, stage, film and TV over the years. Eventually, as Forbes' career and brand evolved, Florida-based HSN became the primary working location for Forbes, keeping her far away from those children for far too long. Then, a comment from her wise-beyond-her-years very young daughter, Makenna Riley, went something like: "Mom, you travel so much because you don't like us very much."

A punch to the gut for any mom, that comment was the catalyst for the whole family to rapidly pack up and move to the other coast! Though they relocated, Forbes maintained her home in LA for many years, still deeply attached to friends, family and colleagues in California—she just expanded her heart to include Florida, too. As Forbes settled into her St. Petersburg community and planted roots, she built Forbes Riley Studios, and this is where I met Forbes Riley. I really didn't want to meet her at all—I was dreading it. No, seriously!

My publisher painted a picture of some high-energy, nit-wit fitness instructor who brainlessly pitched products on home shopping, and she made lots of money doing that, so she built a film studio nearby.

Okay, to be fair, that's not what he said, but that's exactly what I concluded from his pitch of Forbes. My then publisher desperately needs to take Forbes' Pitch Mastery class, because nothing could have been more inaccurate!

My publisher asked me if I've ever heard of the fitness product: the Forbes Riley SpinGym? I replied, "I'm a 200 lb. opera singer who doesn't spend much time thinking about fitness products. So, no."

Anyway, I showed up for the interview at this film studio, which was still finishing up construction, and I tried to interview Forbes. I tried! The interview didn't exactly happen...

Let me explain, I'm a professional writer—this is all I really did at the time.I'd sit down with people, collect their stories, do research, sometimes in the opposite order, then I'd sit alone, and I'd create

magic—I'd tell compelling stories in books and articles; create multi-million-dollar winning proposals; build brands; develop company verticals; create nonprofit programs and services; acquire funding, partners and collaborators and generally level-up ideas and make them come to life—for others.

So, on the day of the interview, I met Forbes sitting behind her newly-constructed reception desk at the entrance of her studio, and I was instantly spellbound as she began speaking. I was swept away by this wildly brilliant, exquisitely well-spoken, polished, huge-hearted, beautiful person who took me on a journey through her dreams and visions and stories and life, and I was so entranced I literally forgot to conduct the interview!

That doesn't happen to me. Not ever. I'm a silent observer—a deeply inquisitive passerby who doesn't engage; I don't buy-in; I don't get involved—I observe, ask questions and connect dots. Not this time. I had met my match!

It's not that Forbes wasn't very warm and happy to answer questions; I was too captivated by her and everything that she was saying to ask anything. By the end of our scheduled hour together, no interview conducted, all I knew was that I wanted, somehow, to be a part of her world. At some point, standing in front of the greenscreen in her soundstage, I felt my spirit jump out of my body, run up to her and exclaim: "There you are! I've been looking everywhere for you. Let's go play!"

And that's how I Forbes'd my best friend, Forbes Riley. Over the years, we've built extraordinary things together, had crazy fun, many long days and nights staring into laptops on a race to meet deadlines. And, our friendship grew, mutual trust and enormous amounts of respect built, and we've supported each other through a lot of life's pain and challenges, powered through successes and disappointments, and we continue to look ahead at new adventures and challenges we can conquer together and apart. We've also had our arguments, caused pain for one another, let misunderstanding grow to ridiculous proportions and all else in between the hard times and the triumphs. We've weathered

through it all as the best friendships do, and I'm humbled to be a part of this magic that she's creating. I so look forward to everything that's yet to come—things we haven't even dreamed of yet and all that we have. Thank you, Forbes Riley.

Lesson #1: Remain Open

There are opportunities preparing themselves for you beyond your wildest dreams! Even our own dreams can be a limiting belief; they can get in the way of more incredible things wanting to break through our walls and open up to us. We can end up too focused on what we think we want, that we block out greatness from entering our lives.

Forbes Riley wanted to be an actress, with all of her heart, and she is a wonderfully talented actress with a very credible resume. Yet, because she remained open to the opportunities that were unfolding before her, her legacy now will be far greater than merely appearing in roles on stage, film and TV. She is empowering people across the globe to transform their lives—to overcome trauma and adversity, giving them permission to live their lives amplified and purposeful.

Likewise, I began the first leg of my life as an opera singer. I had some success singing professionally, but I remained open to greater opportunities that I could have never dreamed up myself, and today I am creating new worlds for people and attracting the resources they need to them, helping them amp-up their game in their businesses. And, we're both just getting started! There's so much more to come. I promise not to get in the way of the biggest possibilities as they continue to unfold, and I'll let these other dreams take flight! I don't even know what they are yet, but I know they are going to be great—I can feel it.

Here's an example: I love being on stage, and I have missed it. Yet, I've spent considerable time nurturing these awesome skills that function behind the scenes, adding immense value to everything I touch. At first, I thought these things were mutually exclusive—that I'd have to give up one to pursue the other, but I eventually learned that these areas of expertise would merge as I begin teaching my skills to others. In fact, just a few weeks ago, Forbes Riley asked me to teach voice production and stage presence during her pitch it on camera class. It's certainly a

subject that I have years of professional experience, training and formal education in—so I'm more than capable of teaching it to a room of aspiring speakers and marketers. We especially had a great time when I abandoned my script and just opened up the lesson to addressing specific pain-points for participants in the audience.

If I had stayed rigid in my particular expertise of the moment, maybe discounting in my head all that I have spent more than a decade committing my life to—voice and performance—just because it had been so long since I had actually done the work, I would have cheated the audience of my knowledge and myself from having the honor of sharing it.

Remaining open to possibilities is key to success. Throughout your life, you'll develop many different skills, gifts, knowledge and experience that you have the privilege of carrying with you, wherever you are, to use however you choose. Just because it doesn't make sense at the moment, doesn't mean you should immediately ignore the universe when it starts tapping on your shoulder, offering up something amazing. There's a difference between being distracted from your dream by playing it too safe or too small and ignoring greatness when it's asking you to step up. There's no way to teach discernment between the two—just pay close attention, and you'll know.Some people call it their gut, intuition, little voice, the Holy Spirit, God, the universe, energy... it's known by many names, but it's one thing—your destiny.

Lesson #2: Ask for help

It's not enough to just accept help when it comes to you, and even that can be challenging for the most prideful among us. We must seek out help. We must deliberately hunt for the right help, from the right source, and ask specifically for what we want and need. Honestly, it was easier to begin doing this on behalf of clients—I'd look for the perfect resource for them, then approach with a mutually beneficial "ask" or pitch. I did this time and again, literally raising millions of dollars in contracts, in perpetuity in some cases, for my clients, while I was barely able to pay rent on my apartment downtown at times. Hang on—what?? Yes, you read that correctly. I landed millions of

dollars' worth of contracts for my clients, and I wasn't earning enough from putting those deals together to even support my modest lifestyle. I needed some serious help of my own. The first step required me to get honest about my situation. Then, I used my resourcefulness to ask for help. It worked.

I have a lot invested in several projects that are currently cooking, so I'm not looking for huge income that could distract me from these heart-centered ambitions. Meanwhile, though cashflow isn't awesome, I'm living in a five-bedroom house in a coveted neighborhood in my native Florida, 15 minutes away from the best beaches on Earth, surrounded by completely awesome people, access to world-class museums and fine and performing arts, access to exclusive clubs, sailing, literary activities, travel and just about everything else anyone could want, with modest earnings... for now!

All of this is my reality because I asked. I asked, and I've built and put immense value on relationships, and I always, always, always give back in whatever capacity I have. To whom much has been given, much is expected. Likewise, whomever gives of themselves, they get an ROI in the bank. Giving, though, has its own balance sheet that can get complicated for novices: it's never point by point equal, and it's never from the same source showing up exactly the same way. You'll be tremendously hurt and often if you keep expecting everything to work out equally with people.

Here's an example: maybe you gave $1,000 to your friend who was going through a tough time, and you're becoming really upset that they never seem to get their finances straightened out. However, you're probably overlooking what your friend gives back to you in loyalty, support and thoughtfulness—priceless gifts. Then, maybe your parents decide to pay your kids' college tuition, releasing you from a huge financial strain. See? It came around, not exactly the same way from exactly the same source, but it came around.

So, ask for help, be open and value relationships and people over money and things, and you'll find yourself blessed beyond belief.

Lesson #3: Money is an illusion; only value is real.

Money is information: it is impermanent, only somewhat agreed upon, representation of the information surrounding what a product or service, or—in some cases—even what a person, a pet or a memory is worth.

Let that sink in.

If you don't find that disturbing, you should. Value, on the other hand, is priceless—it's a relationship, it's loyalty and trust that has been earned, it's hard, compassion, kindness and generosity. Value is everything that matters.

I was raised with money—my mom had two trust funds, so with that type of resource, your experience with money growing up isn't like most other people's. My mother never had to save to buy a car or to put a down payment on a house or to purchase designer clothes, or pay for medical expenses, etc. We requested that out of principal from the trust. I grew up surrounded by original artwork, silver, china, and crystal that had been in the family for generations along with newer acquisitions because my mother was also an art and antique appraiser, and my dad was an artist—a painter who hailed from a long line of other celebrated American artists.

Then, the market crashed, the investments were nefariously managed and lumped into triple A stocks and bonds that were stacked with many of the bank's own investments and a bunch of those subprime mortgage notes. Yeah, it all crashed down. We went broke. My mom lost her house and had to rent an apartment for the first time in her life, which wasn't so bad except that no amount of logic could break her of the thought that haunted her—in her head and heart, this was all her fault. She took on that weight like a planet she felt obligated to carry around on her back. The thoughts that plagued her were that she was a failure, that she lost her family's money, that if she had just done this, that or something else, she wouldn't have disappointed or embarrassed everyone. Even the dead relatives were certainly ashamed of her—especially the dead relatives.

As for my brother and me, we saw what had been happening with the investments. We saw this coming. We tried to prepare our mom, but

she was already shutting down psychologically and couldn't make the smallest decisions to help prepare for the inevitable. Since she was 22 years old, she had owned her own home—not her husband, not her parents—her. And she was going to lose it all. She started selling off the more expensive works of art and antiques at a fraction of their value to keep paying a mortgage on a house that she could no longer afford. She felt guilty about not being able to leave these things to my brother and me as our inheritance. I promise you, we didn't care at all about the stuff.

My brother, John, and I are very different in many ways, but we agree at all times on the most important things. The value we place on stuff is nearly non-existent. But, of course, that doesn't mean that we don't care about or understand the monetary significance of some stuff.

I was always taught, even as a child, that I would not have to worry about paying for college, and likely there would be plenty of money in the family to even have a modest income and pay for a car, down payment on a house, etc. just as we witnessed with our mother growing up. So, I was never taught everyday financial planning and financial literacy. I learned how to manipulate a trust instrument, and I learned about stocks, bonds, treasury notes and other investments, but not anything about simple savings accounts or IRAs and retirement plans.

My mom passed away in 2016, and there was no money in her estate, and few possessions left. Honestly, that's fine. I taught myself advanced budgeting—from personal finances to complex multi-million corporate nonprofit fiscal management. I read like mad, asked many questions and sat down and learned from some of the most brilliant CFOs I could find, and I learned all I could. I'd still never hire me as a bookkeeper let alone a CFO, but I can put together some of the best, most comprehensive project budgets with multiple variable adjustments you've ever seen!

Also, because of my childhood experiences, I don't crave possessions or ownership of anything, really. I've had some of the best of everything, I've seen some of the best of everything, I've tasted the best food and wine and liquor, and I've been a guest in the most exclusive clubs and so forth. It's all very nice and comfortable, but I don't crave any of

it. In fact, I crave the opposite. I even had a big townhouse with three fully decorated bedrooms, gourmet kitchen, three libraries and art and antiques splashed around—all very impressive if that's what you're into. I felt like it was all strangling me—I was stuck being responsible for all of this stuff.

My dream was to rent a one-room dwelling in a small Costa Rican fishing village and write strange fiction novels whilst selling tacos and rum and wander the globe on occasion, writing about all that, too.

The point is that money has very little to do with my dream—next to nothing, really. Believe me, I prefer it versus not having it, because it's just easier when you have it. However, it doesn't buy anything of real value. I can't buy my friends, my peace of mind, my health, my curiosity, my intellect and my heart and understanding of others. If I had all the money I was promised, I wouldn't have learned what people experience when they struggle; I wouldn't have worked in the trenches with people fighting for their very lives with addictions, mental illness, homelessness or kids who are acting out, stuck in the juvenile justice system, because they feel so lost and hopeless and they crave belonging and validation at all costs—even at the cost of their freedom and very lives.

There's no way I would have learned about the business of nonprofit development that exists to help address these devastating social problems, providing critical resources to the mere fraction of individuals who do the work to find a way into recovery and a healthier future. There's no way I would have found my most valuable mentor to date, Jackie Griffin, who believed in me more than I even believed in myself and coached me professionally, sometimes kicking and screaming, so that I now have all of the skills I have to offer today. And, there's no way that I would understand the tremendously deep impact Forbes Riley's Forbes Factor work has on all those touched by her extraordinary gift, if it were not for all of these humbling experiences.

I'm one grateful friend, and I can't wait for the next chapter to emerge.

This book has been compiled by Forbes Riley, and these stories are comprised of extraordinary individuals who have each participated in

one or more classes of Forbes, particularly her Forbes Factor Live event. These are stories of strength, fortitude, lessons learned, heartache, triumph and success. In part, readers will find business tips. Mostly, you'll find life-hacks to get you through some really tough spots or maybe just give you a little perspective when it seems you're up against insurmountable odds.

Each participant agreed to contribute to this publication, and most were interviewed while a few wrote their stories on their own. I, the editor, created these chapters from the interviews conducted or edited the written drafts submitted, which you see within these pages. My goal was to capture the heart of their stories, clearly, while not interrupting their unique voices and spirits that truly make these chapters beautiful.

It has been a distinct honor to take part in this project, and mostly I feel so blessed and humbled to be entrusted with a collection of stories so vivid and personal. My sincere thanks goes out to each author featured in this book. You are all extraordinary, your stories are harrowing and your lessons are profound. Blessings to you all!

P.S.

Story Contributors: Your stories are categorized alphabetically via your first names. As irreverent as that may seem, it was at the insistence of our fearless leader, Forbes Riley, because as you know, she feels that each of your names are very important. Plus, she knows you, and you all know each other, best by your first names. She wants your stories to be easy to find.

Cheers!

—*Daphne Taylor Street*

SPECIAL **FREE** BONUS
Gift for YOU!

www.Free**Gift**fromForbesRiley.com

Enjoy my Video Training Series & Resource Guide"
designed to show **YOU** how to leaverage your
expertise, achieve your goals fast and create true
abundance!

**FREE
$797
VALUE**

Reach for the stars!

Jorbes Riley

I hereby gra... ...OU

> PERMISSI... <

to _____

What would YOU Like PERMISSION to do?

I hereby grant YOU
> PERMISSION <
to _____

This card never expires. It's replaceable, transferable and may be used at any time, as often as needed.

CAUTION: This card is to be used for good, not evil.
"Be careful what you wish for!" *Forbes Riley*

If you'd like to grant PERMISSION & obtain additional cards, please contact us
www.ForbesFactorLive.com
727-954-7071 x20

Get YOUR STEEL PERMISSION cards ...
Experience FREEDOM, GRATITUDE, POWER
and watch YOUR LIFE begin anew!

I hereby GRANT YOU

PERMISSION

to enjoy YOUR life to the fullest

to be yourself

to love yourself

to eat, breathe, move, think & sleep at the highest level

to give back and honor those around you

and to Forbes ANYTHING & EVERYTHING your heart desires!

GRANTED BY

www.ForbesFactorLive.com

Our deepest fear is not that we are inadequate
Our deepest fear is that we are powerful beyond measure

It is our light, not our darkness that most frightens us
Your playing small does not serve the world

There is nothing enlightened about shrinking
so that other people won't feel insecure about you

We were all meant to shine
It's not just in some of us; it's in everyone

And as we let our own light shine
We unconsciously give other people permission to do the same

As we are liberated from our own fear
Our presence automatically liberates others

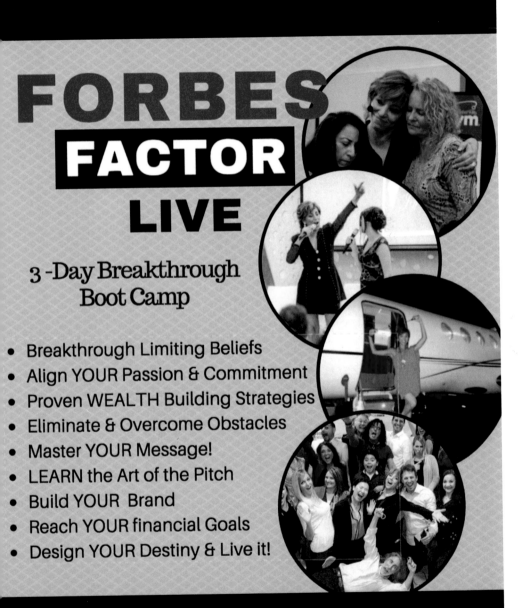

What Have You Forbes'd Lately?

½
4

Forbes'd {verb}

Means to MANIFEST something into your life…
especially when NO ONE else believes it's possible.

Examples from students, friends and co-authors include:

- I Forbes'd becoming a fashion designer after a childhood of bullies making fun of my clothes in school.
- I Forbes'd my way out of the trap of poverty into a running a 7 figure business.
- I Forbes'd being a world champion bodybuilder after a past filled with loss and uncertainty.
- I Forbes'd getting into college with bad grades and no money - and then got my MBA!
- I Forbes'd losing more than 100 lbs after finally understanding and deciding that I mattered.
- I Forbes'd a life dedicated to achieving my dreams after years crippled with anxiety and insecurity.
- I Forbes'd leaving an abusive relationship to finally find a partner who truly cherishes me.
- I Forbes'd becoming a pro tennis player after an accident when doctors told me I might never walk again.

SO, the question is…

What Have You **Forbes'd** Lately?

Forbes FACTOR LIVE

Book a Forbes Factor Live event in your town or
attend an upcoming event
at Forbes Riley Studios in St. Petersburg, FL
www.ForbesFactorLive.com

This training provides grit, wit, insight and wisdom—but most importantly it gives participants tools to shape their mindset and concrete strategies to break free from the ordinary and live extraordinary lives.

Improve your heart, head and business success through this immersive experience.

What Have YOU Forbes'd Lately?

Copyright © 2019 Forbes Riley

What Have You **Forbes'd** Lately?

Cover Photo Credit: Michael Helms

Quantity sales special discounts are available on quantity purchases by corporations, associations, and others. For details, contact the publisher at the address above.

Orders by U.S. trade bookstores and wholesalers. Email info@ BeyondPublishing.net

The Beyond Publishing Speakers Bureau can bring authors to your live event. For more information or to book an event contact the Beyond Publishing Speakers Bureau speak@BeyondPublishing.net

The Author can be reached directly BeyondPublishing.net/AuthorForbes Riley

Manufactured and printed in the United States of America distributed globally by BeyondPublishing.net

BEYOND

New York | Los Angeles | London | Sydney

ISBN Dust Jacket: 978-1-949873-86-3

ISBN Hardcover: 978-1-949873-97-9

ISBN Softcover: 978-1-947256-54-5

What Have You Forbes'd Lately?

A Collection of Success Stories from 36 Entreprenuers who MANIFESTED their DREAMS against all odds.

Created by Forbes Riley
Edited by Daphne Street & Tim Hodgkiss